D1590470

THE DYNAMICS OF WORKING-CLASS POLITICS

THE DYNAMICS OF WORKING-CLASS POLITICS

THE LABOUR MOVEMENT IN PRESTON, 1880–1940

MICHAEL SAVAGE

University of Sussex

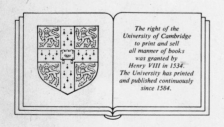

The right of the
University of Cambridge
to print and sell
all manner of books
was granted by
Henry VIII in 1534.
The University has printed
and published continuously
since 1584.

CAMBRIDGE UNIVERSITY PRESS

Cambridge
New York   New Rochelle   Melbourne   Sydney

Published by the Press Syndicate of the University of Cambridge
The Pitt Building, Trumpington Street, Cambridge CB2 1RP
32 East 57th Street, New York, NY 10022, USA
10 Stamford Road, Oakleigh, Melbourne 3166, Australia

First published 1987

Printed in Great Britain at the University Press, Cambridge

British Library cataloguing in publication data
Savage, Michael
The dynamics of working-class politics:
the Labour movement in Preston 1880–1940.
1. Labor and laboring classes – England –
Preston (Lancashire) – History
2. Socialism – England – Preston
(Lancashire) – History
I. Title
335'.1'09427665   HD8397.P7/

Library of Congress cataloguing in publication data
Savage, Michael.
The dynamics of working-class politics.
Bibliography.
Includes index.
1. Labor and laboring classes – England – Preston
(Lancashire) – Political activity – History.
2. Preston (Lancashire) – Politics and government.
3. Labour Party (Great Britain) – History. I. Title.
HD8397.P74S28   1987   322'.2'0941   87–14636

ISBN 0 521 328470

VN

Contents

Tables

Maps

Figures

viii

Preface

The decline in Labour's share of the vote in Britain over the past twenty years has made any simple association between social class and political party look increasingly problematic. Indeed, a number of writers have argued that in contemporary society class is giving way to other political cleavages: new social movements, local social movements, consumption-based cleavages and the like.[1] Arguments such as these, however, often rely on a stereotypical view of what working-class politics have been in the past. Compared with modern complexities, politics in the past seem to have revolved around class identities in a straightforward way: most working-class people voted Labour (regardless of their occupation, gender, ethnic background or location), and voting Labour was primarily a means of defending the working class's economic interests within the overall framework of a capitalist society. Yet there are remarkably few studies actually analysing in detail the dynamics of the Labour movement in this century which show that this is an accurate picture.

This paucity in part reflects the interests of historians in socialist and left-wing movements, rather than in the Labour party itself. There are studies of areas where the Communists were strong, and of industries and occupations known for their radicalism.[2] Yet the vast majority of members of the working class, who did not support organisations to the left of the Labour party, tend to be overlooked in such accounts. Some useful general accounts have appeared which are beginning to rectify this,[3] but these pay inadequate attention to the precise nature of the extent of popular participation in the Labour party, and to the extent to which local Labour politics differed from the well-known concerns of the national parliamentary leaders.

This book aims primarily to present a detailed account of the nature of the Labour movement in the North Lancashire town of Preston between 1880 and 1940. Preston was chosen for solidly pragmatic reasons: it is accessible, and there are some good source materials to draw on. The main concern is to interrogate the relationship between the changing social structure of the town and its political alignments, through detailed accounts of both. In the early stages of my research I was interested in examining relations between the Labour party and other left-wing organisations: in the course of my research this came to be less important (given the weakness of left-wing organisations in Preston) and the pivotal question became the need to explain the local party's political strategies, and the way in which these were related to the type of people active in Labour politics.

It is this issue which is developed at length in the book. In any detailed case study it is easy to stress complexities and ambiguities not captured by generalisations, and inevitably the last chapters 4–7 of the book which present the research on Preston do just that. My aim however is not merely to do justice to the complexities, but to present an analytical framework with which to conceptualise working-class politics more generally. Of prime importance here is the need to conceptualise the political strategies of local political parties, and the way these relate to working-class interests and capacities, based primarily at the local level. This is the subject of the first three chapters, and while it is in the main derived from studies of the British working class between 1850 and 1950, it is hoped that the ideas presented have a more widespread applicability.

Although the chapters 1–3 may attract sociologists and chapters 4–7 historians, it is worth emphasising that they should be read together. The arguments advanced in the first part of the book serve to pinpoint the features to be examined in the material on Preston, but they are only fully demonstrated, I think, by reference to it. Similarly the chapters on Preston do not contain a general social and political history of the town, but concentrate only on those issues which have been developed in the first three chapters.

Acknowledgements

This book has drawn on a great variety of intellectual disciplines, from labour history to political sociology and historical geography. I believe this has been a fertile encounter and reflects the fact that I have studied in a variety of academic environments: departments of history, social history, sociology and urban studies. My fascination with the minutiae of Labour politics on the one hand, and Marxist theory on the other, owes much to my old friends at the University of York: in particular Daniel Benjamin, John Moorhouse, Jon Smith and Paul Wild. A year studying social history at the University of Lancaster also provided a focus for these concerns in the study of Lancashire and the cotton industry: Mike Winstanley and John Walton were helpful here. It was the years spent at the sociology department of the University of Lancaster which gave me the opportunity to consider in greater depth the theoretical issues raised. Alan Warde must get the most thanks here: he managed to find the ideal blend of encouragement (when my confidence was low) and constructive criticism (when my confidence was too high). The other members of the Lancaster Regionalism Group (Dan Shapiro, John Urry, Sylvia Walby and Annie Witz) helped provide the ideal environment for discussing many of the issues which interested me. In particular Jane Mark-Lawson's work has influenced me more than she probably thinks. Numerous conversations with Brian Longhurst as well as with other colleagues mentioned above have advanced my understanding of general sociological concerns. Finally, since moving to Sussex I have benefited from discussions with members of the staff of the urban studies department, particularly Simon Duncan and Pete Saunders.

A large number of institutions have helped me in my detailed research. In particular, the Harris Library in Preston (always an interesting place to work), the Lancashire County Record Office, Preston, the Labour Party Archive in London, the Public Record Office at Kew and the University Libraries at Lancaster and the London School of Economics should be singled out.

In putting this book together Alan Warde, John Urry and Pete Saunders have given me invaluable advice and guidance. Whereas its earlier manifestations owed much to the work of several typists (Heather Salt, Maeve Connolly, Wendy Francis and Kay Roberts), in its later stages my thanks are due to those people (especially Andy Clews and Mary Galgani) who kept the somewhat temperamental wordprocessor on the boil, and to Ginny Catmur, for her diligent copy-editing. A number of people have helped me on specific points: in particular Elizabeth Roberts, Jonathan Zeitlin, Joseph Melling, Alan Fowler and Steve Constantine. Needless to say the mistakes are mine.

1

Political practices and the social structure

1.1 The question of working-class consciousness

In 1922 Jeremiah Wooley, leading officer of Preston's largest union, the Weavers', and the town's first Labour mayor, spoke of his vision of socialism. He defined it as a situation in which 'a man should have work . . . he should be paid for his work . . . he should have a decent house . . . he should have sufficient leisure to enjoy life . . . he should have clothes fit to wear, and . . . he should have a little spending money in his pocket.'[1] This statement is a good example of the limited vision of the Labour movement, an instance of what many writers have seen as the characteristic of the Labour party in Britain: its embodiment in a defensive working-class consciousness. This interpretation owes much to the work of Ross McKibbin who argued that the party's rise was caused by 'an acutely developed class consciousness', but of a defensive and non-socialist kind.[2] For many writers, examination of the Labour party revolves around showing the relationship between this defensive consciousness and its political institutions.

A similar emphasis has informed many of the most important sociological accounts of political change in modern Britain. Perhaps the most influential of these was the debate around Lockwood's arguments showing how different types of occupational and community relations gave rise to particular kinds of 'images of society'.[3] Lockwood distinguished three main types of class imagery, based on a reading of various English studies of workers between 1945 and the middle of the 1960s. Firstly there was 'traditional proletarian' imagery, whereby workers had very strongly defined conceptions of class based on a belief that social advantages were based on power. There was also, secondly, a 'traditional deferential' imagery, whereby workers recognised that a certain elite should rule by virtue of its status attributes: and finally there were 'instrumental' workers, who had less clear conceptions of class,

1

seeing society as composed of differentiated groups with different amounts of money. These forms of imagery could be related to the environment surrounding the workers: in occupational communities and industries where workers exercised autonomy in the workplace the traditional proletarian imagery was most likely to develop; in situations where workers lived and worked near their employers, deference was likely to develop: whilst in the high-wage but tedious mass-production industries workers were most likely to be instrumental.

In order to understand the political propensities of the working class it was necessary to ascertain which of these types of imagery pre-dominated. Clearly it seemed easy to relate the hold of the Labour party to the existence of occupational communities with their 'traditional proletarian' imagery, though Lockwood did emphasise that political behaviour could not simply be read off from these images of society and indeed, with Goldthorpe, argued that instrumentalism may be as likely to lead to support for the Labour party as is traditional proletarian imagery, at least in the short term.[4] Nonetheless the general thrust of Lockwood and the sociological school was to examine the relationship between social structure and political partisanship through the medi-ation of these images.

One of the strengths of focusing on forms of class consciousness is that it allows political forms to be tied to people's everyday life. This approach takes people's beliefs about specific daily practices, such as work or 'community', and then relates them to political practices by emphasising an internal logical connection between the different belief elements. The *coherence* of belief systems is therefore an enduring feature of these accounts. Thus in Lockwood's typology a worker with personal ex-perience of workplace conflict is likely to develop an image of society in which class hostility is pervasive in all matters. An explanation of politics can hence be provided which is firmly based in the social structure.

An interesting recent example of this is Patrick Joyce's account of working-class passivity in mid-Victorian textile Lancashire.[5] Joyce wanted to explain why textile Lancashire, the first regional base of industrial capitalism, failed to give rise to a radical working class. He stressed the role of the local social structure, notably the dependence of workers on employers in the labour market, the significance of rejuvenated patriarchal relations, and the hold which employers could exert in small mill-town environments. The critical link between these specific features and political passivity, however, was provided by 'deference' which, while arising out of everyday work and neighbour-hood relations, then carried over into the political realm. Joyce links together deferential relations in the workplace with deferential political attitudes, encapsulated in working-class Toryism, which were also linked to patriarchal values, patriotism, racism and Anglicanism, so that all are linked in a seamless web of 'deference'. Hence a certain principle is singled out which appears to act as a unifying axis for a range of more specific beliefs about work, the home and politics. It is this which is frequently referred to as 'culture', being understood, in Raymond Williams's definition, as 'a whole way of life'.[6]

The emphasis on working-class consciousness has therefore generally gone hand in hand with attempts to relate changes in the social structure with changes in political alignments. Consciousness or culture is the main link between the two. As such, analyses of popular politics tend to be collapsed into studies of working-class culture. This concentration on questions of culture has, I will contend, been profoundly unhelpful in advancing our analysis of the dynamics of working-class politics. There are three main reasons for this. Firstly there are almost insurmountable problems in ascertaining the precise nature of working-class consciousness in historical periods. Secondly, political practice and action are strongly related to questions of strategy and tactics rather than to moral issues or perceptions of the nature of society. As such the nature of working-class consciousness rarely explains why particular courses of political action are embarked upon. Finally recent work suggests that the category 'culture' simply will not stand the weight put upon it. People have a variety of beliefs about different elements of their lives, and there is no reason to suppose that there is any coherence about these beliefs.

In some ways the first point is relatively minor, but it is necessary to emphasise the practical difficulties in researching working-class consciousness in past times. There is a very strong temptation to concentrate on the articulate minority, the people most likely to leave historical records, and who were also most likely to be involved in political action. This line of reasoning is implicit in books such as E.P. Thompson's *The Making of The English Working Class*, in which analysis of working-class consciousness is primarily inferred from studies of radical texts and speakers. More recently the recognition of this problem has led historians to infer forms of consciousness from various practical activities. Stedman Jones, most notably, has deduced the existence of a defensive working-class consciousness from the content of music hall songs, while Joyce has deduced working-class deference from popular religious behaviour, voting patterns and popular leisure.[7] Contemporary sociologists have emphasised, however, how difficult it is to undertake this sort of operation, since people performing the same activity may have different perceptions about it. There is no reason to suppose that this would have been any different for earlier periods.[8] Finally, for more recent periods at least, oral history has been used. However the problem is that respondents' past beliefs are always interpreted by them through their present perceptions and values, and may not be a good guide to their previous consciousness.[9]

Put simply, it is enormously difficult actually to find out what people in the past believed. One alternative may be to examine popular practice in its own right, rather than use it to infer particular states of consciousness. This procedure has frequently been neglected, since the tendency has been to examine popular practices only in order to illuminate a common cultural framework held to underpin them. This forms the basis of my second reason for finding unhelpful the cultural approach to working-class politics. The precise form of popular action tends to be reduced to a common set of values, but (and this is the problem) the same set of beliefs can be held to underlie a number of different forms of political practice.

Williams offers an especially blatant example of this when he argues that working-class culture, in his terms 'the basic collectivist idea', has produced 'the basic democratic institution, whether in the trade unions, the co-operative movement or a political party'. This implies that it is a matter of little importance which actual form 'the basic collectivist idea' takes, yet for the analysis of Labour politics it is precisely this which is of major importance.[10]

Consider the work of historians of the Labour party. Many have seen the party, in Winter's words, as 'infused with the spirit of a defensive and politically inert working class consciousness'. Stedman Jones's work is well known in this regard, with his observations that from the latter part of the nineteenth century a home-based lifestyle generated a defensive culture which culminated in the Labour party.[11] Yet this is still compatible with a 'proletarian' imagery. The working class recognises the existence of power-based divisions in society; yet is driven by this belief not into revolutionary politics, but into defensive struggles to gain what can be achieved within the existing system. The problem raised is that a certain set of beliefs appears able to generate different forms of political practice: revolutionary movements in some cases, social democratic politics in others, or simple apathy and hopelessness in others. If this is so, the precise nature of working-class consciousness is perhaps of relatively small importance in explaining political alignments.

Many writers are coming to recognise the complexities of this problem of relating forms of consciousness to forms of practice, yet argue that the way to proceed is further to conceptualise the nature of class consciousness. As Winter put it: 'Class consciousness points in more directions than simply towards apathy or militancy. Indeed in most periods it points in both directions at once.' Hence there is a need 'to look at multiple meanings of class consciousness'. The answer to the problem, then, is to look for yet more adequate theorisation of class consciousness, as Winter makes clear in his argument that labour history should be about 'questions of the nature of class consciousness and its political manifestations'. Stedman Jones's recent attempt to emphasise the significance of analysing 'languages of class' also exacerbates this tendency.[12] In fact this seems a most unpromising way to proceed – and this forms the basis of my third reason for finding unhelpful analyses of working-class politics which concentrate on questions of culture. Recent work indicates that people's day-to-day practices are only weakly affected by any wider cultural values. Some writers, drawing inspiration from Gramsci, have attempted to break down any necessary unity to cultural systems and stress the need to examine practical beliefs in much greater detail. Gramsci's distinction between common sense and philosophy stressed the closer connection of the former to the material world. 'In common sense', he wrote, 'it is the realistic, materialistic elements which are predominant, the immediate product of individual sensation.'[13] Forms of common sense came into contact with more general 'philosophies' which attempted to latch on to forms of common sense. The essential point however is that the relationship between common sense and the material world is more significant than that between different elements of a culture. Gramsci's work has had considerable impact in this regard on Marxist conceptions of culture and ideology.[14]

A similar sort of distinction has been made more recently by Giddens in his separation of practical from discursive consciousness. The former Giddens defines as 'those things which actors know tacitly about how to go on in the contexts of social life without being able to give them direct discursive expression'.[15] Giddens's point is that there is no necessary tie-up with discursive consciousness in which agents have to give an account of their activities. Whereas Lockwood saw solidarity in the workplace (practical consciousness) as leading to wider political and social awareness (a form of discursive consciousness), Giddens's distinction suggests that there is no necessary relationship. Therefore Joyce's argument, that the experience of worker dependence in the labour market led to a set of deferential belief systems with wide-ranging applications in all spheres of life, can be seen as conceptually misleading. Forms of practical consciousness associated with particular activities need not have any implication in other contexts.

These types of distinctions can be usefully applied to many of the concrete studies of worker consciousness and practice. Newby's account of deference among East Anglian farmworkers in the 1970s is a case in point. Newby stresses that deferential relationships between farmer and farmworker were established in the course of their everyday interaction and that deferential attitudes applied only in these contexts and need not be generalised into a more general deferential world view. The farmworker was in a position of powerlessness in the labour and housing markets and was hence forced to rely on the farmer for work and security, and this form of dependence was acknowledged by the farmworkers. Thus 73 % of them agreed that 'workers should always be loyal to their farmer, even if this means putting themselves out quite a lot'. These views, developed in the work situation, did not carry over into their wider political outlook. Only 36.9 % felt that 'the aristocracy are born to rule and workers should follow their lead; 28.6 % felt that 'public [fee-paying] schools are the best part of our education system'. The most striking finding was that 43 % of Newby's respondents failed to have a single image of society in Lockwood's sense, but instead had a set of conflicting images, whilst only 15 % evinced deferential imagery.[16] Hence there are no clear connections between 'deference' as practical consciousness and deference as discursive consciousness.

Another good example of this point can be seen in Burawoy's study of a piece-rate machine shop in Illinois, USA, also in the 1970s.[17] He argues that ideology should be conceived not as abstract thought autonomous from lived relations, but rather as firmly based on 'lived experience'. For Burawoy, the shopfloor 'lived experience' created the ideology of 'making out'. In order to impose meaning on dull and boring work, the operatives played 'games' to see if they could meet particular production targets they set themselves, and to see if they could take short cuts in their work. This ideology of making out was firmly linked to the nature of shopfloor life, and would have little relevance outside the workplace. Burawoy discusses this in relation to racism. Racist beliefs developed outside the workplace, mainly in education and housing, had no impact on shopfloor practices in the course of which black and white workers might co-operate in their aim of making out. Racist beliefs, whilst firmly held outside the workplace, held no purchase on activities on the shopfloor. It seems equally valid to reverse this argument and suggest that the practice of making out would not necessarily have any impact outside the working practices on which it was based.

This point is of major importance in analysing the development of the Labour party in Britain, in which many historians have attempted to make firm connections between work experience and political and social practices. Price, for instance, argues that there is an inherent conflict in the capitalist labour process between capital and labour over the question of control. Therefore rank and file workplace militancy have been an enduring feature of British industrial relations, and in specific periods (he cites the early nineteenth century, the period 1880–1920, and the period from 1960) will lead to a capitalist backlash as the employers attempt to restore profitability. 'At these moments', he writes, 'resistance to subordination becomes the central problem to be solved and a battery of weapons – industrial, social, cultural, political and legal – are employed to attack formal subordination, and restore real subordination. Under these circumstances, resistance to subordination . . . moves out of its local workshop environment to enter the wider dynamic of labour's history.'[18] There are a number of studies which support the general argument that changes in work relations were of considerable significance in the growing politicisation of the skilled sector of the working class after 1900,[19] yet the pivotal importance given to work in this account seems theoretically unwarranted; indeed comparative analysis of the American case, where far more intense changes in working practices were being introduced but where no working-class political movement emerged, shows that these connections are far from clear. Rather it is necessary to ground any examination of forms of working-class politics in a study of diverse social practices, with their attendant forms of practical consciousness. It is important to know how specific practices relate to each other, and in particular how forms of political practice are related to more mundane practices of work and leisure, given that it is unfruitful to see them as linked in a common culture, or as based in one experience alone.

1.2 *Political practices and the autonomy of the political*

One of the main needs of political analysis is to come to terms with the diversity and lack of connection between political and other practices. It is misleading to give them a spurious unity by connecting them to an over-arching belief system. Yet if without such a spurious unity all that is left is a whole range of social practices, it is unclear how political practices are to be defined, and how they can be distinguished from other social practices. One solution to this problem would be to define political practices as all those which further the interests of their participants. Furtherance of interests can also provide the mechanism by which the social structure generates political action. People engage in various forms of action because it is in their interests to do so. The use of some notion of interests to link social structure and political action lies at the heart of political sociology, yet the concept of interests is a hotly contested one and needs considerable discussion.

It was the American pluralists of the 1950s who used the concept of interests most clearly, and the legacy of their interpretation has affected other works. The pluralists argued that political movements could be classified into pragmatic interest-based politics (manifested most notably in social democratic parties) and moralistic mass politics (such as Fascism or Communism). They argued that the former was linked to the centrality of class politics, since class divisions provided basic economic interests around which people could organise, while the latter was linked to status politics in which people acted not pragmatically but for irrational reasons of status anxiety.

The sort of politics which these writers felt could best be related to interests were peaceful formal pressuring and party organisation. The significant effect of this interpretation was to link formal political alignments in liberal democracies to the class structure in a fairly mechanistic way. Lipset for instance stated that 'on a world scale the principal generalisation which can be made is that parties are primarily based on either the lower class or the middle and upper class'. Alford elaborated on this point: 'A relation between class position and voting is natural and expected . . . given the character of the stratification order and the way political parties act as representatives of class interest it would be remarkable if such a relationship were not found.' The rise of the Labour party in Britain could easily be interpreted in this way as the normal development of an interest-based party.[20]

The problem with this definition of political practice as interest-based was that it could not come to terms with various forms of activity that did not appear to be pressing for the advancement of interests within the existing order. Class interests could be held to account in a fairly simple way for the existence of orthodox 'reformist' parties or moderate political alignments. Class interests were not however responsible for other 'mass' forms of political action, which were explained not in social terms at all, but in terms of the isolation of individuals from society. Where individuals were isolated from society their irrational unconscious impulses could emerge and would therefore produce moralistic 'mass politics'. Fascism was explained by reference to the authoritarian personality which could develop where there were large numbers of self-employed businessmen and farmers not integrated into industrial society.[21]

Mass society theory has been heavily criticised[22] largely because the distinction between interest-based and mass politics seems impossible to draw: on close inspection most 'mass' movements are concerned with basic economic issues which can be linked to various interests. Halebsky for instance stresses that many forms of mass politics, such as Nazism, are to be explained in the same terms as other more 'orthodox' political forms. Halebsky's critique of mass society theory argues that diverse forms of party political mobilisation are to be understood not in terms of the extent to which people are integrated into society, but are instead linked to 'political socialisation, group membership, historic loyalties, dominant themes in the national political culture, interest conscious-ness, class divisions, the lack of responsiveness by political elites, the nature of available alternatives and such other political influences that account for most political commitments, radical or otherwise'.[23]

This passage indicates that the critique of mass society theory is in danger of ending up simply in descriptions of various political forms. The theoretical problem can be labelled 'the problem of the under-determination of politics by interests'. A wide variety of forms of political action can be seen as viable strategies to defend or advance interests, in which case the actual specification of these interests seems of relatively little importance in explaining the precise form of action undertaken. This problem is a precise analogue of that discussed earlier where it was seen that a particular form of culture could give rise to a number of political practices: in a like way a given set of interests can give rise to divergent political forms.

In recent years this problem has been approached from a new angle, with stress placed on the autonomy of the political. Since political actions appear under-determined by social interests greater emphasis is placed on how political structures such as the state and party systems may determine the precise nature of political action. This type of argument has been expressed forcibly by Berger. She emphasises that interest groups are not the spontaneous result of socio-economic cleavage but are produced by the political process itself. Attention should be placed on 'the specificities of national historical expansion, the role of the state, and the instabilities inherent in the operation of a representational system'.[24]

The process of state formation is often given key importance in accounting for national variations in forms of political alignment. Interest is often centred on the period at which the franchise was extended to encompass a mass electorate, for the type of parties in existence at this period then have the opportunity to mobilise the new electorate, and maintain themselves in the longer term. Inspired by Lipset and Rokkan's seminal work, Schafter puts it thus: 'the circumstances under which a party first mobilises a mass following has enduring implications for its subsequent behaviour'.[25] The normal argument here is that if the state is slow to extend the franchise after the emergence of industrial or capitalist society, it is more likely that the excluded working class will form its own party to gain entry to the polity. If the franchise is extended early, however, it is more likely that the working class will be incorporated into existing political alignments. Thus the main differences between American and British politics, for instance, lie not in the different class structures or patterns of capitalist development, but rather in the patterns of state development.

This argument has been used to explain the fortunes of the Labour party in twentieth-century Britain by Cronin, who argues that the Labour party's rise between 1900 and 1920 was due to the exclusion of the working class from the existing polity, and that 'Labour became the vehicle of workers' entry into the polity'.[26] Since the Labour party predated the development of the mass franchise and was partly responsible for it, it stood to reap the electoral benefits, and has persisted. Within a similar line of argument Katznelson explains the lack of radical politics in the USA by reference to the early franchise and the autonomy of the states, which allowed local political parties to develop; these organised the new voters in a territorially based patronage system. 'In this politics, workers appeared in the political arena not as workers but as residents of a specific place or as members of a specific (non-class) group.'[27]

The argument that formal political parties operate on the terrain created and structured by the state is a very powerful one, and in later chapters we shall see how the development of the Labour party did link with changes in the national polity. Yet there is a major problem in such state-centred accounts: the set of assumptions concerning people's relationship to the state is very simplistic. It is assumed that people will want to gain access to the state and use it to their own advantage: the way in which this occurs (whether through explicitly working-class parties or patronage-based ones) is deemed to be determined by the nature of the state. In capitalist society working-class relationships to the state are however much more complex than this. A large number of practices which advance one's interests may not involve the state, may involve it only indirectly, or may be actively hostile to it. For instance if working-class people are surviving by relying on money wages provided by capitalist enterprises they may be indifferent to the potential of patronage provided by the state and, no matter whether the state is 'strong' or 'weak', they may not be interested in participating in it. Urry has argued that struggles in what he terms 'civil society' cannot be reduced to struggles in and over the state, though they do have powerful effects on the state.[28] It is therefore vital to distinguish formal party politics, in which parties compete to gain access to the state, from what I shall term 'practical politics', in which struggles to defend or advance one's interests may not make direct demands on state agencies. This point will be elaborated at length below, but a few illustrative examples are useful here. In the British context historians such as E.P. Thompson have argued that the early radical movement was not simply trying to get access to the British state (or 'Old Corruption' as it was frequently termed), but was fundamentally opposed to it, and struggles were concerned with minimising its hold on society. More precisely Phillips and Whiteside have shown how dock workers in Britain persistently opposed state intervention which superficially seemed to benefit them by de-casualising labour, because it actually undermined their own informal patterns of work sharing and labour market control.[29]

These points can be elaborated by discussing Katznelson's emphasis that the federal character of the American state was a factor behind the weakness of class-based political alignments in the USA. It does indeed seem that those countries where party alignments are long lasting and not easily changed are characterised by federal state and party structures. In the US not only do the individual states have considerable autonomy, but local government is also less centralised and more fragmented than elsewhere, while the parties hardly function as unified national machines except in the nomination of presidential candidates. In these circumstances new social forces and movements find it very easy to win over and change the character of local political parties, and in turn to be incorporated into the older party framework. Thus in the US it is well known that in some areas the Democrats are the 'progressive' party and in others (notably the South), the Republicans are. Similarly Democratic city politics have massive local autonomy, so that in some cities the Democrats are based on ethnic machine politics, in others on more popular mobilisation, and in others on elite dominance. While it is true to say that the character of the US state does account for the nature of formal party alignments, it tells us very little about the *substance* of practical politics: the type of interests the party advances, the character of the activists and the like. On the other hand in more centralised states local political mobilisation is much more likely to be forced to work outside the pre-existing party system since the centralised party structures are much less easy to win over. This is one reason why wars are so important in realigning formal party alignments; for in wartime the centralised state holds full sway, and existing national parties are usually co-opted into the national state. Under these conditions it is virtually impossible for them to be used as agents of popular political practice, and new parties (most famously the Communist parties of Italy and France in World War II) can emerge under these conditions.[30]

While the character of the state is very significant in affecting the character of formal political organisation, it is less clear how it affects the 'practical politics' which I have argued are an essential element of working-class politics. People need not have a uniform desire to use the state for their own advantage, since they may be more likely to benefit through other means. Yet it will not have escaped the reader's notice that I have yet to define how we can identify interests, which I have taken to lie behind practical politics. These will be discussed now.

1.3   The sociology of working-class interests

The argument advanced so far can be summarised simply. Working-class political practices are not to be understood as umbilically linked to working-class life more generally by their embeddedness in a common cultural framework. They should be conceived as those practices which advance the interests of the participants; but there is the problem that a given set of interests can lead to a massive diversity of political actions to defend or advance them. Yet to see political practices as structured by the state and the political environment is too restrictive, since important practices to advance the interests of people may not involve the state, except in an oblique way. To advance the argument further it is necessary to consider in more depth the nature of interests.

There have been some notable attempts in recent work to argue that a proper appreciation of material interests can be used to develop a fuller analysis of working-class politics than the one I have presented so far. This approach lays great emphasis on the inherent individuality of social action, and on the potential tension between individual and collective action. Olson stresses that people's greatest self-interest is gained from securing the benefits of collective action whilst expending as little effort as possible themselves in achieving them. Thus the maximum self-interest of a worker lies in reaping the advantages brought by trade unionism whilst doing as little as possible personally to support it. Olson stresses that this tension necessitates coercion on the part of trade unions to force individuals to join. Other writers in the same vein emphasise the importance of a creation of a collective identity which allows people to assess the reasons for joining organisations on a non-instrumental basis.[31]

One of the most interesting recent accounts of the dynamics of working-class politics is that of Offe and Wisenthal.[32] They argue that there are fundamental differences between the capacities of capital and labour to recognise and act upon their material interests because of their respective structural characteristics. They observe that for the working class the exercise of labour power is inextricably linked to the individual labourer. Working-class action is therefore always based on an association of separate individuals. This leads to problems of collective action as discussed by Olson. For Olson individuals who rationally pursue their maximum self-interest will tend to refrain from collective action since their maximum self-interest is gained by securing the advantages of collective action without having to expend any effort in achieving them. Thus workers will attempt to secure the advantages of trades unionism without becoming involved themselves. This is the problem of the free rider. Clearly, if all workers follow their maximum self-interest no trade unions will ever be formed. Capital on the other hand can be accumulated and hence action can be based on the aggregated capitals in the firm rather than on the individual. Hence a hundred shares can be organised and directed more easily than a hundred workers.

There is also another side to Offe and Wisenthal's argument. Because workers cannot be separated from their labour power it is unclear what precisely their interest lies in: whether to improve wages, working conditions or employment security. Their activity as people cannot be separated from their activity as workers and hence their precise interests as workers are unclear. On the other hand the interests of capital – to accumulate profit – can be separated from those of individuals and hence more easily acted upon.[33]

These writers have effectively turned the older assumptions on their head. 'Reformist' working-class political action to defend working-class interests, far from being regarded as normal, is now seen as difficult and unstable. Offe and Wisenthal stress that workers are forced to develop dialogical forms of activity in which a collective identity is formed so that they do not assess the value of collective action from the point of view of their individual self-interest, but from the perspective of a particular group. Dialogical action is distinguished from monological action (characteristic of employers) because it does not simply 'aggregate and transmit' interests, but also 'plays an active role in defining and transforming members' interests'.[34] Offe and Wisenthal do not however discuss the conditions under which these dialogical forms of activity come into being.

Within this perspective the attribution of collective interests to members of the working class is not relevant in explaining their political action. It should be noted that Offe and Wisenthal would not necessarily argue that social groups do not have 'real' interests. They emphasise merely that these interests do not in themselves provide a mechanism which links social structure to political action. Yet there are some problems with this. For example, it is unclear why collective working-class struggle has been such an enduring feature of all capitalist societies. However, the main weakness of the work of Olson, and Offe and Wisenthal lies in their excessive voluntarism. The tension between individual and group interests discussed by these writers is applicable only in situations where the groups concerned *initiate* action. Thus Olson argues that class-conscious workers will not risk their lives or resources to carry out a socialist revolution because they would rather gain the benefits of action carried out by others. This however assumes that the existing regime is not currently threatening their lives, wages, property or whatever. In such a case the logic of collective action is somewhat different. If workers are faced with a government that is cutting all wages by, say, 10 % it seems perfectly rational for workers to act to prevent this. In defensive situations no one stands to benefit by not engaging in collective action. Olson's arguments really apply only to initiatory actions where there is no real antagonist. Thus in the case of a works outing, for instance, everyone would benefit (supposedly) by one being arranged, but no one would want to put in the effort of organising it (the free rider problem again). If an individual acts, other people will benefit who have put in no effort and the individual concerned will therefore think twice about becoming involved. Yet in defensive situations the free rider problem takes a rather different form. In this case the free riders are those – other groups whose wages are not being reduced, shareholders or whoever – who stand to benefit at the workers' expense, and the free rider problem encourages collective action: workers feel that if they do not act the free riders will benefit at their expense. The same point can be made in relation to Offe and Wisenthal's arguments. While it may be true that the precise nature of what one should be struggling for is not prescribed by the nature of class, nonetheless attempts to take something away can always be seen as detrimental to one's interests. Thus it may be unclear whether a worker will benefit more by a wage increase than by better housing, and this may make a definition of interests difficult. But in a situation where wages are reduced (or more commonly, are not kept up with inflation), or housing subsidies are lowered one cannot be in any doubt that this is against one's interests. What recent accounts of the theory of collective action fail to recognise then is that people are not only actors but are also acted upon.[35]

A slightly different approach to conceptualising class and politics which attempts to dispense with the notion of interests has been developed explicitly within a realist framework, whereby classes are held to be 'social entities' possessing causal powers, powers to generate 'empirically observable events'.[36] Whether or not these powers are realised depends on the particular context in which that class exists; furthermore, the same social class can have a number of different causal powers. This complex schema tends to evade the central problem, namely of how these causal powers are to be identified, and it is by no means clear that a notion of interests can be dispensed with for this purpose. Thus, in referring to the causal powers of the service class, it appears that Abercrombie and Urry list those powers which further that class's *interests*. Interests hence appear to remain the key causal mechanism. Unless it can be shown that a class's causal powers may be against its interests it is difficult to see how reference to causal powers in itself aids analysis. It may of course be argued that the pursuit of a class's short-term interests, for instance to gain reforms within a capitalist society, may be against its long-term interests, by making capitalism more secure perhaps, but this point can be accommodated simply by talking about possible tensions between short- and long-term interests.[37]

Some notion of interests linked to the social structure must remain if an adequate analysis of working-class politics is to be carried out. The precise definition of these interests will always be contested,[38] and in what follows I will argue that it is most useful to conceptualise working-class politics in terms of reducing working-class insecurity.

There are two main ways of conceptualising working-class interests. A Hegelian approach posits general human interests (such as freedom) and then assigns the realisation of these interests to a particular social group by virtue of its social position. On the other hand interests can be related directly to the structural position of certain social groups. The most recent defender of the first position is Wright[39] who attempts to show how types of class exploitation generate class conflict as they strike at the human interests of the working class. Wright argues that class conflict is based on the process of exploitation in capitalist society. There are three broad conceptions of exploitation. The first of these is absolute exploitation: a worker can be said to be exploited if he or she gets below a certain minimum level necessary for 'civilised' life. As Marx argued, however, exploitation may also be occurring if a worker in fact receives a wage allowing him or her to live well above subsistence level, since the value of his or her work to the employer remains well above that which is paid back in wages. This argument depends on the labour theory of value, however, a concept which has fallen into disfavour in recent years because of the problems in distinguishing productive from unproductive labour. Wright, following Roemer, therefore uses another relative concept of exploitation, whereby a worker can be said to be exploited if he or she would be 'better off' if he/she withdrew from existing social structures and developed alternative, but feasible ones, while the employer would be worse off.[40]

I do not propose to discuss whether or not this is a useful theory of exploitation but simply if it can be seen as the basis of working-class interests and hence as the underlying spring of action. Here Wright runs into problems. He states that people have 'an interest in expanding their capacity to make choices and act upon them'.[41] This refers to general human interests rather than class interests. It is not however clear that these interests should in any way explain why exploitation will lead to resistance or struggle. The problem of using a relative concept of exploitation as Wright does is that it is possible to increase one's capacity to make choices *within* continued exploitative relations. It is also true that one's capacity to make choices can be increased by rejecting exploitative conditions. Whether or not a struggle against exploitation ensues cannot then be accounted for by interests; some other factor must be brought into play. To give an example of my argument: factory workers have an interest in increasing their capacity to make choices. This may involve revolutionary struggle; it could however merely involve what Burawoy has observed in a Chicago machine shop: workers 'making out' by setting production targets for themselves (rather than having them imposed by management) and enhancing their autonomy on the shopfloor within the capitalist enterprise. Given the bedrock of workers' general interests, it is not clear what class relations based on exploitation actually show about how people go about acting to advance such interests. Hence, while exploitation, in Wright's relative sense, undoubtedly exists, it seems difficult to derive any useful notion of interests from it which can help illuminate political practices.

Given these points it is essential to fix interests not to general human ones, but to class-specific ones, and also to recognise that not all interests are class interests. Working-class people, like other people, are strongly affected by a general human interest to increase their income (which is interpreted broadly to include income in kind as well as money). This however overlaps with, but is separate from, the class-specific interest to reduce the insecurity inherent in wage labour. The central feature of capitalism is the separation of workers from the means of production, so that they can subsist only by selling their labour to employers. Hence they cannot subsist without engaging in social relations with other social agents: capitalist employers who provide wages in return for labour; husbands who provide subsistence to wives in return for domestic labour; the state which may provide benefits, and so forth. The central point is what is distinctive about capitalist society: the extent to which workers cannot be self-dependent. In societies where labourers are not separated from their means of subsistence self-exploitation is a continuing option.[42] (By self-exploitation I mean the practice of people of working long hours perhaps under poor conditions for meagre rewards by their own choice and under their own direction.)

I would argue that in capitalist society the working class can be broadly defined as all those people separated from their means of subsistence. Hence working-class interests lie in the reduction of the insecurity which results from this separation. It might however be argued that it is not only labourers who suffer insecurity, but also their employers, for in any system based on a market certain forms of insecurity are inherent. The continued existence of capitalism depends upon profits being made and hence for employers the need to reduce insecurity is secondary to the need to make profit, and indeed greater profitability is usually the means by which insecurity can be reduced, in extreme cases through the creation of monopolies. Similarly, for petty capitalists, insecurity can still be dealt with through self-exploitation. But for labour, the reduction of insecurity is tied up with the need to undermine the commodity status of labour power, and it is this which must be seen as the class-based interest on which practical politics are based. It primarily involves three elements: the need to detach income from the 'law of the market'; the need to ensure job security; and the need to make the reproduction of labour power non-dependent (or less dependent) on market-based services. If wages are derived not from the market value of labour, but from the powers of workers to force employers to pay more, or if services are provided as of right then the commodity status of labour cannot but be undermined. Practical politics are composed of all those practices designed to reduce working-class insecurity along these axes.

These working-class interests are often in conflict with individual ones to increase individual income by selling labour more expensively. In fact much wage bargaining, concerned with securing 'a fair day's wage for a fair day's pay', is not in my terms part of practical politics, since it deals with the price of labour as a commodity rather than with its very status as a commodity.[43] Practical politics, concerned with reducing the commodity position of labour, is an initiatory struggle (whilst wage bargaining is as much defensive as initiatory, since two parties at least are engaged in a bargaining process). There is therefore no inevitability about practical politics taking place: the mere fact of class does not guarantee this. However, since a wide range of individual life chances do depend on practical politics, they are likely to emerge whenever the problems of collective action discussed by Offe and Wisenthal (the free rider problem) can be overcome. Wage bargaining, on the other hand, does not face the same problems of collective action: instrumental, individualistic workers can act together over this without any major 'dialogical' forms of consciousness. But it is vitally necessary while examining practical politics to study the processes which can bind workers together to allow them to engage in initiatory collective action.

The interests of the working class to reduce insecurity by undermining the status of labour as a commodity are class specific, but my use of the term 'working class' must be borne in mind. It is based on the separation of workers from the means of production, and hence subsistence, rather than on their precise relationship to the creation of surplus value. Clearly the working class as I have defined it is a heterogeneous group, with differing degrees of separation from the means of subsistence. However, different groups within the working class have differing degrees of separation from the means of production. Workers who own a plot of land can produce certain of their means of subsistence and are differently positioned from those workers who depend entirely on the labour market. People have different degrees of dependence on the capitalist labour market, and this is of vital importance in conceptualising their position within the working class. Fundamental to this is the need to recognise the significance of gender relations within the household as affecting types of dependence on the labour market. In patriarchal situations where women are confined to performing domestic labour for their male relatives, a number of services (such as cooking and cleaning) can be carried out in a non-commodified form and this may lessen degrees of dependence on the labour market. This point is of central importance: it is not possible to study working-class politics in isolation from gender relations.

Gender is not an extra 'variable' which adds a little to the type of issues struggled over, but is centrally implicated in the very formation of all types of working-class politics, as much of the rest of the book will show. The actual degrees and types of dependence of particular working classes on the capitalist labour market, which I take to lie at the heart of class analysis, has been far less well researched than have the working classes' relations in the workplace. It is, for instance, unclear how recent trends in Britain are likely to affect this. Several commentators have discussed the rise of a 'self-service' economy, in which large sections of the population perform much of their own servicing, through purchase of certain goods such as washing machines and cars which might appear to reduce their dependence on bought services (and hence indirectly on the labour market). Since this depends on purchasing expensive capital equipment and on replacing, repairing and buying routine goods for them it is by no means certain that this will occur.[44]

In this chapter I have argued that working-class political practice is not merely structured by the polity alone, but needs to be grounded in a correct appreciation of working-class interests arising out of the need of workers to reduce the material insecurity inherent in capitalist society. Political practices do however need to be divided into *formal* politics, the character of which is affected by the nature of the state and existing party structures, and what I have termed *practical* politics, which form the issues over which formal politics can operate but which are much more closely tied to the social structure. Later in the book it will be argued that the Labour party in Preston was stronger when campaigning over practical politics than when involved merely in wage-bargaining disputes. But this is jumping ahead: in Chapter 2 I shall indicate how working-class interests may lead to diverse forms of practical politics.

2

The diversity of working-class politics

In this chapter I shall argue that three distinct types of working-class practical politics may develop out of the interests of the working class to reduce material insecurity. These can be seen as attempts to reduce the insecurity inherent within the capitalist labour market by trying to move out of it, by struggling within it to weaken employers' discretion to treat labour as a commodity, or by forcing the state to alter the structure of the labour market in some way advantageous to the working class. More exactly these types of struggle can be identified as, firstly, 'mutualist', in which workers struggle to establish their own independent provision of jobs and services; secondly, 'economistic', in which workers struggle to force employers to guarantee job security; and finally 'statist', in which the state is used to establish measures of security. In each case these struggles may take patriarchal or non-patriarchal forms,[1] and collectivist or individualistic forms; the focus of this chapter will be on collectivist forms. The struggles are all 'rational' responses to the problem of insecurity, yet it is vital that these are not conflated, for they do not entail each other; and, in ways which will be discussed below, they may also be incompatible with each other. It is important to establish this point in order to emphasise that there is no one 'natural' way by which working-class interests manifest themselves in political action. The under-determination of political practice by social interests must be recognised here.

2.1 *Types of working-class struggle*

In mutualist struggles workers attempt to reduce the insecurity inherent in capitalist society by developing their own provision of jobs and services. In the labour market the most significant instances of this occur when workers move away from dependence on capital for employment to work provided by the worker or workers themselves, the most notable collective examples being co-operative production or associated forms of enterprise. The importance of these has been well recognised on the European mainland.[2] In France, for instance, in 1849–51, 300 co-operative associations with 50,000 members were formed in Paris alone and 800 further projects were launched in the provinces. Although never thoroughly examined, there have also been many manifestations of this type of struggle in Britain, for instance the Chartist Land Plan, which aimed to buy land in order to settle workers on it, or the attempts of Lancashire cotton workers to control some cotton firms through the early joint stock companies, especially in Oldham. It surfaces also in Owenism, with its stress on producer co-operatives, and in the Co-operative movement based mainly though not entirely on retail co-operation which developed after 1850 and its generally thought to have reached its peak in the inter-war years.[3]

In civil society more generally these associations were also important. Members of the Centre for Contemporary Cultural Studies argue that working-class attitudes to education vary between 'substitutionist' and 'statist' ones. 'Substitutional strategies concentrate on building an independent popular educational provision more or less in contestation with philanthropic or state agencies. The solution is to do it ourselves drawing on resources that already exist within communities, but improvising new more flexible forms.'[4] These could be seen in some Sunday schools, where parents had popular control over the running of the school, and in independent adult education which, in the form of the Workers' Educational Association or the Plebs' League, became significant at the turn of the century.

These same elements can be seen in Friendly Societies and mutual aid societies which provided a mutualist solution to health care problems, and in some building societies in which workers provided housing through joint finance. These societies differed in important respects from conventional insurance societies or contemporary building societies. Whereas the latter provided help on a strict actuarial basis, many of the former did not and in the case of financial shortfall relied on one-off collections from members who would be prepared to contribute. In addition, much of the running of the association was in the hands of lay officers and members rather than paid officials. The activities of the associations could not therefore rely on instrumental support of subscribers and they depended on more committed members in order to function. As a result members had effective control over the associations.[5]

Some of these mutualist associations were highly patriarchal, with male workers using them as a basis for closure against women. The French mutualists supported resolutions that women should not work outside the home.[6] In contrast other forms of mutualism, notably Owenism in Britain, had a strong commitment to the equality of the sexes. There is therefore nothing inherently patriarchal or non-patriarchal in mutualist struggles, but, as I shall argue below (see Section 3.2), which form these struggles take depends on other contingent factors.

It is important to distinguish between two forms of mutualist struggle which I shall call 'substitutionist' and 'strategic'. In the former attempts are made by workers to become directly independent of capitalist social relations through the provision of viable alternatives. Owenism is perhaps the clearest example of this: workers built their own community, established their own workshops, and lived almost entirely apart from wider society. On the other hand, workers engaged in strategic struggles recognise that capitalism cannot be entirely superseded and the main focus of strategic mutualist struggles is to emphasise the *potential* autonomy of labour, so that the security of workers within capitalist employment may be improved. The possibility of leaving the capitalist system is in this case used as an important lever for securing more rewards within it, but it does not directly counterpose itself to existing society.

I have mentioned only collective forms of mutualist struggle. Individualistic forms of substitutionist struggle are not really mutualist at all, but may in some cases rely on wider mutualist provision. Take for instance the concept of self-servicing which has become familiar to social scientists through recent research on the 'informal economy': individuals or households can choose to perform their own servicing functions in certain circumstances rather than to rely on the market.[7] Some writers see this as essentially household based, with individual households planning how to best organise their work strategies given the general social constraints which surround them. Successful self-servicing, however, frequently relies on general neighbourhood support, in terms of access to appropriate specialised skills and/or tools. Individualistic substitutionist struggles are often most successful where there is this collective back-up: an important example of this is the case of workers who become self-employed often relying on the support of their acquaintances to make their businesses viable.

Yeo argues that these mutualist struggles are essentially anti-state.[8] While this element is important in distinguishing them from statist struggles, nonetheless they are concerned with the state in some respects. Mutualist associations cannot but exist within a broader capitalist economy, and in this situation they are subject to economic constraints – the principal of which is shortage of capital. One vital element of mutualist struggles is an attempt to rely less on capital and more on the voluntary labour of members, or on the mutual support of consumers, yet this rarely provides a sufficient counterweight. The result is that many mutualist associations have been interested in developing state-based sources of credit or capital, or in using the state more generally to ease their financial burdens. Hence Proudhon's concern to establish state credit institutions,[9] and the Co-op's concern in early twentieth-century Britain to be made exempt from income tax. The state is seen to be important in providing an alternative source of capital to that available on the private market, and in certain cases there may be a recognition that this will entail special recognition by the state of the particular status of mutualist associations. It should be emphasised that there is little concern that the state itself should be directly redistributive; rather that as an agency it should provide the facilities for making credit available, though for this to be self-generating finance. From the mutualist point of view, therefore, the state is seen as having a positive role to play in the circulation of money and perhaps of commodities, but in nothing else.

The second form of struggle can loosely be called economistic, although I use that term with reservation because of its Leninist connotations. This form of struggle basically works within capitalism and attempts to improve working-class conditions by struggling with capitalist buyers of labour to undermine its commodity status.

In Britain the main instances of economistic struggles are linked to the growth of trade unions and collective bargaining, whereby the autonomy of capitalist employers to treat labour as a freely disposable commodity is challenged through the creation of organisational procedures to reduce employers' discretion. This may involve procedures for disciplining workers, for reducing the employers' autonomy to hire, promote and fire, or for paying wages not on the basis of 'what the market can bear' (as was advocated by many nineteenth-century unions with their support of sliding scales whereby wages were automatically adjusted to market conditions), but on the basis of the workers' needs. Not all trade unions are economistic in this sense, however, nor are all workplace-based struggles economistic. A considerable number of union-based struggles to increase wages on the basis of the market value of labour are not part of the practical politics being discussed here, though they frequently overlap with economistic struggles. Furthermore, some trade unions have been keen advocates of mutualism, whilst others have been concerned to develop state intervention in industry and employment. Finally, struggles within the workplace itself may relate to different forms of practical politics. Rather than see all these as based around attempts to secure 'work control', it is useful to distinguish craft control from work control. The former emphasises the autonomy of workers' skills from the employer, and can best be seen as a form of strategic mutualist struggle; work control is not concerned to defend monopolies of skill, being linked instead to a variety of factors, not all of which are part of practical politics, such as making work bearable.[10]

Economistic struggles can take either a collective or a sectionalist form. In a sense all struggles are sectionalist since no struggle has ever spanned all workers, and hence a demand from one union will always place it at a different level from other workers. Nonetheless there is an important difference between those struggles waged directly against other sections of the working class in order to reduce the free competition of labour on the labour market, and those waged against employers (which may still have sectionalist effects). The latter usually require greater measures of organisation whilst sectionalist ones may rely on informal struggles and pressures, exercised in a number of environments. One of the most important forms of sectionalist economistic struggle is patriarchal, since one way in which male workers can try to divorce their wage from the market value of labour is to demand a 'family wage' which is necessary to support wife and children. Patriarchal struggles are also directed against women's entry into, or at least equal participation in, the labour market, such as the well known opposition of printing trade unions to the employment of women.[11] Such struggles may take either a formal or an informal form. Hartmann and Barrett emphasise the struggle of men through trade unions and political campaigns to establish a family wage. Brenner and Ramas have recently argued that these struggles should not be overemphasised, bearing in mind the small numbers of unionised male workers in Victorian times. They rehearse the traditional argument that there was then a more harmonious division of labour between the sexes with women, being biologically suited for childcare, staying out of the labour market and allowing males to avoid female competitors.[12] Such biological determinism is problematic, however, if we bear in mind that the most advantangeous situation would surely have been for both men and women to earn full wages, and for childcare to be carried out collectively. It seems more helpful to focus on informal forms of struggle which may be viable even when work-based organisation is weak.

In the economistic type of politics the emphasis on increasing money wages and security within the labour market entails a lack of interest in providing services for unemployment, poverty and health on any other than a market basis. This characteristic of economistic struggle distinguishes it from both mutualist and statist struggles where the attempt to de-commodify labour power often involves making workers less reliant on market provision of services for their subsistence. Usually there is reliance on the provision by women of those services which can be provided through the household (e.g. childcare, cooking, cleaning), and on market or charitable provision of other services (certain forms of health care, housing etc.). Yet it is possible to find workers engaged in economistic struggles in the labour market who support mutualist or statist demands over the provision of services outside it.

For my purposes the relationship between these struggles and the state is especially important. Whilst there is no attempt to use the state directly as a tool to de-commodify labour it frequently appears in two main roles. Firstly, given that workers attempt to negotiate with employers to enhance their condition, there is an essential need to ensure the 'neutrality' of the state so that it does not pass legislation giving undue advantage to employers. This may involve securing immunities for trade unions. Economistic struggles are based on workers fighting employers 'freely' to secure gains, and if the state is held to prevent this then the working class will struggle to gain equality in the face of the law. In this respect these workers may support the liberal–democratic rather than the corporate state.[13]

In the second place, cases may arise when the capitalist enterprise becomes unviable economically and some forms of external support become necessary to sustain it. Economistic struggles attempt to divorce wages from market value, and any successful economistic struggle may lead to the unprofitability and lack of competitiveness of capitalist firms. Hence it is common for the state to be seen as having a role in *regulating* the capitalist labour market. The focus here remains on the need for secure employment by reducing the discretion of employers in the labour market, but this may now need state backing to help provide various services and functions without eroding the viability of the buyers of labour. This is the classic form of 'reformist' struggle, with the state itself not seen as having any wealth-creating (or distributing) role. In Britain the strongest instance of this is in state regulation of health insurance, first introduced in 1911 and existing in a modified form today. Contributions were provided mainly by the worker and the employer (and, as was widely recognised, these would be passed on to the consumer), and the state's main role was a regulatory one to ensure that all designated workers were covered and could not opt out. In this context the payment of health insurance benefit remains dependent on workers' participation in waged employment. The struggles behind the nationalisation of industry in Britain have often fitted this pattern of economistic regulationist struggle, since state ownership is primarily regarded as an agent of efficiency and does not directly intervene in the structure of the labour market.[14]

Finally to the third type of struggle, the statist. The key element here is that the state itself directly intervenes to reduce working-class insecurity and to de-commodify labour. The distribution of economic rewards of the capitalist system may be maintained, but struggles are concerned to de-commodify labour by establishing a social wage whereby various services are provided by the state, so making labour less dependent on the capitalist labour market. These are paid for, to a lesser or greater extent, through money raised from wealth holders. Some means of subsistence become 'guaranteed' by the state, and need not be paid for on the market. As the Labour party of Poplar put it, early in the twentieth century: 'Decent treatment for the poor outside the workplace and hang the rates'.[15]

In the first place, statist struggle may take on a welfarist form. Examples of this can be found in campaigns to expand state services, and because of the way the British state raises its revenues these often take on a local form as working-class forces struggle to increase provision by local authorities. The main finance for the expansion of the provision comes from local rates (property taxes), a redistributive tax which falls more heavily on the rich than on the poor, and from central government grants which are also derived from the wealthy (although this is less true now than it was in the inter-war years, before the working class began to pay income tax). Struggles over the local state rarely testify to any commitment to local self-government or autonomy but are in the British case one of the most effective means of conducting statist welfarist struggles. It is worth noting here that the famous conflicts in the early 1920s over the levels of spending on poor relief by some Labour-controlled local authorities did not result in these authorities asking for self-government in all matters, since one of their main demands was that the central state (and wealthier local authorities) should provide more financial resources.[16]

Secondly, statist struggles may attempt to reduce labour market insecurity by providing employment directly, or by providing financial support to those in the labour market who hence become less dependent on it. Here the labour market itself is being undermined. Important examples of this can be seen for instance in the policies of Labour councils in East London at the turn of this century in the provision of alternative employment to the existing casualised labour force through a works department and extensive public relief for the unemployed and under-employed.[17] It is not uncommon for economistic regulationist struggles to lead on to this form of statist struggle if capitalist waged employment proves unviable.

Whether these struggles are patriarchal or not depends on the service being provided. If the state intervenes in services which would otherwise be provided through the household by and/or for women they are generally non-patriarchal, since they tend here to relieve women of a burden of work for which they would otherwise be responsible. In those cases where state intervention is geared to non-household services, or to services used primarily by men, or to the labour market security of male workers, these struggles may, however, take on a patriarchal form.

The discussion above has been somewhat abstract, and I will now clarify the general issues and add some detail. I am not suggesting that these struggles in any simple way cause effects (of the type 'statist struggle *causes* the welfare state to come about'). The working class is not the only class to struggle, and any concrete historical interpretation of developments must examine all the contending forces. What I attempt to do here is to describe in greater clarity the range of issues with which working-class practical politics are concerned, in order to emphasise the under-determination of politics by interests. While many writers recognise this complexity there is a tendency to assume that there is a historical progression from mutualist to economis-tic and then to statist struggle, and that earlier struggles are superseded by later ones. Such an account is misleading, however, since it makes the error, discussed in Chapter 1, of reading off political forms from the strategies of political parties and organisations. To put it bluntly: in periods when national working-class political parties are weak or non-existent mutualist struggles at the local level are easily observed; but when Labour movements develop a national presence it is easy to assume that the national campaigns and policies in some way represent working-class aspirations, and so it is easier to overlook local mutualist struggles which may still be going on. Concentration on national politics tends to obscure a due recognition of those struggles not concerned with the state, or which are concerned with the state only obliquely.

At the local, everyday, level there remains a much greater diversity of struggle. It is indeed at the local level that these forms of politics are rooted, for reasons to be elaborated on in the next chapter. The relationships between these different types of struggle are extremely complex, and will be explored in detail in the rest of this book. There are important interdependencies between them. Thus, for instance, mutualist organisations help to organise workers collectively, and it is then possible for these collective organisations to struggle for state intervention. In a similar way successful statist provision (which may be in part caused by statist struggle) may facilitate forms of substitutionist provision (though, and this is more likely, such provision may be of an individualist type). Thus, for example, public provision of roads allows people to rely on their own forms of transport in cars.[18] Economistic struggles may lead on to statist ones (when capitalist enterprises become non-viable). There is considerable flux in the struggles adopted, and at any one point in time the working class in different localities may adopt different strategies.

One feature of my discussion is to take the emphasis away from wage struggles, which have attracted the most attention from historians. Indeed the various types of mobilisation discussed above may seem to be relatively unimportant historically: that is to say that people have not been especially enthusiastic to involve themselves in them. If this is true it would seem most difficult to argue that formal party politics gain support by taking action on these issues. In the rest of this chapter I shall draw out these neglected forms of struggle for certain services in the period 1900–40. I shall concentrate on a number of areas which reveal the points especially clearly: South Wales, Sheffield, East London, and the area to the west of London.

2.2   Health care, 1918–39

The tendency to examine changes in popular health care through 'Whig' spectacles, whereby mutualist forms of provision are seen as leading up to the creation of a free, universal and centralised health system in 1948, has led to an over-concentration on temporal change to the detriment of local shifts in popular struggles over health. It is usual to emphasise the reliance on mutual provision (primarily through Friendly Societies) until the National Health Insurance Act of 1911 was passed: this regulated health provision through the state to the benefit of groups in regular paid employment (the central principle of the Act being the provision of medical care through a state-administered system into which workers, employers and the state all contributed). The National Health legislation of the Labour government of 1945 can be seen as developing a fully statist form of provision with treatment based not on contributions of workers but on need. The recent revisionist 'anti-Whig' interpretation (particularly that of Green),[19] whereby the pre-1911 period of mutual provision is seen as the Golden Age, although salutary in some respects, does little to remedy the over-emphasis on temporal change without looking at local variations in forms of medical provision. There was anecdotal evidence of local variations in some forms of health care. In 1910 for instance a government report discussed the considerable variations in the use of 'unlicensed' providers of health care. Chemists were widely used for general consultation in South Wales and West Yorkshire, while for herbalists the climate was particularly congenial in Lancashire, West Yorkshire, Nottinghamshire and Derbyshire.[20] It is more important, however, to point out how these local variations can be interpreted by reference to the typology developed above.

Mutualist provision was not entirely ended by the 1911 National Health Insurance Act. Before this date much popular health care was based on Friendly Societies (or the Mutual Aid Societies in South Wales) which had grown out of work-based provision of medical facilities after 1900 as workers demanded direct control over these societies and most employers gave way. These sorts of society generally charged a fee of 2*d* or 3*d* a week and provided a range of medical services. They hired their own doctors and medical staff and the members' annual meeting would elect a general council to look after all weekly business. The 1911 Act, in providing for state administration of contributions from workers (and from employers and the state), appeared to undermine their autonomy, but in fact it allowed for their continuation as it placed the administration of the collection of fees and the provision of health care under approved societies, which could be trade unions, commercial insurance companies or mutual aid societies.[21] Mutualist provision was permitted (though hardly encouraged) and took two main forms: the old works-based Medical Aid societies, or the Friendly Society-based Medical Institutes (in which groups of Friendly Societies banded together in particular places to employ full-time medical officers). In the inter-war years these types of provision retreated to areas in which they had been strong in the pre-war period and they were not especially significant in terms of the national proportion of the population they covered (perhaps half a million) but they remained extremely important in those areas where they were strong.

The heartland of the Medical Aid Societies was South Wales. Although

Earwicker shows that there was a drop in the membership of some societies as a result of the 1911 Act,[22] others were actually set up to become approved societies. The Llwynypia Medical Society was formed in 1912 in order to formalise arrangements whereby employees of the Glamorgan Coal Company had previously paid 3*d* a week to ensure the services of three doctors. These associations spread outside the coal-mining valleys. The Neath and District Medical Aid Society was formed in 1914 when 'negotiations with the medical gentlemen of the district having failed, we, with much trepidation but with the greater courage, determined to establish a Medical service for insured persons and their dependents and other people not entitled to medical treatment under the Insurance Act'.[23]

These societies remained mutualist. They were run by an elected committee from which the medical profession was excluded, and they hired their own medical staff and in some cases ran their own hospitals. In 1938 a doctor was dismissed by the committee for disparaging the organisation of the Neath and District Medical Aid Society; up to 500 members (out of about 2,500) attended the annual meeting.[24] It was not uncommon for secretaries of societies to provide their own medical help, and special contributions to pay for certain forms of expenditure could still be requested. It would be more precise to term these 'strategic mutualist societies'. Such a large number of workers supported their own provision of health care because in order to obtain sickness benefit a certificate testifying to sickness had to be produced. Clearly this would be much easier in an association which they controlled than in one where the medical profession held full sway. Indeed the Welsh Board of Health made many complaints over this issue. In 1938 64 % of the cases referred to the Regional Medical Officer for full certification by the Neath Society were found to be not ill enough to have time off work. In this context it can be seen that the workers' control of the Society gave them leverage over absenteeism and claims for sickness benefit.[25]

These societies did not go into any obvious decline in the inter-war years. This was especially true of the best known society, the Tredegar Medical Aid Association, to which over 90 % of the local populace belonged in 1944. For other societies moderate growth was not unknown. Contributions to the Gawr Medical Aid Society rose from £4,640 in 1924 to £5,500 in 1947, and it diversified its supporters from the collieries to the Royal Ordnance Factory and employees of the Urban District Council. The Mid-Rhondda Society's contributions rose from £2,894 in 1931 to £4,817 in 1947. The Neath Association claimed that whilst only seventy members attended meetings in 1914 over 500 did in

1938. The societies were geared to the (male) wage earner and can therefore be considered patriarchal, though most did cater for the dependants of the wage earner in return for his contribution. Midwifery was usually provided free of charge, though the quality of the service remains uncertain. South Wales had a very low level of childbirth in hospital: in 1927 only 5 % of births were in hospitals compared with 15 % in England and Wales.[26]

The other mutualist bodies, the Medical Institutes discussed by Green, survived (with a very slight growth in numbers after 1918) predominantly in medium-sized free-standing towns. The largest was in Norwich (where one-seventh of the population were members) and there were other notable Institutes at Leicester, Luton and York.[27]

Outside these distinct areas, however, new demands for state health care were being made. Earwicker points to the development of local initiatives in health care in the inter-war years, although central government legislation did not permit total autonomy. He cites Sheffield as a city where the Labour movement struggled for state provision. Demands for municipal health facilities were evident before 1914, with the local Labour party pressing for public baths, a sanatorium, public control over food, and maternity and child welfare provision. In 1921 the party stated that 'the health and medical services, a vital matter to the whole nation, should be financed and controlled by the community through local and national administration'.[28] When the Labour party won control of the town in 1926 it introduced frequent checks on the quality of milk, built public abbatoirs and a fever hospital for tuberculosis cases and made various provisions for maternity and child welfare. The Sheffield case is an interesting example of how statist provision may be patriarchal in character. Despite superficial appearances, mentioned by Earwicker, the maternity and child welfare service remained very poor, a point emphasised by the Ministry of Health Inspector in 1932. He complained that there were inadequate facilities for ante-natal care, that health visitors did not follow up cases, and that the weighing room at the hospital was too small. The Town Council, however, refused to co-operate in improving matters. Most damning of all, there were only about seventy lying-in beds, whereas the Inspector felt 250 were needed, and he concluded his report by noting that 'the maternity services of the City are at present inadequate'. This apparent neglect was in stark contrast to the provision of facilities for tuberculosis sufferers. In this respect Sheffield displayed a number of novel features: it rehoused infected people to reduce the risk of infection, it had twenty-seven health visitors for tuberculosis, there were 208 beds for tuberculosis patients, and all children showing the slightest sign of the disease were treated immediately. One new hospital, the orthopaedic, was, according to the Inspector, 'of the highest class; the accommodation, general management and specialist treatment and facilities appeared exceptionally good'. It is interesting to note that in Sheffield, much more than elsewhere, tuberculosis was a predominantly male disease because of the risks faced by grinders in the cutlery industry. 1,144 men per million had the disease in Sheffield compared with 641 women (the average for all County Boroughs in England and Wales being 1,163 and 821). The treatment of venereal disease was also gender related: whilst the facilities for men were reasonable, the Inspector had no hesitation in saying 'the arrangements for the treatment of gonorrhoea in females were entirely unsatisfactory, both from the point of view of the facilities provided and possibly also of the quality of the treatment'. In particular women notified to the venereal diseases clinic by the maternity service during childbirth were not contacted.[29]

In the case of Sheffield, therefore, statist struggles to provide health care primarily for the male disease of tuberculosis did not necessarily carry over into other forms of provision. However, other areas which also developed strong forms of statist struggle were not patriarchal. The town of Nelson in North Lancashire, where there was exceptionally good provision for maternity and child welfare, or the London Borough of Poplar are examples.[30]

Whilst some localities saw the development of working-class struggles for statist provision of health care, other areas saw few attempts to interfere with provision by the market. In the context of the National Health Insurance Act market provision existed in cases where a commercial company was the main approved society, with hospital services being obtained primarily through insurance schemes whereby workers paid 2*d* a week to guarantee them care. Less research has been carried out on the development of this commercially-based provision than on other forms, but it does appear that in many of the rapidly growing industrial areas of southern England, particularly around West London, these held strong sway. One of the largest societies, the Pearl Assurance, noted in 1930 that West London had for many years been one of its biggest growth areas, and also detected strong support in Birmingham ('a great storehouse for Pearl Progress in the past') and Reading ('another centre which has always been looked upon as singularly productive').[31] It is however not possible to determine whether these advances were made at the expense of other societies or whether they testify to the general strength of these commercial societies. In Slough, the most dramatically expanding town in inter-war Britain, the local authority made relatively little provision for health care, and the local Labour movement did not attempt to develop the service;[32] much of the provision lay in the hands of voluntary bodies run by employers, doctors or other leading notables. In 1932 a Medical Club was set up in Slough under the aegis of the British Medical Association to provide medical services to non-insured people on commercial lines, with adults paying 3*d* a week and children 2*d*. By 1934 it had 1,000 members.[33] In 1938 the employers were instrumental in setting up an industrial health scheme, with clinics based in the workplace, which had the support of the local Labour movement. This scheme, however, allowed employers to record the length of sickness of particular workers and the extent of malingering: a far cry from the levels of autonomy present in South Wales. It does appear that when economistic struggles predominated, as they did to the west of London, mutualist campaigns over issues such as health care were weakened.

2.3   Housing provision

Mutualist provision of housing, as of health care, was extremely important in South Wales before World War I. Daunton indicates that in certain areas, such as Merthyr Tydfil, over 50 % of houses were built through building clubs. In such clubs each member would hold a share and would pay a monthly subscription until enough capital had been raised to commence building – at which point lots would be drawn to determine the order in which members would move into the houses – and the club would disband when all the members (rarely more than fifty) had been housed. In addition to this there was also a considerable amount of conventional 'self-building', with workers contracting a builder to build for them, though it is very difficult to estimate its extent.[34]

The economic recession and out-migration from Wales in the inter-war years considerably reduced the demand for new housing outside the main cities, and these schemes died away. The inter-war years saw the emergence of speculative building for sale (rather than rent), with finance generally being provided through permanent building societies, on strict actuarial principles. Though aimed primarily at the salaried employee, in some areas this form of housing provision was more widespread, for instance in the railway town of Swindon where 60 % of residents were owner-occupiers by 1930.[35] These market-oriented societies waged bitter campaigns against mortgages provided by the

mutualist societies well into the period between the wars. Friendly
Societies, although geared primarily to various forms of life insurance,
still provided mortgages, and were often prepared to grant 95 %
mortgages – in contrast with the permanent societies, which felt such
lending to be financially unsound and offered only 75 %. Some trade
unions also gave cheap mortgages to their members which, the building
societies argued, came out of the general fund.[36]

The main battleground for housing lay in the state provision of
housing which increased dramatically after 1919, especially as a result of
the slum clearance of the 1930s. It is important to resist the idea that all
working-class demands for state housing should be regarded as statist,
however.[37] Certain forms of public housing consisted simply of the
provision of houses to be let at an economic rent by the local authority,
given the lack of interest shown by private builders. In particular it
should be emphasised that because of the peculiar nature of the provision
of finance for public housing, whereby the central government gave
various subsidies to local government, a whole range of local interests
stood to gain from council house building since it increased the rateable
base of an area without the local authority bearing the full cost. In some
areas, therefore, Ratepayers' Associations were keen advocates of
council house building since they felt that the attractions of a larger
rateable base would not be detrimental to their overall concern – the
reduction of the rates. A leading example of this was in the rapidly
expanding town of Slough where the Ratepayers' Associations were the
leading forces behind the implementation of a wide-ranging council
house building programme in 1930, yet they insisted that such houses
should be available only at 'economic rents' (i.e. without subsidy from
the rates). Their interest in public housing was fuelled by their belief that
private tenants could often not pay their rates because of the high level of
private rents.[38] (An 'economic' rent would have been about half of that
charged in the private sector.)

In cases where public housing was conceived as filling the gaps left by
private building, working-class demands for state housing can be seen as
evidence only of *regulatory economistic* struggle. *Statist* campaigns
demanded extra elements: either the provision of council houses at a low
rent so that the tenants were effectively being subsidised by the state; or
the building of the houses through schemes of direct labour which
undermined the casual nature of the building labour market. It is
therefore the management of housing and the means of construction
which were the key political issues, not the mere fact of building.

If this is borne in mind some interesting points can be revealed. In some areas, most notably in South Wales, even though there were Labour councils there were few attempts to introduce rent rebate schemes or to implement low rents on council housing. The public housing stock was not seen as having any redistributive role. Government files show that no Welsh authorities contested the rent levels suggested by the Ministry of Housing and Local Government on stock built before 1926. In 1936 a survey of local authorities showed that only Milford Haven, Newport and Cardiff Rural District ran rent rebate schemes.[39] In this area the mutualist tendencies already described for health care were such that the state was not regarded as having a more positive role.

The situation was very different elsewhere: Labour councils used public housing as a direct means of reducing working-class insecurity. Dickens *et al.* show that this is true in Sheffield, where council houses were built by direct labour, and where the Council attempted to set low rents for public housing.[40] The same is true in Glasgow and parts of East London. Norwich is also a particularly clear example. The Authority built large numbers of good-quality houses, yet also attempted to set very low rents. In the pre-1923 houses it proposed to set rent levels at 6s compared with the Ministry's recommendation of 10s and it also introduced comprehensive rent rebate schemes in the 1930s. Local authorities devised a number of different systems of rent rebate for tenants who had been cleared from slums in the 1930s, ranging from Carlisle's policy of charging one-fifth of a household's income as rent to more common schemes whereby 3d or 4d in the shilling were deducted from the rent for every shilling by which household income fell below a specified minimum.[41]

It is notable that many of the areas which witnessed statist campaigns over health care saw similar struggles in housing. Economistic working-class struggles were more characteristic of those areas where the Labour movement pressed merely for 'economic' rents on council housing or was concerned to make the best of private provision. The expanding West London area, stretching out to Slough and along the Thames Valley, is an example of this. In Reading, for instance, the Labour party did not appear to be concerned with the issue of low rents as much as with the quality of the houses.[42]

In situations of chronic housing shortage private builders found it profitable to build speculatively for working-class owner-occupiers. Building societies in Slough were prepared to offer mortgages to anyone with a £25 deposit (on houses costing about £500) with repayments taking up to one-half of household income. Others forced to rely on private tenancies found themselves paying 25*s* a week for a house, when the average income was 50*s*.[43]

The situation became more serious after an economic downturn in 1930 when many mortgages could not meet repayments and nearly all building societies tightened their lending policies, usually asking that the monthly repayment should represent no more than one week's income. Yet the noteworthy point is that there were no concerted working-class campaigns for statist (or mutualist) housing provision. To pay the mortgage many households relied on individualist strategies of buying a house and then subletting a room at an exorbitant rent.[44] It was the Ratepayers' Associations, with only passive support from the Labour movement, which were responsible for the building of over 2,000 houses in Slough in the early 1930s.

The Ratepayers' Associations could however be defeated by concerted working-class pressure on economistic issues, which were clearly more central to these workers. In 1932 Langley Ratepayers' Association opposed the siting of a factory near a residential area. This led to a considerable and successful campaign to build it, with one speaker at a public meeting stating bluntly that 'he represented the tradesmen and the working classes and he could visualise what it would mean to the worker if factories were built in Langley'.[45] And on this occasion the factory was built. There were also successful efforts to get local labour employed (by private contractors) on council house building sites. Clearly the working class in Slough did have a voice, but it was not generally used in support of statist housing provision.

The implications of these struggles for gender relations are complex. In some places the provision of good housing was regarded by men as a means of reinforcing women's domestic position, yet in others women were to the fore in statist struggles (particularly in Glasgow).[46] The provision of housing was a less significant factor in structuring gender relations than was how the houses were lived in.

2.4   Conclusions: working-class practical politics as market strategies

In the inter-war years at least there were notable local differences in the types of politics pursued by the working class, and certain areas do appear to be dominated by particular forms: South Wales by mutualism, Sheffield and East London by statism and West London and Slough by economistic struggles. Such types of political strategy are not, however, easily revealed by concentrating on political organisation alone (although in the course of my presentation I have had to draw on evidence from the pronouncements and actions of such organisations). Particularly in terms of voting patterns, South Wales and Sheffield were both Labour strongholds, yet they pursued different types of politics. It is important to separate out formal political organisation from the 'practical political struggles' which, while present in the strategies of local Labour movements, may also be articulated outside them. These considerations strongly indicate that it is advisable to dispense with vague, all-encompassing notions used to describe the politics of an area. Terms such as 'radical', 'deferential', 'paternalist', 'Red islands' and 'Little Moscows'[47] conflate orthodox party politics, voting patterns and certain types of practical politics in unhelpful ways. This is not to argue that there are no relations between these spheres, but they need to be explored at a concrete rather than an abstract level, and this will be a major theme of the second part of this book.

I have not yet attempted to explain these variations in practical politics. What can account for these differences? The most immediate answer might be that they reflect the character of markets in the area. It might be assumed that if a service can be provided cheaply on the market then economistic struggle will be the natural form of practical politics. If it is not provided cheaply workers may have to provide it themselves if they have sufficient wages to do so, or if they earn low wages they may be forced to struggle for state support. So these types of struggle can be seen as rational responses to market opportunities. Such an account is in fact singularly unhelpful in explaining the differences I have outlined above, as I shall show with reference to housing. In this case it might be assumed that if cheap housing was not being provided for rent then workers would turn to the state (if poor) or build houses themselves if they had the income. Table 2.1 uses details from the 1906 Board of Trade inquiry into the cost of living to probe this issue. Now if the market interpretation is correct it is difficult to explain why people in Merthyr, where rents were amongst the lowest, should have been so concerned to develop owner-occupation. Furthermore it can readily be observed that Sheffield was the wealthiest town: its wages were only 10 % below London levels, yet its cost of living was much lower, and its engineering wages in particular were the highest in the country. One might suppose that this should lead to economistic politics, since Sheffield workers were in the best overall position to buy services on the market. And what are we to make of Reading, where wages were low and cost of living extremely high, yet where no demands were made for statist provision? These figures do not of course prove everything (in particular they do not allow for the quality of houses for rent though they do take into account

Table 2.1. *Local variation in wages, rents and prices, 1906*

Town	Wages (skilled)	Wages (unskilled)	Rent	Cost of living
London	100	100	100	100
Merthyr	83	83	50	88
Sheffield	90	88	55	83
Reading	84	85	58	92

Note: Wages: skilled = median of skilled engineering and building wages; unskilled = median of building and engineering wages. The cost-of-living index includes rent.
Source: Report of an Enquiry by the Board of Trade into the Cost of Living, BSP 1906, Vol. CVII.

the number of rooms), and they refer to a period before the onset of mass unemployment in the inter-war years. It would appear however that high real wages do not in themselves lead to economistic politics. In fact upon consideration it might be that low wages are more conducive to economistic struggles since there seems so much more to gain by trying to raise wages. The main feature of high wages is that it is possible for greater financial resources to be devoted to whatever type of struggle emerges.

We cannot rely on simple arguments about workers pursuing market-based interests. I argued in Chapter 1 that practical politics tend to be initiatory, which means that the problems of sustaining collective action, notably in binding together groups of workers whose labour is inherently individual, are especially apposite. For this reason, workers' struggles depend on the local context in which specific groups of working-class individuals find themselves. Different elements of the local social structure provide various capacities for the maintenance of particular forms of collective action. While it is wrong to tie the formal political alignments of a locality to the nature of local social relations (we should not overlook purely political factors) this should not obscure the point that there are very important connections between elements of local social relations and practical politics. It is by separating out different elements of the 'political' that firmer connections can be made between certain of its aspects and the social structure. I shall spell out the nature of these connections in the next chapter.

3

The local bases of practical politics

I have argued that practical working-class struggle can best be conceptualised as based around attempts to reduce insecurity through the de-commodification of labour. Which class one belongs to does not, however, entirely determine the type of struggle in which one engages. In order to explain which struggle ensues it is necessary to focus on how workers draw on resources and capacities to generate particular forms of struggle. These capacities in some way bond individuals together, so that they are less likely to consider actions from the point of view of their own immediate interests and more likely to act as a group. In this chapter I shall discuss the most significant types of these and indicate how they tend to facilitate collective action, and to lead to one or other of the types of struggle discussed above.

How are these capacities to be conceptualised? Lash and Urry have argued that people can draw on two main types of resource to sustain collective action. Firstly there are cultural resources, which refer to particular conceptions of justice and languages of opposition (in C. Tilly's words). Lash has argued that these considerations may explain differences in worker militancy between France and the USA.[1] Since I have already drawn attention to the problems of deriving particular political forms from abstract belief systems, however, this argument does not appear helpful for our purposes. In particular Lash emphasises only the national dimension, which is understandable since national languages and media are very important constituents of these cultural resources, yet this is less relevant to our task of analysing *local* variations in political strategies.[2] Lash and Urry's second type of resource is organisational: political parties, unions, general strikes and so forth. While these are clearly very important, it is necessary to explain how they can have more effect in some environments than others: in other words how they interact with other forms of social life.

Wright develops the concept of capacity to explain why in certain

39

contexts the working class appears to have been better able to act in its interests than in other cases. Wright defines class capacities as the 'social relations within a class which to a greater or lesser extent unite the agents of that class into a class formation'.[3] Like Lash and Urry he refers to organisational capacities, but more importantly he also refers to structural ones. These fall into two types: those based around the unification of workers in large mass-production factories (the 'collective worker'), and those based upon community ties. The reasons why these appear to facilitate working-class action are because they allow face-to-face contact to develop between working-class individuals thereby undermining individualist actions.[4]

The recognition of capacities based on face-to-face interaction is of profound importance for it is primarily at the local level that such interaction occurs for working-class people (this is not always so for members of other social classes).[5] It entails a clear recognition that it is at the level of the locality (defined as the physical area within which people travel to work, which is the area within which most face-to-face contacts occur),[6] rather than at the level of the nation or region, that working-class practical politics are generated. It is however essential to realise that the mere fact of face-to-face interaction guarantees nothing, since it may lead to antagonism as much as to solidarity between the various agents, as Olson's discussion of the free rider problem makes clear (see Section 1.3). Instead capacities can be said to develop when certain elements of the local social structure facilitate co-operative interaction. I shall elaborate below on how this takes place. The concept of capacity refers to the *potential* for collective action alone: people need not actually make any use of it. It is essential to avoid an overly deterministic account whereby the existence of particular capacities necessarily leads to particular forms of political mobilisation. Nonetheless, given the general need to reduce insecurity (by de-commodifying labour) in order to realise a great number of individual projects, it is highly likely that people's practical politics will be affected by these capacities – though formal politics need not be so strongly determined.

These capacities not only aid collective (rather than individual) action, but also in this very process tend to favour particular types of struggle from among those I discussed above. The different types of struggle are not simply the product of tactical and strategic thought, but are brought about primarily by elements of local social relations (which allow one form of struggle to take place rather than another). To elaborate this point I shall focus on three main features of local social relations: firstly on the way in which particular forms of skill harbour certain capacities for different types of practical politics; secondly on the way in which forms of gender solidarity based on labour-market and household structure affect political forms; and finally on the way in which local social structure is an important determinant of the possibility of the formation of class alliances, with subsequent effects on the nature of working-class politics.

3.1   *Skill structure and working-class politics*

One of the most influential approaches to historical studies of the working class and its political forms has been based around a 'labour aristocracy' theory. This is primarily a debate among labour historians seeking explanations for the weakness of labour politics in Britain in the years between 1850 and 1900. One of the main confusions generated by this debate is over the precise claims being made by various writers. The central point being emphasised was the existence of a distinct working-class elite, which earned higher wages and enjoyed more secure employment than the majority of workers; yet there was uncertainty about what this should imply. Some writers saw the existence of this elite as a satisfactory explanation for the lack of a revolutionary working-class politics in the years after 1850 and the 'incorporation' of the working class,[7] while others saw it merely as a reason why the elite itself was relatively conservative.[8]

The confusion engendered by this debate is testimony to the need to separate out different elements of the 'political', as I have done in earlier chapters. The critics of the labour aristocracy theory have successfully shown that as a theory of the failure of a revolution it is deeply flawed, since it does not explain why the politics of the labour aristocracy should infect the politics of the rest of the working class.[9] While this criticism is largely justified, it is important not to lose sight of the theory's explanation of how the 'labour aristocrats' themselves may be affected by specific features of their social context, regardless of their impact on the rest of the working class. In particular many of the historians of the labour aristocracy have indicated how the practical politics of these groups relate to their occupational position.

In this case, however, the exact nature of the labour aristocracy is rather imprecise. Generally, most writers emphasise the role of skill in the formation of this group, but skill is never fully defined. Hobsbawm tends to equate it with high wages, implying in a rather simplistic way that wage levels are a reflection of skill; Gray and Crossick tend to identify skill with the existence of trade unions, thereby suggesting that skilled workers are self-defined.[10] There is a certain vagueness as to whether skill is synonymous with craft skill, and whether all craft workers are skilled. The definition of skill is an important matter since we need to know what it is about skill that produces political effects.

There are in fact a number of different types of skill which may be significant. Hanagan, referring primarily to French workers, argues that artisans can be distinguished in three ways: firstly in the 'ability of the worker to participate in the production of the total product'; secondly in 'the presence of considerable skills which give the worker some sense of creative participation'; and finally in the 'existence of a skilled work hierarchy which is not directly controlled by the employer'.[11] The first element seems unhelpful in the British context where artisans often seem to have established themselves in industries with a considerable division of labour, such as shipbuilding, building, printing and much engineering. The second rather begs the question of how skills are to be defined. The final element is in my view of major importance, however, for it points to the significance of skills necessary for production which are not controlled by the employer (i.e. after recruitment) but are passed on by workers themselves.

In Britain skills were chiefly acquired through apprenticeship whereby young workers learnt a trade by copying a fully trained worker. The transmission of skills was entirely carried out between workers and the next generation of workers. In Victorian industry foremen played a significant part in that they could ensure that apprentices were passed round to a variety of workers in the shop, ensuring that the apprentice had an all-round training. Since foremen at this time were frequently closer to labour than to capital the overall point still holds.[12]

Some writers have argued this point in a particular way, noting that the definition of skill is dependent on the ability of workers' organisations to define a job as skilled. H.A. Turner is the most notable exponent of this view, especially in his much quoted observation: 'from the point of view of trade union development at least workers are thus "skilled" or "unskilled" according to whether entry to their occupation is deliberately restricted and not in the first place according to the nature of the occupation itself'.[13] This statement is rather ambiguous, however, in that it argues that while the social definition of skill is subject to negotiation between employers and workers (i.e. about whether a specific job should be graded as skilled or unskilled), it is less clear that the actual objective skill content of a particular set of work tasks is affected by such tensions. In fact it is this objective nature of the occupation which is of great importance. Here More's arguments are of considerable relevance.[14] He argues that craft skills did not depend on craft union organisation for their existence, and indeed the majority of apprenticed crafts could not have ranged behind them a strong enough union organisation to be able to sustain craft production processes if employers had been interested in changing them. In this he reasserts the arguments of the Webbs, who in the early 1890s argued that only 15,000 workers were strong enough to enforce effective restrictions on entry, while another 575,000 were members of unions able partly to restrict entry.[15] The fact that craft apprenticeship was so common is therefore evidence of the fact that many employers were happy to accept it.

In certain contexts, as Stinchcombe pointed out long ago, employers may have been keen to allow craft skills to remain regardless of the strength of unions. In situations of irregular work it was often beneficial for employers to subcontract to workers directly; craft apprenticeships in addition had the advantage of being relatively inexpensive for the employer, since no specialised training staff were needed, and the wages of apprentices were very low.[16]

More notes that not all workers were trained through apprenticeship. Some were trained by 'picking up', 'following up' and 'migration'. The key difference was that employers had much greater control over the skill acquisition process. Not all workers would be given the opportunity to learn new skills (a very different situation from apprenticeship, in which all entrants knew that if they served their time and were competent they would become full craftsmen), and some would normally stay at the lower levels. Skill acquisition was dependent on conformity and frequently took the form of patronage. This type of training was most common in forms of work which were regular and stood to gain nothing by maintaining craft apprenticeship; in Victorian times these included railways, the Post Office and iron and steel production.[17] These skills can best be referred to as 'factory skills'.

This distinction is important when analysing these workers' receptiveness to different types of practical politics. Craft workers are continually receptive to mutualist struggles, because they do not rely on employers for their skills and are consequently able to perform their skills either within or outside the capitalist enterprise. Their capacities to engage in mutualist struggles are directly linked to the character of their skill. This tendency is strengthened by other features of the craft workers' position. Generally they have little prospect of a career within capitalist firms. Once they have become fully qualified craft workers, usually at the age of twenty-one, they have relatively little chance of promotion except for becoming foremen – a possibility open only to a few. In the sample of fitters studied by Davis, only 15 % expected to become foremen in the future.[18] Craft workers are hence forced to rely on their own resources if they are to improve themselves.

It is indeed a general point of agreement within industrial sociology that craft workers have a distinctive outlook linked to these features. Wedderburn and Crompton noted that in the Seagrass chemical complex the tradesmen 'felt they could get a job anywhere', and that 'the tradesmen were expressing a sense of their own worth and independence which stemmed from their consciousness of their own skill'. Sabel also emphasises the distinctiveness of the craft worker, albeit in a rather romantic way. 'The portrait of the craftsman that emerges from all these studies', he observes, 'is that of a man proud of his fellowship with companions whose skills he respects; a man hesitant to forgo that fellowship for a place in the world whose values he mistrusts.'[19]

The key question of course is how these outlooks are related to various forms of practical politics. Labour aristocracy studies are useful in revealing some connections here. Since many historians of this theory tend to focus on the 'cultural' aspects of politics discussed in the first chapter they disagree about whether this belief in 'independence' should be linked to bourgeois ideas (as Gray and Foster argue) or to working-class ones (as Crossick suggests). Yet the practices they describe are much less ambiguous. Crossick, discussing the engineers, shipbuilders and builders of Kentish London noted the rejection by them of patronage organised from above. They organised their own education in the Greenwich Mutual Improvement Society and they had a strong co-operative movement. The weak hold of religion in the area could be explained by the artisan rejection of bourgeois-dominated churches.[20]

Gray attempts to show how the labour aristocracy of mid-Victorian Edinburgh (by which he primarily means the craft-skilled engineers, printers and miscellaneous artisans) was incorporated into a form of bourgeois hegemony, but nonetheless his analysis of its practices differs little from that of Crossick. Gray notes that 'certain voluntary organisations in the city had a distinctively artisan character combining high participation by skilled groups of the working class and considerable participation by business and white collar workers'.[21] By business Gray does not mean employers – though his occupational classification is confusing – but petit-bourgeois self-employed groups. Craft workers, along with the independent middle class, engaged in mutualist provision of various services. Gray notes that 37 % of the officers of the Mechanics' Library were skilled workers, 62 % of the members of the Bruntsfield Links Allied Golf Club, and 59 % of the prizewinners of the Working

Men's Flower Show. Most of the rest were petit-bourgeois and white-collar workers.[22]

Similar points can be made about health care in Edinburgh. The Friendly Societies had high levels of craft involvement. In one lodge of the Oddfellows' Friendly Society 71 % of members were artisans – more specifically, the artisan elite of engineers, masons, joiners, shoemakers and gold beaters. On the other hand the Savings Banks run by local businessmen had lower levels of artisan support (52 % of depositors 1865–9, and 37 % 1895–9), and these tended to be the more marginalised craft workers.[23]

A final example mentioned by Gray was the volunteer movement (a corps of volunteer troops recruited from the town). The artisans refused to mix with other occupational groups, and instead formed their own corps, composed entirely of artisans, with 712 members in 1868.

Gray also refers to the occupational sub-culture of each group and admits that these workers were hostile to patronage and employer-led initiatives: 'the more direct forms of patronage and control from above [were] typically resisted by artisans who insisted on the autonomy of their institutions'. In relation to religion Gray also notes that 'attachments to bodies of the patronage type are likely to have been limited, with considerable calculative element'.[24]

Gray's observations are in fact very similar to those of Crossick. The capacity of craft workers to engage in mutualist struggles is considerable but not inevitable. In some contexts purely individualist struggles may develop as these workers attempt to become self-employed. According to McKenzie's study, 25 % of craft workers in Rhode Island in the 1960s had worked for themselves at some earlier time, 10 % were currently doing so, and 25 % hoped to do so at some time in the future. Only a minority had always worked for capitalist employers and expected to go on doing so.[25]

These tendencies may not, however, lead to collective mutualist struggles. Historically the possibility of geographical mobility by these craft workers is also important. Their general all-round skills mean that their labour is in general demand, and it is possible for them to move to a location where such labour commands higher wages. Alfred Williams noted the astonishing extent of geographical mobility by craft workers at a Swindon railway factory in the early years of this century. One smith had been an apprentice at Cheltenham, became a journeyman at Gloucester, and then worked in Birmingham, Sheffield, Liverpool, Lancaster, Rotherham, Durham and 'several other manufacturing centres' before coming to Swindon.[26] The practice of 'tramping' remained common until the late Victorian period, and certain craft industries such as shipbuilding were noted for their migrant workers. Before World War I migration between the major yards on the Clyde, the Tyne, the Mersey and in Barrow-in-Furness was common.[27] This was ended only during World War I when the trade card scheme prevented workers from leaving their employment without consent, which provoked considerable unrest.

This discussion can be summarised as follows. Because of their command of general skills craft workers have the capacities to engage in mutualist struggles, which will tend to be *individualist* if a craft worker needs little capital to set up on his own account in his or her trade. The most powerful forms of *collective* mutualist action take place when the entire local labour market is dominated by craft processes. The South Wales coalfield is an excellent example of this, since recruitment processes were primarily based on a form of apprenticeship with trainees learning from hewers and becoming fully fledged hewers in their early twenties, a different system from that which prevailed in the North-East of England.[28] In particular the practical politics of South Wales mining can be characterised as strategic mutualist: given the extent of capital needed to work a mine, the prospects of direct worker production were slim, but nonetheless the potential autonomy of workers from capitalist social relations was a weapon frequently used to enhance conditions within the capitalist enterprise, as I have illustrated in Chapter 2 (Section 2.2); and their industrial struggles had strong syndicalist overtones, rejecting collective bargaining and state nationalisation, and advocating industrial democracy with the mines controlled by the workers themselves.[29]

One of the distinctive features of British industry is that craft workers have been able to re-establish themselves in many industries with a considerable division of labour, often performing specialised tasks such as tool fitting or maintenance. This is a rather different situation from that found on the European mainland where most craft workers are employed in small workshops with a relatively limited division of labour and where they have found it difficult to re-establish themselves in mass-production industries. As a result many British industries are characterised by having craft and other workers working alongside. In these industries craft workers are slightly less receptive to mutualist struggles since they frequently find it easier to use their relative indispensability to the employers to increase their wages, at the expense of the other workers in the plant. Economistic struggles frequently become more viable than mutualist ones, though strategic mutualist struggles, emphasising the potential autonomy of the craft worker, remain an important tool in forcing the employer to recognise his or her significance in the production process.[30]

The situation is more complex than this would imply, however. In cases where craft workers are responsible for the total product mutualist struggles are viable since it is not too difficult for them to establish production outside the capitalist enterprise. When the employer attempts to impose a more extensive division of labour, craft workers tend to respond with sectionalist struggles, imposing a variety of labour market controls against the introduction of new workers. Once it is clear, however, that these new workers have become permanently established the craft workers will frequently ally with them in a collective economistic struggle in order to improve the wages and conditions of the newcomers so that they compete less successfully with the craft workers. Williams shows how these tensions worked in the Manchester tailoring trade. The craft tailoring unions attempted to exclude Jewish 'slop' tailors until 1890 but, after this date, recognising their permanence, they encouraged their unionisation so that their wages and conditions would be improved, making them less competitive vis-à-vis the craft workers.[31] Similar processes are at work in relation to female labour, with male hostility to female labour changing to support for its unionisation in order that it does not compete with male labour once it is established.

The situation in industries with mixes of craft and other workers is therefore conducive to economistic forms of struggle, but these are not inevitable. The alliances needed between these working-class groups are more easily forged in some circumstances than others. Hanagan shows that in countries where there is universal suffrage these alliances are more likely to develop because considerable muscle can be exercised through the ballot box if both groups vote together. On the other hand where only skilled workers have the vote (as in nineteenth-century USA, where many ethnic-minority workers were excluded, or in late Victorian Britain) an alliance is less advantageous to them.[32]

Earlier in this chapter I discussed workers whose skills resulted from promotion on an internal labour market under employer direction: workers with 'factory skills'. These workers have historically displayed different patterns of practical politics from craft workers, engaging, in general, in profoundly economistic struggles. As More points out these 'factory skills' occupations have been less well studied than crafts and there is an unfortunate tendency for them to be conflated with crafts, particularly if they were well unionised. The best examples of such occupations are to be found in the railways, where workers started as engine cleaners, would then become firemen and finally engine drivers, with several intermediary stages. In iron and steel production there was a similar procedure: at the open hearth furnaces workers moved from being chargewheelers, to third, second and finally first melters and then possibly sample pressers or foremen.[33]

For these workers advancement and the gaining of greater measures of security were dependent on the internal labour market. Their careers tended to be linked to specific firms. The type of skill they exercised tended to be plant-specific, linked to a knowledge, for instance, of one furnace, and this accentuated their geographic immobility and their dependence on the viability of the capitalist enterprise.[34] The potential for mutualist struggle was thereby undermined since improvement rested upon the viability of the existing firm, and independent provision might have endangered prospects for promotion. Statist provision might also have undermined the existing enterprise. On the other hand their relative indispensability for specific employers gave these workers some potential for negotiating with them to reduce insecurity by, in many cases, lessening the employer's discretion over promotion – an economistic struggle – with frequent attempts to develop rules of seniority defining the order by which workers could be promoted.

Historical studies suggest that labour markets characterised by these sectors rarely give rise to mutualist or statist struggle. The town of Reading, for instance, was dominated by Huntley and Palmer's biscuit factory and other food-processing companies characterised by non-craft skills. More notes that biscuit-making was learnt by workers progressing from simple to more complex tasks; they were moved on to a variety of jobs by the employers. In Reading associational life was based around the 'vice-presidential' charity rather than the autonomous working-class institution examples of which, Yeo notes, could be seen only in the co-operative stores, the pubs and the corner shops. The mutualist Friendly Societies were upstaged by employer-sponsored societies. George Palmer, the leading employer, created a 'Help Myself Society' (!) which had 1,125 members by 1895.[35]

Another relevant case is that of Lancaster which was dominated by the linoleum industry, an industry again characterised by More as one where workers progressed if they were 'up to the mark'. Here again there was little evidence of campaigning for either state or mutual provision, the paternalist provision of many services being relatively unchallenged by the local Labour movement.[36] These two examples are however inconclusive, for Reading and Lancaster were characterised not only by these specific forms of skill, but also by having the local labour market dominated by large firms, and it might be this which is the crucial factor in explaining their specific patterns of working-class struggle. There is however considerable confusion about the precise nature of the 'size effect'. Traditional accounts of industrial sociology argued that increased plant size should lead to increased radicalism, or at least to alienation from employers. Recently however some writers have argued that the dominance of one firm in the local labour market will tend to lead to greater dependence and workers' 'deference'.[37] This in itself suggests that there is no clear size effect. Dennis Smith's account of the differences between the politics of Sheffield and Birmingham in the nineteenth century adds further weight to this argument. In both these towns small-scale industry predominated (until the 1860s in Sheffield when the steel works began to expand) based on cutlery in Sheffield and iron ware in Birmingham.[38] Smith points to the independence and mutualism of the artisan cutlers of Sheffield which lasted down to the 1870s in contrast to the weaker forms of independent action, greater wealth of charitable provision and more economistic struggles prevalent in Birmingham. Smith explains this in terms of class alliances, yet it might be worth considering also the different types of skill in the two towns. More points out that the 'Birmingham trades' were learnt through 'picking up and promotion', especially common in precious-metal working, brass casting and moulding, tin smithing and sheet-metal working,[39] whilst in Sheffield the cutlery industry was based upon extremely strong craft unions, which in the 1860s were at the centre of national attention because of their intimidation of workers who did not observe craft practices.

In local labour markets dominated by these types of industries struggles generally revolve around the securing of full unionisation (a situation achieved in Reading around the time of World War I, but never fully achieved in Lancaster). Economistic struggles in such local labour markets tend to be collective rather than sectionalist, since there are no permanent barriers between different grades of worker – these instead reflect stages in the lifecycle. Whereas the children of craft workers may often start as apprentices in their turn, the children of workers with factory skills must start at the bottom with everyone else. Most of the industrial unions in Britain which attempt to organise all workers in the industry regardless of grade have developed in sectors dominated by factory skills, with the railways (the National Union of Railwaymen), gas (the unionisation of which in the 1890s was very important in the wave of 'new unionism' based on non-craft workers), steel (the Iron and Steel Trades Confederation, though there are also some craft unions in steel), and the Post Office[40] being notable examples. The steel unions for instance were early supporters of nationalisation conceived as state regulation, rather than as part of a fully fledged statist strategy.[41] These types of industry became common in the inter-war years, and I have pointed to the economistic nature of struggles in this area in Chapter 2. These industries are also those most likely to see a shift to regulatory struggles, primarily through nationalisation, where the state intervenes to prop up high-waged work.

I have so far concentrated on particular forms of skilled worker, yet large numbers of unskilled, casualised workers also exist. These are often located in large urban labour markets and possess neither prized autonomous skills which allow them to engage in mutualist struggles, nor ties to particular firms which allow them to engage in economistic ones. Some writers have seen them as profoundly apathetic, as Stedman Jones argues, in the case of the casualised workers of Victorian East London.[42] It is for these workers that the problems of collective action raised by Olson and discussed in Chapter 2 are most relevant. Any worker who becomes militant can easily be dismissed and the tension between collective and individual action is at its greatest. Therefore sectionalist economistic struggles, aimed not directly against employers but against other workers, are especially frequent in cases such as these. These sectionalist conflicts often take an ethnic form, since ethnic identities will do most to help redefine collective interests and hence overcome the free rider problem. Several writers have pointed to the link between 'the politics of ethnic exclusionism' and casualised labour markets. In Liverpool, which was exceptional in that over half the working population was engaged in casualised dock-related work in the Victorian period, strong ethnic tensions between Protestants and Irish-Catholics were endemic. These persisted well into this century, with the Labour party finding it very difficult to win the support of both the Catholic and Protestant working class.[43]

In certain cases, however, statist struggles do develop in such areas, as is indicated by my references in Chapter 2 to the politics of East London, another casualised docking area. Where problems of collective action in such labour markets can be overcome, clear advantages accrue to workers who force the state to intervene to restructure the labour market in situations where they do not have the capacities to do so themselves and cannot rely on internal labour markets of capitalist enterprises.

Table 3.1 indicates the broad connections which can be made between forms of skill dominant in different places and the form of practical

Table 3.1. *Skill structures and practical politics*

Local occupational structure	Type of practical struggle	Examples
Craft/small scale	Mutualist	Sheffield cutlers pre-1870
Craft/large scale	Strategic/mutualist	South Wales 1900–40
Craft/other workers	Economistic (sectionalist/ collective)	Midlands 1900–40
Factory skills	Collective	Reading 1900–40
	Economistic	Lancaster
Casualised	Sectionalist or statist	Liverpool 1870–1960
		E. London 1914–40

politics likely to result. I have chosen places which are distinctive in having large numbers of the types of workers which I have singled out, and the situation is rarely as clear elsewhere. In many towns there are mixtures of different types of these workers, and each group may conduct its own practical politics; alternatively, connections between the different skill groups may lead to the dominance of one form of practical politics. These connections may be made through common forms of gender solidarity or other forms of local social relations, notably those arising from neighbourhood structure, and these will now be discussed.

3.2   Gender and practical politics

Gender solidarity can be deployed not only against the other gender but also to unite gender groups in pursuance of other practical struggles. It is an important means by which problems of collective action can be solved, as it leads to strong forms of collective, rather than individual, practical struggle – particular forms of action (such as supporting other workers in strikes) are defined as 'manly', for instance. Patriarchal relations are inextricably linked to gender solidarity: they are, according to Hartmann, 'a set of relations between men, which . . . establish or create interdependence and solidarity among men that enable them to dominate women'.[44]

As I argued in Chapter 1 gender relations affect the conditions under which both men and women sell their labour power and hence affect the types of struggle which may be pursued. Let me develop this point by considering three basic types of gender relations which may be present in different areas: firstly where gender divisions correspond to divisions between waged work and non-waged work so that very few women are in paid labour while the formal labour market is composed almost entirely of men; secondly where there is relatively little difference between the participation of men and women in either economy, formal or household; and finally where relatively large numbers of women are in paid employment but their work is strongly segregated (horizontally or vertically) from men's.[45]

Mining areas are classic examples of the first type of area, with very low levels of women's work outside the home, especially after the 1842 Coal Mines Act prevented women from working underground. In the Yorkshire mining village of 'Ashton' in 1935 there were only six insured working women to every hundred insured working men compared with a national average of twenty-five. Male solidarity was based on the workplace and on social life more generally. In the 1950s there were six working men's clubs with 6,884 members, and since there were only 4,824 adult men in the town nearly every man must have belonged to a club and some indeed to more than one. Women members were banned, being allowed in only at the weekends as guests. The clubs cemented male solidarity which was formed in a variety of contexts: 'The men conversing have often been life long acquaintances; having been at the same school and played together as children they now, as adults, work in the same place and spend their leisure time together in such places as the club.'[46] Women on the other hand had little institutional life of their own. Nonetheless they were not without some forms of their own solidarity based on home and neighbourhood.

These solidarities are an important element behind the strong collective politics of these areas; as a result, though, male concerns tend to take priority over female. In South Wales, where mutualism was dominant, most of this provision was geared to the male wage earner, as I showed in Chapter 2. In other mining areas economistic struggles were the norm, since male solidarity forged in the workplace could best be mobilised over immediate work-based issues. Campbell has illuminatingly contrasted the militancy of miners over wage and job issues with their long-standing apathy over basic social services, such as the provision of pit-head baths.[47] For male workers provision by the state or voluntary agencies of household services was not an issue since such services could as easily be provided by their wives. The women themselves were in a paradoxical situation, for although their restriction to domestic labour was symptomatic of their patriarchal subordination, nonetheless the status they could enjoy was linked to their competence as housewives. Their existing status in mining towns might have been undermined by official or charitable provision of services since this might remove the one area of social life where they held sway.

For this reason when women did become active in these areas it was generally over the same sorts of economistic and wage issues that the male workers were also concerned with. Female solidarity could be used to support economistic struggles which did not endanger their position in local social life. Smith and Francis's account of the South Wales mining area is an example of this. Women were involved in the wage issues which dominated political life in the inter-war years. When the miners held a massive 'monster campaign' against non-unionism in 1929 a great stress was put on involving women in order to encourage them to force their husbands into the union. 'Miners' wives especially invited to co-operate', ran the words of one poster. In the General Strike of 1926 women were also active in the protest. 'An edge was provided by the involvement in the disturbances of married women who inevitably felt the hardships most acutely.' [48]

There are some exceptions to this argument. Although women might not have wanted to politicise issues over welfare or services which might jeopardise their position, there were some forms of service which could not be provided entirely through the household, yet which were essential for women to carry out their domestic labour. Housing is the best example of this, and women could become politically active over housing (and to a lesser extent education) while still seeing themselves as housewives. Many areas with major campaigns over housing were those where there were few women in paid employment. Glasgow, which saw a major rent strike largely organised by women in 1915, was a notable example. In a similar way Barrow-in-Furness, a town with a large number of men in shipbuilding, developed a very strong women's politics based upon the need for good housing to meet the chronic shortage in the early years of the century.[49] In these forms of struggle statist demands did come to the fore, and they are examples of the way in which male economistic campaigns could co-exist with female statist ones.

The second type of area is an almost complete reverse of the first: here men and women are relatively unsegregated in paid employment. Historically these areas are few and far between and I discuss this case more to develop some analytical issues than because of their typicality. The weaving areas of North-East Lancashire can, however, be characterised in this way, for men and women would generally perform the same sort of work, cotton weaving, for generally the same wage. The 'weaving family' was quite common: husband, wife and children, possibly with other family members, would work together on neighbouring looms.[50] Although evidence is scanty, domestic labour seems to have been equitably arranged. Gittins, in an admittedly brief survey of families in Burnley, found that where both husband and wife were weavers family arrangements were remarkably egalitarian, with both partners sharing domestic labour.[51]

The result of these relations was that solidarity was not specifically based on gender. There were few separate spheres of men's and women's political activity; rather, joint action was the norm. Jane Mark-Lawson shows how in Nelson women's politics were based in the Independent Labour Party and Weavers' Unions rather than in the Women's Sections of the Labour party (as in Barrow). In Burnley women were active in the trade unions and the left-wing Social Democratic Federation at the turn of the century alongside men.[52] The relative strength of religious non-conformity could be explained by the greater role women played in it compared with Anglicanism or Catholicism. The cross-gender movement which emerged was strongly concerned with women's issues, notably women's suffrage.[53] This campaign was based on the Labour movement rather than being separate from it, and indicates a less differentiated politics than that found, for instance, in mining areas.

Mutualist struggles were common in North-East Lancashire for much of the later Victorian period, since the undermining of women's sole responsibility for household duties facilitated various forms of collective provision. These tended to lead to statist struggles after 1900. Since women were employed in the formal economy their position in society was not based on their domestic role and they were more likely to campaign to get state support in welfare issues. In a similar respect, because men did a certain amount of domestic labour, they were more likely to be concerned about these issues also. They would have been less concerned than men in other areas with maximising their money wage, but would have had an interest in increasing their leisure time by forcing state intervention in this sphere. This form of statist politics extended beyond welfarism, for North-East Lancashire was in the inter-war years the only textile area strongly to support nationalisation.

Finally, I shall discuss areas where women are in paid employment but in segregated forms of work, confined to a secondary labour market with low wages and casualised work. In Victorian Britain the most extreme place of this type was Dundee, a jute town, which was unique in 1901 in having more women in paid employment than men. Unlike North-East Lancashire, however, women did not work in similar occupations to men

Table 3.2 *Local gender relations and practical politics*

Local gender relations	Practical politics	Examples
Male-wage based	Economistic	Yorkshire mining areas 1900–40
Household-wage based	Statist or mutualist	N.E. Lancs. textile areas 1870–1940
Segregated employment	Economistic	Dundee 1900–20

but were concentrated in female-only activities, jute spinning and weaving. Men were normally employed in the skilled craft and supervisory jobs.

The numercial imbalance between the sexes created a situation in which many women lived independently of men, and did not live in family households. Walker notes that

Dundee was not a city where the male breadwinner acted as head of household and agent of moral and social training within the family . . . it was not uncommon for Dundee girls to desert the family home or for women who presumably despairing of the marriage market, or anxious to share housing costs, resolved by 'co-operation to keep house and home . . . over their head'.[54]

Female independence appears to have been an important element in Dundee. There was a vibrant female social life. In 1875, 1885, and 1891 more women were accused of offences of 'Assault, Breach of the Peace and Disorderly Conduct' than men. Between 1889 and 1898 40 % of the apprehensions for drunkenness were of women.[55] In these conditions Walker makes it clear that women did not display the apathy over trade unions which was alleged to be the case in other areas, and indeed after 1900 were generally much more ardent unionists than men. In these conditions female gender solidarity helped bring about strong collective mobilisation, geared however to economistic rather than statist politics, since as industrial workers sometimes living independently of men many of their concerns could be met through improvements in employment. The years up to the major strike of 1922 were characterised by growing industrial tension and periodic disputes yet, despite the appalling social conditions in the town, the Labour movement remained relatively unconcerned with statist concerns.[56]

These examples (summarised in Table 3.2) show that it is not possible to detect any general effect of gender on types of struggle. There is nothing pre-determined about women's struggles, with women being inherently more likely to struggle over state welfare, for instance. The types of struggles conducted by women and men were instead linked to the precise structure of local gender relations, manifested most notably in labour market and household relations. In this respect it is misleading to claim, as Lewis does, that it was general for women to be opposed to state intervention in the late Victorian period. While this was true in coal-mining areas, it was not true of Burnley or Nelson.[57] Where women were independent wage-earners they became involved in economistic strug-gles (or mutualist struggles if they worked in craft sectors, though this was rare), yet where they were wage-earners within a strong family framework they were active over statist forms of politics.

Analysis of local gender relations is not however easy: once again I have illustrated my arguments with extreme cases. In particular it is not possible to read off the character of local gender relations simply from the number of women in the labour market. This must be supplemented by analysis of the capacities of all workers for collective action in the labour market. This returns us to the discussion above: the critical element is the nature of the skills which workers possess and the extent to which they themselves transmit them to new generations of workers. Furthermore relations between men and women in household and neighbourhood are of vital importance, as we shall see in the case of Preston.

3.3   Local social relations and practical politics

A number of writers have argued that central to any understanding of collective working-class action is the way in which 'community' ties may provide the bonding necessary for sustained organisation. This argument developed out of a critique of mass society theory which argued that radical politics were linked to the decline of community and subsequent isolation of individuals from society's values. In particular several writers have related the decline of Labour voting in Britain to the decline of the community. Leaving aside the question of whether 'traditional working-class communities' have declined in the way suggested, it is quite revealing that few of the well-known studies of such communities actually say very much about politics.[58] Willmot and Young, for instance, state baldly that

every constituency in East London returns a Labour member of parliament and every council is controlled by the Labour Party . . . the people share their politics; they speak the same language with the same accents; they work with their hands; they have in short the same way of life.[59]

In their study of 'Ashton', Dennis, Henriques and Slaughter suggest that the Labour party's local hegemony was based on its 'serious concern over the miners' predicament, and a determination to seek out its cause'.[60]

These vague observations do not really carry much weight, however. Should a serious concern for the miners lead to statist or economistic politics? A greater theoretical development of these points has been made by Calhoun. Following Olson, Calhoun argues that it is difficult for classes to act collectively. Hence collective action depends on communal bonds which integrate individuals together. 'Small stable groupings . . . may act in concert fairly readily. Large groupings tend to be only latent collective actors.'[61] Calhoun therefore argues that communities are needed for collective action and that many instances of radical politics (he refers to English radicalism of the period 1780–1850) should be conceptualised as community rather than class action. Calhoun uses the concept of community extremely vaguely, however, to refer not only to the neighbourhood but also to workplace relations; indeed at times the concept seems to be synonymous with the 'social foundations on which to organise collective action'.[62] Calhoun's argument appears to be circular: communities (defined as any form of social bonding) create the social foundations for collective action. Calhoun argues that bonding develops where relations are dense, corporate and multiplex. By density he refers primarily to the scale of the community (the smaller the better); by corporateness he means the linking of individuals to groups and groups to each other; while multiplexity refers to the overlapping of different relationships. This only describes again the conditions needed for social bonding, and it is not clear what will actually help bring about these conditions. Thus in the 'traditional working-class community' physical density of population is as likely to lead to antagonism as to co-operation. There needs to be an extra element which leads to co-operative interaction. Calhoun recognises this implicitly since he notes that 'communities' need to be based on 'tradition', and were hence most common in old pre-industrial villages. There are considerable empirical problems here, however, for Calhoun argues that the outworking industrial villages of handloom weavers were the main supporters of traditional populist radicalism in early nineteenth-century Britain in reaction to the growth of industrial capitalism which threatened their way of life. These villages were not however traditional pre-capitalist creations, but had come about with exceptional rapidity in the previous century as a response to the expansion of domestic production by earlier capitalist development. They were not traditional feudal relics, but newly formed villages.[63] 'Communities' are hence not the property of any one historical period, but are constantly being formed and re-formed, regardless of whether there are traditions or not.

Since the concept of 'community' is so vague it will not be used here. Its value in pointing to social relationships not based on the labour market can best be considered more specifically by discussing neighbourhood capacities and the significance of local social relations in shaping these. One plausible line of argument might be that large cities are characterised by statist struggles to force the state to intervene in various services, given that the city is too complex for mutualist provision, and market provision may be unprofitable.[64] On the other hand small villages may be more likely to give rise to mutualist struggles in that the small scale of operations might make it easier for people to provide their own services. Such attempts to relate the type of struggle to urban form need to be treated with care, however: the inhabitants of small villages may be more reliant on state services than urban dwellers (say in transport or health provision).

The most fruitful way of conceptualising the relationship between local social relations and practical politics is in the way in which local, small-scale bonds may be created partly by internal neighbourhood elements, and partly by the way in which a particular local area can be unified in the face of external agents. It is the external relations of neighbourhoods, as well as their internal density, which help generate forms of capacity and collective action. The nature of local social relations hence helps to constitute the solidarities of the working class and also shapes the type of struggle. The main features affecting the internal solidarity of working-class neighbourhoods are connected with residential turnover and the type of sites within these neighbourhoods where regular interaction takes place.

The stability of neighbourhoods in British cities remains under-researched. Victorian cities were characterised by extremely high rates of residential mobility, hindering the formation of face-to-face neighbourhoods. Pooley found that only 18 % of Liverpool residents lived at the same address after ten years. Joyce's study of the Blackburn electorate, in which he compared the 1868 poll book with the 1871 census, showed that only 55 % of the electorate were living at the same address in both these years.[65]

In certain areas where there was more stability greater collective action was possible. Sometimes this was linked to the existence of working-class owner-occupiers, who were less likely to move than private tenants.[66] High levels of neighbourhood solidarity resulted.

Daunton contrasted the situation in Cardiff where only 7 % of houses were owner-occupied with that in some mining valleys of South Wales. Daunton emphasises that in Cardiff 'generally the working class did not provide institutions for itself',[67] but in the valleys, as I have noted, mutualist self-provision was rife. Similar contrasts can be drawn between the Lancashire towns of Blackburn and Burnley, the latter having high levels of owner occupation, and a strong culture of self-help.[68]

Having referred to the high levels of residential turnover before 1914, it is important to note that many tenants moved only a short distance. Pooley noted that 70 % of moves in Liverpool were of less than 2 km, a figure which rose to 80 % in the case of working-class residents.[69] It may be that institutions and voluntary associations were important as permanent bases of social life, even with people moving house quite frequently.

This raises one of the longest-running subjects of inquiry in sociology: the significance of voluntary associations in social life. Mass society theory saw the membership of these as antagonistic to community ties, being instrumental rather than affective, and Calhoun restates this view. In fact, it may well be the case that 'community' sentiment depends on these associations, especially in situations of residential turnover. Calhoun in fact ignores the existence of voluntary associations in many of the radical communities he examines, which Thompson argues had great significance for focusing loyalties. Joyce has noted how political clubs and churches set up by local notables for particular purposes can also become the centre of affective ties in a neighbourhood.[70] The central point is that the institutional sites through which regular interaction takes place may be of vital importance in facilitating collective action. In turn the type of institution is tied to social relations more generally in the neighbourhood.

This point can be developed by considering accounts emphasising the significance of institutions based on the petite bourgeoisie in working-class neighbourhoods. These, particularly the 'corner shop' and the pub, were very important in the later nineteenth century. Crossick and Haupt argue that in the nineteenth century such institutions helped bind the two classes together, with the result that 'the neighbourhood was a fundamental unit tying together working class and local petit bourgeois within a social milieu that was plebeian rather than proletarian'.[71] These sites were pivotal channels through which information about local residents flowed, and gave the petits bourgeois considerable power through their discretion to grant credit. The petit-bourgeois groups were of added importance since they frequently had more autonomy than other workers and could therefore lead agitation, and arrange their working times more easily (for instance to attend meetings). Hobsbawm and Scott have drawn attention to the role of shoemakers in radical agitation in the nineteenth century, largely because of their frequent contact with large numbers of the population, and their literacy.[72] In many areas shopkeepers were active leaders of local Labour movements.[73] In these situations neighbourhood capacities based on petit-bourgeois sites could help collective action to come about, but in an economistic form. The main interest of the petits bourgeois was in the existence of a wealthy clientele and so they tended to be concerned with economistic measures, or even wage bargaining, since mutual or state provision might well undermine their role as dispensers of services. Hence while there is ample evidence concerning the role of petit-bourgeois militants in many industrial disputes, such as the general strikes of 1842 and 1926, they were frequently hostile to other types of working-class struggle and tended to pull it in an economistic direction. This was especially true because of the extent to which petty property owners were affected by rate demands, which generally made them hostile to the expansion of the local state.[74]

This situation can be contrasted with those where contact in the neighbourhood is based on institutions controlled by the workers themselves. This became increasingly common in working-class areas in the twentieth century, as we shall see in Preston, with the development of the co-operative store, clothing clubs and working men's clubs. These were more conducive to mutualist struggles, since they provided a basis for mutual provision, but they could also be used to support statist demands.

It is also necessary to examine the relationships of working-class areas to outside groups, for these help to generate particular types of struggle. Recent accounts have emphasised the ambiguous effects of residential segregation on collective action. Some writers have argued that working-class militancy is likely to be fuelled if there is a local elite resident because of feelings of deprivation that this will engender, whilst others have emphasised that working-class militancy is most likely in one-class environments where no elite exercises its control.[75] In cases where working-class neighbourhood cohesion is weak, the existence of a local elite may well forestall working-class collective action: where strong, however, the existence of an elite can do little to prevent collective action but may influence the type of struggle engaged in.

A salient point here is the existence of a local bourgeoisie, who employ considerable numbers of the local working class. In those cases where capital appears immobile and rooted to one place there seems to be less concern to find alternatives to it (through employment based on the state or co-operation) and more concern to increase security by economistic means. Where capital is mobile, however, workers will be aware that economistic struggle may simply cause the disinvestment of a firm from a locality, or its closure following loss of profitability, and so there is a greater concern to find alternatives to capitalist employment. Trodd's illuminating comparison of political differences between the Lancashire cotton towns of Blackburn and Burnley in the later Victorian period shows that in Blackburn, where the local elite was composed of the principal industrialists, working-class politics were based on trade unions, and labour-market conflicts, yet in Burnley, where the elite was composed of landowners and there was a less distinct local industrial bourgeoisie, there was a greater concern with mutualist provision before 1890 and statist provision thereafter.[76] Places like Lancaster and Reading, which were discussed above as instances of areas with economistic struggles, also had large active employers in the Victorian period, and this accentuated their economistic tendencies. On the other hand the absence of a capitalist elite in many South Wales localities helped the tendency to mutualist provision.

Where a local elite is primarily composed of a 'service class' located in public sector professions, this may be an extra impulse towards statist struggles through some form of alliance between the elite and the working class, as both will benefit from demands for further state employment. Stedman Jones has argued that at a national level these alliances have been one of the major factors behind the fortunes of the Labour party in the twentieth century. Certainly London's East End, one of the early strongholds of the Labour party, saw a considerable degree of involvement by middle-class professionals based on the contacts engendered by the various church missions, and it was also an area characterised by statist working-class politics.[77]

3.4   *Concluding remarks: Preston in the analytical context*

Accounts of working-class politics tend to focus on the relationship between three elements: social structure, belief systems and political mobilisation. In the first three chapters of this book I have argued however that working-class politics need to be analysed with reference to *four* main elements. Working-class *interests* must be seen as the basis of political practice, but the type of politics they lead to are mediated by the role of *capacities*, anchored in the local social structure, which facilitate some types of political mobilisation rather than others. Working-class politics themselves can be divided into two elements: *practical politics*, based around those activities generated by the need to reduce insecurity; and *formal politics*, which are strongly affected by purely political factors, but which operate by campaigning on the issues current in practical politics. It is the relationship between practical and formal politics which needs much closer, concrete, examination, and this will be the task of the remainder of this book.

The arguments developed in the last two chapters all point to the conclusion that the relations of independent working-class political parties to their social base rely on the mediation of practical politics. The rest of the book will examine this process in Preston, North Lancashire, between 1880 and 1940, using the analytical schema developed above. My aim here is to provide more detailed indications of the relationships between locality and practical politics (and hence to confirm the ideas presented hitherto) yet also, and more importantly, to show how formal political parties draw upon these forms of practical politics to develop their own constituencies of support.

A main concern will be to argue that the rise of the Labour party owed little to intensified workplace conflict between capital and labour, or to a growing homogeneity of the working class; rather it was based to some extent on purely political developments, and to a greater extent on the changing character of skill-, gender- and neighbourhood-based capacities. Even in the apparent hey-day of class-based politics, the Labour party relied not on a simplistic class loyalty, but on the conditional allegiances of different working-class groups allied together.

The next two chapters discuss the changing character of working-class capacities in Preston, Chapter 4 concentrating on the labour market and workplace, and Chapter 5 on the neighbourhood. The principal aim here will be to argue that the capacities before 1900 were such as to favour economistic politics, but by the 1930s these had changed considerably, making possible the emergence of statist practical politics. Chapters 6 and 7 show how formal political parties acted on the terrain of practical politics, with the Conservative dominance of the town before 1900 being explicable in terms of that party's skilful articulation of an economistic politics, and the emergence of Labour after 1900 being due to the abdication of the Conservative party from this position. I also show in Chapter 7 how the Labour party was able to re-orient itself from sectionalist economistic to statist politics in the course of the 1920s, so bringing in a short-lived period of Labour hegemony. Throughout these chapters my aim will be to show how successful parties can operate only by articulating particular programmes which, in harnessing various capacities and practical struggles, gain popular support. In Chapter 8, Conclusions, I shall show how such an appreciation helps a proper analysis to be made of the history of the Labour party in Britain.

4

Labour market structure in Preston, 1880–1940

Preston has proved to be one of the most adaptable of northern England's towns. It was one of only four Lancashire towns to be a royal borough in medieval times, and its guild, originally held to grant the freedoms of the borough to new generations of citizens, is the only one surviving in Britain.[1] In the nineteenth century, however, Preston became a major industrial town based on the cotton trade, and was regarded as an archetype of the industrial town by writers as diverse as Charles Dickens, Lewis Mumford and Michael Anderson. Michael Anderson, in his study of the effects of industrialisation on family structure, chose to study Preston as it 'was in most relevant ways typical of the larger towns of the area'.[2] Yet Preston, unlike many other industrial towns, was able to diversify away from its reliance on an export-oriented staple industry, and in this century has been relatively successful in gaining new branches of industry (British Aerospace and British Nuclear Fuels Ltd became major employers after World War II), and in becoming a regional service centre (it houses the headquarters of Lancashire County Council), and Preston's unemployment rate remained somewhat below the national average during the recession of the 1980s.

This transition has not however been a smooth one. Indeed the later nineteenth century was a period of considerable economic recession in Preston, which was of great importance in affecting the capacities of different occupational groups in the town. Change to Preston's major employer, the cotton industry, was of the most far-reaching importance in this respect, and this will be discussed below.

4.1 Preston's economic decline, 1850–1900

Preston, like most Lancashire towns, was overwhelmingly a cotton town before 1914 (see Table 4.1). In 1891 28 % of all males over ten and 42 % of all women over ten worked in it. In 1911 45 % of the occupied population

Table 4.1. *Preston as a Lancashire cotton town, 1901*

Town	Occupied population in cotton (%)	Cotton workers who were males aged over 25 (%)
Burnley	53.2	23.7
Blackburn	52.1	21.3
Oldham	41.7	22.9
Preston	40.8	17.7
Bolton	35.4	19.4

Source: 1901 Census.

worked in the industry. Yet such stark figures fail to convey Preston's distinctive characteristics as a cotton town.

Although the cotton industry continued to dominate the regional economy of Lancashire until 1914, the major period of innovation and mechanisation was completed by 1850 with the introduction of the power loom and the self-acting mule, and thereafter expansion was based upon an increasingly intensified division of labour, with each factory specialising in a particular process (spinning, weaving or finishing) and a particular cloth geared to a specific market. Particularly in spinning, this allowed production runs of single types of yarn to be very long and weaving firms, which usually relied on a variety of yarns for their cloth, could then purchase the required amounts of each type from separate firms. Such tendencies resulted in the increased hegemony of the small firm: the larger firms found their more general products undermined by smaller specialised producers, and could adapt only if they were able to establish themselves as known brands.

These specialisms had very notable spatial manifestations. The two major cities housed relatively little of the production process: Liverpool imported raw cotton and exported finished goods, Manchester became primarily a financial centre and centre of the dyeing and finishing branches. The fairly capital-intensive spinning processes became concentrated in the immediate surrounds of Manchester, especially in Oldham and Bolton, whilst weaving, the last branch to be mechanised and remaining the most labour intensive, became focused in the initially un-unionised North Lancashire towns of Burnley and Blackburn. Each town had its own speciality and its own markets, Burnley for instance concentrating on cheap narrow cloth, while Blackburn relied on coarse goods for the Indian market.[3]

Preston was distinctive in that it had developed in the later eighteenth

Table 4.2. *Type and size of firms in Preston's cotton industry,*
1883–1911

	Spinning	Weaving	Mixed	Total	Number of workers	Average number of workers per firm
1883[a]	13	23	20	56	27,519	491.41
1891	9	21	17	47	28,681	610.23
1901	8	21	15	44	24,956	567.18
1911	11	23	15	49	28,171	574.92

[a]These figures are not strictly comparable with the others because they
include some firms with mills outside Preston. They are more accurate than
those derived from the Census.
Source: 1883: Hewitson, *A History of Preston*; 1891, 1901, 1911: Censuses.

and early nineteenth centuries a less fragmented industry geared
towards high-quality production, with the home market being of
considerable importance. Preston's most famous firm, Horrockses,
started by carrying out spinning in factories, and building special houses
for its handloom weavers. With the mechanisation of weaving Preston
became noted for its 'combined' firms, which both spun and wove their
cotton (and in the case of Horrockses finished the cloth, and marketed it
as well). As a result firms were much larger than was general in
Lancashire, and Horrocks, Crewdson and Co. was the largest cotton firm
in England, employing 3000 workers in the 1880s. There were also two
other major firms specialising in fine production: William Calvert and
Sons, who employed 2,218 workers in 1883 at its mills in Preston and
Walton-le-Dale 3 km away, and G.R. Dewhurst and Co. with 2,030
workers in 1883.[4] Table 4.2 shows that after 1850 these large combined
firms were declining in number, however: Preston's was in no sense a
dominated labour market (as nearby Lancaster's was) and firms had to
compete for labour.[5]

The spinning sectors of these combined firms came under steadily
heavier competition from the specialised spinning mills of South
Lancashire which could carry out long production runs of single kinds of
cotton yarn. Horrockses still prospered since its spinning mills were large
enough to allow a variety of counts of cotton to be spun, and its
extremely fine cotton was difficult to obtain on the yarn market: indeed
the company even built a new spinning mill in 1895, raising the total
workforce to nearly 4,000. The smaller combined firms found it cheaper
to purchase their yarn from the specialised mills than to produce their

Table 4.3. *Employment in Preston's cotton industry, 1901 (percentages)*

Age	All men	Occupied men	All women	Occupied women
10–15	15.88	45.79	30.77	86.62
15–25	23.27	23.93	61.64	71.96
25–45	21.10	21.43	34.82	69.15
45–65	16.13	17.30	13.46	44.58
65 +	7.23	12.23	2.44	32.88
Total	20.54	22.52	36.33	68.32

Source: 1901 Census.

Table 4.4. *Sexual division of labour in spinning and weaving in Lancashire, 1901 (percentages)*

	Cotton workers in spinning sector[a]	Weavers[b] who were male	Weavers who were males aged over 25
Oldham	67.12	7.39	5.95
Bolton	57.65	13.30	9.20
Preston	21.65	20.71	10.19
Blackburn	11.53	30.68	17.02
Burnley	8.07	39.16	21.90

[a]Defined as those working in card and blowing room processes, and spinning processes, in the 1901 Census, and discounting cotton workers in undefined occupations.
[b]A small number of 'weavers' were in fact ancillary workers in weaving sheds, and these were nearly all male.
Source: 1901 Census.

own (with the attendant needs to stop production frequently to change the counts being spun), and they increasingly disposed of their spinning sector. Between 1850 and 1890 Preston lost 500,000 spindles, about one-fifth of its 1890 total, and the town became increasingly dependent on weaving.

Cotton weaving continued to expand, as it did throughout North Lancashire. The number of looms rose from 27,148 in 1862 to 35,000 by 1888 and 60,000 by 1912.[6] The significance of the shift to weaving in Preston lay in the sexual division of labour which emerged (see Tables 4.1, 4.3 and 4.4). In the other weaving towns of Blackburn and Burnley there had not been a major spinning sector before 1850, nor indeed any

Table 4.5. *Spinning and weaving employment in Lancashire, 1901 (percentages)*

	Cotton workers in spinning sector	Weavers who were male	Weavers who were males aged over 25
Oldham	67.1	7.4	6.0
Bolton	57.7	13.3	9.2
Preston	21.7	20.7	10.2
Blackburn	11.5	30.7	17.0
Burnley	8.1	39.2	21.9

Source: 1901 Census.

other major employer of male labour, and so large numbers of men entered the weaving sector in these areas. In Preston, however, at the time when weaving was expanding in the middle of the century, spinning and other male employment remained buoyant and hence very few men entered the weaving sector which became overwhelmingly female.

Although Preston was still a cotton town, it had changed from being a town which combined spinning and weaving to one reliant on weaving. This posed specific problems for male workers. Initially they seemed content to allow women into the weaving sector, but the steady decline of the spinning sector in which they were concentrated left them exposed to unemployment. Not only was the spinning sector declining, but the men's position was further jeopardised by the introduction of ring spinning in place of mule spinning. This developed as a female occupation, primarily because men initially felt it would not compete with their mule spinning. This however was not the case and towards the end of the century several firms began to re-equip. An observer reported: 'One large firm employing 1,442 women told me that . . . being unwilling to turn the men out of employment they had offered to teach them ring spinning and then gave them the same wages as on the mules . . . the men tried it for a time and then gave it up.'[7] Table 4.5 shows that by 1901 the proportion of male weavers in Preston was well below that in Blackburn and Burnley even though the spinning sector, while larger than that in these two towns, was still relatively unimportant.

The situation was exacerbated by the problems under which Preston's engineering industry was labouring. In the early nineteenth century it was common for machine engineering firms to be located in the same towns as the firms for which they were producing, and in Preston a number of noted spinning-mule engineering companies developed, notably Murray, Sleddons, Grundy, and Ainscow and Tomlinson.[8] The mass-production engineering firms became increasingly important after 1840, however, particularly in the production of the new self-acting mules – Platt Brothers of Oldham became dominant in this field – and all the Preston firms closed. The industry was also hit by the failure of the North of England Carriage and Iron Co. This was an extensive railway engineering workshop opened in 1864, but it failed in 1879, as did an attempt to establish iron shipbuilding on the Ribble, and after this date Preston's engineering sector was in a poor state. By 1883 the town's leading historian could refer to 'the wane or stagnancy . . . of its modern commercial and industrial career'.[9]

The erosion of male employment in Preston brought about by trends in the localisation of the cotton industry and failures in the engineering industry left male workers in a potentially serious position. In 1888 the Secretary of the Preston Spinners' Union (Amalgamated Association of Operative Cotton Spinners and Twiners, Preston Branch), Thomas Banks, wrote grimly about Preston's economy:

Naturally we deplore our loss of mules and spindles in Preston because it deprived so many men and boys or young men of employment, many of whom had to seek work in other towns . . . down to the present day a continuous flow of our spinners wend their way to Bolton . . . In Preston there is nothing left for us but to regret the loss of our machine shops. Great hives of industry have all disappeared. Mules, mills and 500,000 spindles destroyed by fire. We are in a retrograding condition.[10]

Several indicators of the weak position of men in Preston's labour market can be found (see Table 4.6). There was a very high proportion of general labourers (twice as high as in Burnley). There were relatively high numbers of male craft workers, but these did not have secure jobs either, many relying on self-employment in the absence of other alternatives. Only the transport sector offered a reasonable level of security. Table 4.7 shows that Preston's wage rates for unskilled workers were lower than those in other comparable Lancashire towns, though the skilled workers (except in engineering) were able to maintain relatively good levels. There was a largely casualised male labour force, but an apparently stable and secure female one in the expanding weaving sector.

Table 4.6. *Some indicators of employment for men in Lancashire, 1891 (percentages)*

	Men aged over 10 in metals[a]	Men aged over 10 in general labour	Men in population (aged over 10)
Oldham	22.52	4.81	47.63
Bolton	17.36	5.33	46.85
Preston	7.65	7.52	44.78
Burnley	6.97[b]	3.40	47.21
Blackburn	6.58	4.08	45.91

[a]Census category 10, numbers 1 and 2, and category 21, numbers 8–12.
[b]There was also a significant coal-mining industry in Burnley. Combined with metal workers, 13.76 % were employed in this sector.
Source: 1891 Census.

Table 4.7. *Comparative wage rates in Lancashire, 1906*

	Building		Engineering		Printing	Furnishing
	Skilled	Unskilled	Skilled	Unskilled		
Burnley	85	87	85		81	84
Blackburn	87	86	89	79	83	81
Oldham	92	92	87		88	83
Bolton	90	94	89	79	85	90
Preston	86	84	82	75	83	85

Notes: London wages = 100.
Printing and furnishing were craft sectors with a high proportion of skilled workers.
Source: Enquiry by the Board of Trade into the Cost of Living, 1906.

4.2   The patriarchal character of Preston's labour market

Two questions present themselves from the discussion above. Why did men not attempt to remove women from weaving and go into it themselves? It is well known that the sex typing of a job at its foundation may be difficult to break in the future, but weaving was never an entirely female occupation, and it is likely that most men would have known it to be a respectable male occupation in other Lancashire towns. And secondly, what were the implications of women's apparent strength in the labour market for women's capacities to organise? These questions necessitate a greater consideration of the internal character of the weaving labour market.[11]

There is in fact a paradoxical conflict between women's apparent strength in the labour market and their position in the household. Most towns with high numbers of women in employment had distinctive demographic structures: generally late ages at marriage and a lower fertility rate. As Elizabeth Roberts's work makes clear, however, Preston was in this respect distinctive.[12] In 1891 women in Preston married at the average age of 25.9, only slightly above the national average. Between 1901 and 1905 women in Preston were more fertile than the national average, and the number of live births per thousand women was over 20 % above that of other textile towns. Roberts argues, furthermore, that values were generally more patriarchal than in the towns of Barrow and Lancaster where far fewer women worked. Thompson's oral history on Preston confirms this impression: 'Everyone to whom I spoke agreed that the status of the woman was little better than that of a servant.'[13] Despite the fact that young women would probably earn as much as young men, it was still customary for the boy to pay for the girl when they went out.

Roberts also argues that women in Preston did not particularly enjoy weaving and preferred to become domestic providers. It is therefore extremely unclear why men did not simply take the place of women in the weaving labour force especially since, as I have argued elsewhere, employers' control over the labour market was limited at this time.[14] In order to probe this paradox at greater length it is necessary to examine women's employment more closely, and particularly the extent to which women's work related to household structure.

Paid employment may have increased women's autonomy from men, and hence their capacities for action might have been enhanced in two ways. Firstly, as Walker notes in the case of Dundee, women may have been able to set up home independently of men. Secondly they may have become the chief wage earners in the household which, although not giving them independence from men, may have allowed them more leeway to challenge household decision-making structures. As Gittins puts it, 'the power relationship would depend primarily on the wife's working or not working'.[15] It was indeed widely believed that high numbers of working women were caused by the lack of remunerative male employ. The Interdepartmental Committee on Physical Deterioration of 1904 examined some towns, of which Preston was one, where

Table 4.8. *Female cotton workers in three areas of Preston not living with related male head of house, 1881 (percentages)*

	Marsh Lane	Canal	Fishwick	Total
Son breadwinner [a]	5.03	3.12	0.88	3.16
Family of female head	14.42	8.91	11.89	11.28
Female householder	7.72	7.13	7.49	7.23
Boarder/lodger	8.05	6.46	15.86	9.38
Total	35.22	25.55	36.42	31.05

[a]Indicates employed adult male son
Source: 1881 Census Enumerators' returns for Preston.

there were high numbers of women in paid work, to examine whether this had any adverse affects on the rearing of children. In discussing Preston the Report noted the relative absence of male employment, but commented that the family structure survived, with the husbands of women workers being 'labourers in intermittent employment' and that 'in all cases where the husband was in regular employment as weaver, platelayer, painter, bricklayer etc., the one wage was insufficient to keep the family in the standard of life they expect'. However, the evidence of the Report is hardly conclusive, since in the male occupations named by the Committee wages were quite high. Elizabeth Roberts, relying mainly on oral evidence (chiefly from a later period than the Victorian one) concurs, noting that 'many women had to work because of thier husbands' low wage rates'.[16]

In order to determine whether female employment led to greater independence more generally I examined three working-class areas of Preston by consulting the Census Enumerators' returns for the 1881 Census, the most recent available in such a form. Full details can be found in Appendix B. It is of particular importance to assess whether access to relatively secure and well paid work allowed women to set up home independently of men, as Walker argued in the case of Dundee. Of the 982 female cotton workers in my sample, 31 % lived independently of a related male head of house. This seems quite a large number but Table 4.8 shows that a sizeable minority of these were dependants of female householders rather than householders on their own account, who represented only about 7 %. In addition, female householders were not especially likely to work in the cotton industry (Table 4.9). Just over a third worked in cotton, despite the abundant market for female labour.

Table 4.9. *Female head of house in three areas of Preston working in cotton, 1881*

Marsh Lane	25 out of 76	32.89 %	
Canal	32 out of 85	37.64 %	37.18 %
Fishwick	17 out of 38	44.74 %	

Source: 1881 Census Enumerators' returns for Preston.

Table 4.10. *Employment and age of female boarders in three areas of Preston, 1881*

	Employment (%)				Median age
	Cotton	Domestic service	Other	None	
Marsh Lane	57.1	9.5	9.5	23.8	30
Canal	74.4	18.0	2.6	5.1	26
Fishwick	70.6	5.9	11.8	11.8	26
Total	66.7	10.9	8.5	14.0	28

Source: 1881 Census Enumerators' returns for Preston.

The single-parent family with the mother working in cotton was not the norm. It was rather more common for the mother to stay at home, performing domestic labour, while her teenage children worked, or occasionally she might work or take in boarders. This clearly was a strategy possible only at certain stages of the lifecycle, and might leave the mother in an insecure position when her children got older.

About 9 % of female workers were boarders or lodgers. Two-thirds of female lodgers worked in cotton, and there can be little doubt that the cotton industry did allow a number of women to live independently in this way (see Table 4.10). Most of these lodgers were more mature women; only sixteen of the eighty-five were in their teens, and the average age was nearer thirty. Not all these lodgers necessarily lodged with households headed by females, however. There was only one case of what might pass as a communal female household, with a number of female lodgers living together.

Hence it is possible to conclude that there was a greater measure of female independence in household arrangements than might have been found in other areas without much female paid employment, but this should not be exaggerated. The majority of women who were not in male-headed households still lived in some form of family unit, and only about 16 % of female cotton workers were totally independent, either as heads of house, or as lodgers.

More than two-thirds of women cotton workers did live with a related male head of household. To what extent was women's economic activity conditioned by the paucity of the male wage? Table 4.11 shows that over a quarter of female cotton workers lived in households where the male head was also a cotton worker, and there were notable differences in the employment of wives and daughters. Table 4.12 shows that employment of daughters did not vary much with the type of occupation performed by the father: virtually every young woman in Preston went into cotton at some time or other. It was very different for wives, as Table 4.13 shows. Whereas the co-residing wives of 59 % of male cotton workers worked in cotton, the wives of only 32 % of railway workers did so. Yet what is remarkable is that it was the less well paid labourers and workers who were least likely to have working wives.[17] The two groups of workers with large numbers of wives working in cotton were cotton workers and metal workers. This suggests that the reason for a wife's working was not economic necessity; it was caused by other factors. These details are so striking that it is worth discussing them in more detail.

Table 4.14 shows that cotton workers at the lower levels, mainly weavers and piecers, who would be on relatively low wages, were exceptionally likely to have a working wife: over two-thirds of them did so. Here this high participation might well be accounted for by the inadequacy of the male wage. Yet cotton workers at the higher levels and supervisory workers were not far behind, and were well above the average for all workers. For these workers (mainly spinners, overlookers, tapesizers and grinders) having a working wife could hardly have been an economic necessity. This group was of especial importance because it formed 60 % of the total. Finally, the wives of cotton craft workers, like those of the craft workers who worked outside the cotton industry, had low levels of participation.

It is more difficult to be precise about metal workers because of the greater range of occupations and smaller numbers recorded. Table 4.15 shows those trades with over six representatives. The labourers, who earned 60 % of a craftsman's wage, were less likely to have working wives than were other better paid iron workers.

It was therefore not the case that wives worked only because of the

Table 4.11. *Occupations of male heads of household related to female cotton workers in three areas of Preston, 1881*

	Marsh Lane		Canal		Fishwick		Total	
	Number	Percentage[a]	Number	Percentage[a]	Number	Percentage[a]	Number	Percentage[a]
Cotton	69	23.15	144	32.00	59	25.88	272	27.87
Metals	37	12.42	24	5.33	11	4.82	72	7.38
Railway	18	6.04	14	3.11	1	0.44	33	3.38
Craft	16	5.37	54	12.00	32	14.04	102	10.45
Labourer	29	9.73	45	10.00	20	8.77	94	9.63
Agriculture	3	1.01	14	3.11	3	1.32	20	2.05
Miscellaneous	10	3.36	15	3.33	8	3.51	33	3.38
Employer etc.	2	0.67	2	0.44	2	0.87	6	0.61
Petit bourgeois	9	3.02	23	5.11	9	3.95	41	4.20
In male-headed households	193	64.77	335	74.44	145	63.59	673	68.95

[a]The percentages relate to all female cotton workers in my sample.
Source: 1881 Census Enumerators' returns for Preston.

Table 4.12. *Occupations of male heads of household with wives and daughters working in cotton in three areas of Preston, 1881*

	Marsh Lane		Canal		Fishwick		Total	
	Wives	Daughters	Wives	Daughters	Wives	Daughters	Wives	Daughters
Cotton	18	51	80	64	34	25	132	140
Metals	18	19	13	11	6	5	37	35
Railway	6	12	6	8	1	—	13	20
Craft	7	9	22	32	8	24	37	65
Labourer	10	19	19	26	8	12	37	57
Agriculture	—	3	5	9	—	3	5	15
Miscellaneous	3	7	5	10	6	2	14	19
Employer etc.	—	2	—	2	—	2	—	6
Petit bourgeois	—	9	2	21	2	7	4	37
In male-headed households	62	121	152	183	65	80	279	394

Source: 1881 Census Enumerators' returns for Preston.

Table 4.13. *Occupations of men with co-residing wives working in cotton in three areas of Preston, 1881 (as a percentage of men in these occupations with co-residing wives)*

	Marsh Lane	Canal	Fishwick	Total
Cotton	36.73	61.07	64.15	58.92
Metal	52.94	46.43	66.67	52.86
Railway	26.08	35.29	100.00	31.71
Craft	29.16	39.62	24.24	33.64
Labourer	33.33	43.18	33.6	38.54
Agricultural	—	33.33	—	29.41
Miscellaneous	21.43	23.81	50.00	29.79
Employer etc.	—	—	—	—
Petit bourgeois	—	4.88	28.57	6.35
Total	31.79	42.99	44.52	39.69

Source: 1881 Census Enumerators' returns for Preston.

Table 4.14. *Percentage of male cotton workers with wives working in cotton in three areas of Preston, 1881, by grade of worker*

		Marsh Lane	Canal	Fishwick	Total
Lower cotton[a]	N=68	50.0	67.7	82.6	69.1
Upper cotton/ supervisory[b]	N=134	33.3	56.7	63.0	57.5
Cotton crafts[c]	N=23	18.2	67.7	33.3	39.1
All cotton	N=225	36.7	61.1	64.2	58.9

[a] Weavers, piecers, labourers, oilers, watchmen.
[b] Spinners, overlookers, tapesizers, grinders, drawers, managers.
[c] Mill joiners, engineers etc.
Source: 1881 Census Enumerators' returns for Preston.

Table 4.15. *Selected metal workers and their wives' employment in Preston, 1880–3*

Occupation	Wage level 1880	Number with wives in cotton	Number with wives not in cotton
Labourers[a]	17s 10d	4	4
Turners	27s 6d–33s 0d	4	4
Fitters	28s 6d–33s 0d	5	2
Moulders	29s 0d–36s 0d	5	5
Blacksmiths	31s 0d	5	1
Boilermakers	32s 0d–40s 0d[c]	4	4

[a]Seven labourers and one blacksmith's striker.
[b]Wage statistics for 1883.
Source: Wage level 1880: Returns Relating to Wages, BSP 5172, 1883; other columns: 1881 Census Enumerators' returns for Preston.

paucity of the male wage. About 60 % of female cotton workers who were married had husbands in cotton or metal production, and the majority of these were very well paid workers. This helps explain why women's participation in paid employment did not lead to independence: since so many of them had husbands on high incomes, they would have been very much the junior partners as wage earners. As Roberts also makes clear, it was where husbands were in skilled and supervisory jobs that they were most likely to be dominant in the household.[18] The fact that working wives were frequently related to elite male workers therefore explains why Preston differed in its demographic structure from many other textile towns.

There remains an equally puzzling feature however. Why should it have been these women who were most likely to work? Why did poorer households have lower proportions of working wives? In order to understand this it is necessary to probe the nature of the weaving labour market in more detail. Production was organised around a 'section' with about eighty looms, and about twenty to thirty weavers. Fully trained adult weavers would work on four looms, being assisted by children (or tenters) in the routine tasks, and there were a number of two-loom weavers intermediate between tenters and full weavers. The bulk of the actual training was done by the weaver (or mistress as she was known if a woman). This form of training was in many ways similar to the craft system I discussed in Chapter 3, despite the lack of formal apprenticeship.

And since skills were transferable workers could move between mills. The problem was how to retain a skilled, low paid labour force working in poor conditions. Such a problem was intense in Preston as weaving steadily expanded after 1850, yet the population began to stabilise at around 100,000. In this situation, as I have explained elsewhere, the employer relied on the overlooker to police the labour market.[19] The overlooker, always male, was in charge of a section, could hire, fire and promote workers within it, and was responsible for loom maintenance and the preparation of looms for weaving as well. These overlookers had originally been weavers, being promoted to their supervisory position from their late twenties, and they were generally from working-class backgrounds and environments. Weaving became an increasingly skilled job as production became more labour intensive, yet since there was no formal training or qualification given to women weavers the only means by which weavers were known as skilled was through personal knowledge or recommendation. This was where the detailed knowledge of the overlooker was so important – he was a key figure in the labour market.

This point answers many of the questions. The overlookers did not want to employ male labour: they knew that any pool of male weaving labour might be used to undermine them since employers could promote them to take their place if they were insubordinate. They would also have had more difficulty in applying patriarchal forms of labour control if there were large numbers of men under them, particularly older men. So the overlookers were concerned to find specifically female labour if they could.

When looking for weavers the overlookers relied on two main sources. They had firstly their own family labour to draw on: perhaps one-tenth of weavers were directly related to overlookers, if the overlookers in my sample from the 1881 Census are typical, and the overlookers themselves claimed that 1,000 members of their families were weavers. They could rely also on informal contacts, often with working-class men. These men, who were often cotton workers working in one of the elite cotton crafts or in spinning, had frequent chances to meet the overlookers to notify them about daughters and wives who were available for work. The labour market was hence largely organised by men and was structured in their interests. It was usual for women workers to be given time off work by the overlookers in the situation of pressing domestic need such as illness. Strict patriarchal control over the behaviour of women was also maintained, preventing the development of female camaraderie or solidarity.

Hence, despite the high levels of female activity in employment, women did not have strong capacities for political action. This is in contrast with the situation obtaining in Burnley discussed in Chapter 3. Men in Preston were polarised between two groups: a group working in secure, remunerative employment in cotton and metals, who were also likely to have working wives and daughters, so leading to a high overall family income, and a group in the large casual labouring sector who were far less likely to have women family members working in cotton and were much worse off, with few of the types of capacities for action described in Chapter 3. This also helps explain why, despite the decline of male employment in Preston, there were no concerted efforts by men to remove women from weaving: those men who had key control over the female labour market were doing extremely well and would gain nothing if existing labour arrangements were altered to accommodate other working-class men; indeed these would benefit at the expense of the overlookers' own female relatives. In any case there is no evidence that working-class men wanted to become weavers. It is to the key male workers with working wives, and their capacities for action, that we now turn.

4.3   *The overlookers: the emergence of craft autonomy*

The overlookers were key figures in the weaving labour market. In the mid-Victorian period they were in an ambivalent position between capital and labour. They generally needed to have an extensive set of working-class contacts in order to do their job well, yet they were also dependent on the patronage of their employers. Male weavers were usually in their late twenties when they were promoted by employers and this promotion was vital for them to get out of the low-paid weaving sector. As Joyce notes, this frequently meant that overlookers spent much time involving themselves in activities connected with church or chapel which might bring them to the attention of their employers.[20] The acquisition of adequate skills was dependent on the employer's patronage. I argued in Chapter 3 that these sorts of skills are closely identified with economistic struggles as workers who are tied to a career ladder seek to achieve the best rewards possible within it. The overlookers fitted this model perfectly. The Preston and District Association of Power Loom Overlookers, hereafter the Preston Overlookers' Union, was formed in 1875, and soon recruited the majority of the trade – about 90 % by 1890 – making them, along with the spinners, the most heavily unionised trade in Preston. The overlookers managed to secure extra payments for certain odd duties connected with their work, which gave them better wage rates. More significant than this, however, was their campaign to undermine the employers' hold over promotion. By 1900 they had enforced the rule that anyone wishing to become an overlooker needed to become first a recognised learner, at the cost of £2. This learner would be recognised only if the majority of overlookers at a shed voted to do so, thereby effectively ruling out any but the relatives and favourites of existing tacklers (overlookers).[21]

In themselves these rules would have been ineffective in preventing employers promoting whom they wanted to. In conjunction with these formal regulations, the overlookers attempted to prevent male weavers learning any but strictly necessary skills so that they would not be competent to become overlookers unless they had served time as recognised learners. This was especially applied against those weavers who had been in the habit of gaiting up their looms themselves (i.e. placing warp in their looms to weave). The union strictly enforced this policy and summoned any overlooker allowing weavers 'to run among his looms' to account for himself before the union committee.[22] Any informal help given by weavers to other weavers was ruthlessly eliminated. In 1912 a weaver, John Wilcock, complained about his sacking:

A weaver named Elizabeth McKeown was putting on a picking leather: on seeing that she had some difficulty with it I went and put it on for her. Just as I finished putting the leather on, her tackler came to see me and asked what I was doing there. I said I was putting her a leather on. He said, 'Well, you have no business here – get back to your alley' . . . I went back to my own alley. Then Dickinson the manager came to me and said, 'You had better put your coat on and go home.'[23]

The result of this was that employers had their hands tied when they came to choose new overlookers: formerly they had had a number of male weavers to choose from, but after 1890 they were forced to choose the 'recognised learner'. This new form of union control was combined with an insistence that no tackler should be discharged without union consent, and that all vacancies were to be filled by union nominees.

These controls were so effective that by 1910 the overlookers were effectively self-recruiting. Many observers felt that this increased their autonomy from management. One critic wrote:

It is not only unfair but it is absolutely unjust to both weavers and employers that a shed should be filled with tacklers who are all relatives to each other . . . The manager is face to face with a body of men who will on many occasions do their own, irrespective of instructions.[24]

Overlookers succeeded in becoming a craft, with self-regulation over entry, and gaining control over the processes of skill transmission. An economistic struggle in and over the labour market had helped create a situation where as craft workers they had the capacities for mutualist politics: a clear instance of the constant state of flux which practical politics undergo. The overlookers were not alone in developing craft barriers; a number of other cotton trades created craft barriers at this time. The tapesizers were a group of workers who prepared the yarn for weaving by covering it with 'size' which was a chemical compound used to soften the yarn and prevent it breaking. There were perhaps two or three tapers to a shed, and they formed a highly cohesive group which, like the overlookers, sought to erode the control of the employers over promotion. By 1900 they were able to select their own learners, and enforced a rule whereby tapers' labourers had to pay them for the honour of being taught. Drawers and beamers fought and won similar battles. These men arranged for threads for new patterns to be put into the looms. As in the case of the tapers this involved a work team of two on each machine – a drawer, or reacher, and a boy assistant. The boys relied on the experienced workers for the acquisition of their skills and it was relatively easy for controls over entry to be developed.[25]

These changes in work practices were of vital importance to the career prospects of male weavers. Before the controls were developed they expected to be promoted to one of the lucrative occupations by their late twenties, especially since there were so few male weavers in Preston. However, this became virtually impossible after 1900 unless a weaver was a relative or favourite of one of the elite workers. The growing tension was revealed in a tacklers' dispute at Brookfield Mill in the 1890s when the overlookers asked for the support of weavers but the male weavers refused it, stating that overlookers had discriminated against male weavers who might have been able to become overlookers. When the tacklers struck, the employers promoted male weavers, and these weavers – all union members – readily agreed to take the job on.[26] As a result the overlookers became more determined to prevent weavers from displacing them. This had a dramatic impact on the Weavers' Union (the Preston and District Power Loom Weavers', Winders' and Warpers' Association), formerly a weak union organising only about one-quarter of weavers, and primarily representing the interests of male weavers. The members initially tried to erect craft barriers around weaving,[27] but this gave way to an attempt to recruit all women members in order to ensure that they were paid full rates, and were not given preference in employment. The male weavers shifted from a position of not bothering to organise women to one of intense interest in their unionisation. The political ramifications of their strategy were of extreme importance, and will be discussed in Chapter 6.

Another occupational group to develop craft structures were workers in the cardroom, who prepared raw cotton for the spinners. These were a diverse set of occupations, but one point of interest was the emergence of the strippers and grinders as a skilled and well-paid group from the 1880s. Before this they had been general labourers, but they were able to take control of the new more efficient carding machines in the 1890s. The reasons for this have been seen by Turner, and more recently by Penn, as being due to the organisational power of the cardroom workers' unions to define this job as skilled.[28] In fact, however, at least in the case of the North Lancashire Card, Blowing Room and Ring Spinners' Association, this union was extremely weak throughout the critical years 1880–1900, being formed only in the late 1880s, and even at its peak in 1892 it organised only 40 % of its potential membership, a figure which fell to under 10 % by 1898 when the union collapsed. It was not the organisation which was the key of the power of the strippers and grinders, but rather their critical role in the labour market. A very high proportion of strippers and grinders had female relatives who worked in the other cardroom occupations. Of the thirteen grinders in my sample of 1881 who had co-residing wives, no less than nine were rovers (a particular type of female cotton worker). Thirty-seven of the eighty-five rovers in my sample were married, and of their husbands no less than twenty worked either in the cardroom or in spinning. In this situation employers were not able to staff the new carding machines with cheaper female labour because most of the available female labour had family connections with male workers able to prevent women from taking on these jobs. As a result of these patriarchal relations the grinders were able to develop apprenticeship regulations and could nominate their trainees.[29]

Let me take stock of a complex argument. There were critical shortages of skilled female labour in the late nineteenth century, which forced employers to rely on particular groups of male workers who had access to female labour either directly through family ties, or indirectly through friends and acquaintances. These male workers exacted a price, however, as their indispensability for the smooth running of the labour market allowed them to define their occupation as a craft one. The overlookers did this by de-skilling male weavers whom they did not want to see become overlookers; the grinders did this by preventing female workers taking on new jobs in the cardroom. All this had a profound impact on their practical politics. Whilst full-scale mutualism was hardly possible given the complexity of the cotton industry, the overlookers became much more active in asserting their independence outside the workplace than had hitherto been the case, and they became extremely active in the Co-op, and to some extent in 'self-building' schemes.[30] In particular six of the Co-op's twelve committee men were overlookers in 1902, including the secretary of the Overlookers' Union, William Eastham, and there was also a tapesizer on the committee. Joshua Wallwork, the secretary of the Tapesizers' Union, Preston Branch, was also a leading proponent of co-operation in this period.[31]

The overlookers and associated crafts witnessed the emergence of craft skills in Preston. The other key group with large numbers of working wives, the spinners, were somewhat different. These have been described as a classic example of the process whereby craft control can be continued into large-scale factory production.[32] This argument is based on the superficial similarity between the division of labour on hand mules and on mechanised self-acting mules introduced from the 1840s, which is taken to indicate that the spinners were able to impose the old working practices on new machinery through strength of bargaining power. In both cases there was a team of three (occasionally four): a spinner, a piecer and a creeler.[33] The spinner had effective control over the work group and earned 28s 11d weekly compared with the piecer's 13s 9d and the creeler's 7s 4d.[34]

The problem which has been inadequately addressed however is why the spinner should have been in such a privileged position. In fact it had nothing to do with craft control, for in cotton spinning skills were learnt through promotion: these were factory skills, in my terms. Two main arguments are used to point to the craft basis of the spinner's privileged position: firstly the survival of sub-contract, and secondly the importance of father–son recruitment.[35] In the sub-contract system wages were paid to the spinner who would then apportion some to the piecer and creeler. Linked to this sub-contract system was the fact that the spinner could choose whom to employ as piecer and creeler. The employer thus had no control over recruitment and the transmission of skills was very much in the worker's hands.

By the 1890s, for Preston at least, sub-contract was relatively unimportant. It remained formally, in that the employer still gave the wage packet to the mule spinner who would then pay the other workers. The mule spinner, however, had little discretion over how much to pay these workers: this was decided by the employers, sometimes in negotiation with the Preston Spinners' Union. In 1898, for instance, when a piecer left work without giving notice, the firm deducted three days' pay. On another occasion spinners were told to pay their piecers and creelers by the day rather than the hour, and spinners were often forced to pay learners as soon as they started work, rather than being allowed to wait until they reached a certain level of competence, as the spinners preferred. When new spinning mills opened the payment of piecers was the subject of negotiation between piecers, spinners and employers. In 1913 when the piecers at Cliff Mill complained of their wages, they were told by the spinners to see the firm.[36] Hence while the shell of the sub-contract system survived the underlying reality was that the wages of all the workers were decided by union–employer negotiation. Preston may be somewhat different from the other major spinning centres of Oldham and Bolton, but even so the wage lists which governed the industry in these areas stipulated the wages to be paid to piecers.[37]

The second element deemed to be important in preserving craft control was the way in which sub-contract allowed spinners to recruit piecers and creelers. This also overstates the importance of sub-contract. Creelers and piecers were employed by the mill and could be moved around the mill to work under different spinners. Spinners did not have to recruit their own piecers, though the firms would not object if they did, bearing in mind the problems of finding enough labour to work in the mule rooms. Spinners could not fire their piecers nor exercise arbitrary forms of discipline over them. Piecers were subject to the general authority of the mule overlooker, not the spinner. In 1914 the manager of Tulketh Mill fined some creelers 6*d* each for damaging a water tap. At Gregson Lane Mill a spinner was sacked when he caused his creeler to leave work by swearing at him, and another was sacked from Horrockses for telling the creelers to stay away from work on Boxing Day afternoon as the spinners intended to. There were numerous examples of creelers and piecers being sacked by mule overlookers.[38]

The promotion of creelers and piecers lay in the hands of the mule overlookers, not the spinners. Some historians have suggested that rules of seniority were a means of control over entry whereby the longest serving piecer was promoted to become a spinner when a vacancy occurred.[39] This, however, did not control entry, just the order of entry, and furthermore these seniority rules did not emerge through the spinners' demands. In the 1890s seniority rules were in fact quite rare. James Mawdsley, secretary of the National Spinners' Union, was emphatic about the freedom of employers to promote whomsoever they wanted: 'For one thing it has been a good job for the cotton trade perhaps, that employers have had a splendid selection and that they select giants . . . they get a good selection.'[40] As late as 1898 the Webbs wrote that 'it is a cardinal tenet of the Amalgamated Association of Operative Cotton Spinners that . . . it is for the employer, and the employer alone, to determine whom he will employ. When a pair of mules are vacant the mill owner may entrust them to whomsoever he pleases.'[41]

Struggles over seniority are important instances of economistic struggles, but in this case the spinners themselves were not great supporters of seniority rules because if it was established that all vacancies had to go to the longest serving piecer it would prevent unemployed spinners from taking these jobs, hence restricting horizontal mobility of spinners between mills. This is why the initiative in establishing these rules came from the piecers. In 1892 there were complaints from Hartford Mill that the overlookers did not promote piecers in order of seniority. In 1890 a deputation of piecers from Park Lane Mill complained of 'the actions of overlookers in putting piecers on sick spinning [i.e. putting them to work on the mules of spinners who were off work owing to sickness] that have only been employed at the mill a few months over the heads of piecers that have worked there 7 or 8 years'.[42]

There is also little evidence that piecers and creelers were the children of spinners. Only ten of the fathers, out of my sample (from the 1881 Census) of eighty-five creelers, piecers and spinners co-residing with their fathers, were themselves spinners. Anyone could become a creeler and then a piecer, and finally a spinner, dependent on promotion by the firm. The Spinners' Union exercised no meaningful labour market controls.

What then explains the spinners' privileged position? The most important point, as Lazonick has stressed, was the functional value which the older division of labour had for employers, even on the new technology of the self-acting mules.[43] The three workers looked after two pairs of spinning mules which would face one another, both about 40 yards long. There were grave problems in co-ordinating the labour process to ensure efficient production. The most routine task was piecing, the procedure whereby the ends of the cotton thread, if it broke, were joined by being twisted together between thumb and forefinger. The mule carriage would move out into the alley and draw out the cotton: this involved the complex adjustment of the quadrant nut by the spinner to ensure that the cotton thread was taken up correctly, but even when it was the cotton thread could still break – hence the need for piecing.[44] To ensure that all the threads were watched, one person (the spinner) had to

Table 4.16. *Industrial mill disputes in spinning, Preston, 1890–1914*

	Total number	Bad spinning disputes	Serious disputes	Strikes
1890–5	109			5
1896–1900	54	24	16	3
1901–5	42	21	13	2
1906–10	61	36	21	—
1911–14	46	30	17	1

Note: Serious disputes are those mentioned more than once.
Source: Spinners' Union, Committee meeting minute books.

instruct the others which part of the mules to watch over. The job of the
spinner was particularly important when excessive breakages occurred,
as it was he who would have to redeploy the workers. Secondly there was
the act of doffing, performed about four times daily: when the reels were
full of spun cotton the mule had to be stopped and the reels removed as
quickly as possible in order to minimise the loss of piece-rate earnings.
Doffing required the co-ordination of the stopping of the mules and the
quick clearing of the reels, and was usually directed by the spinner, since
overlookers might have been busy elsewhere at the time. Finally there
was cleaning. The work team was responsible for this, and it was usually
done by the creeler. He would be told to clean under the mule while it
was in motion, while the spinner gave him the word. This process again
needed someone to clean and someone else to watch the mule and inform
his colleague when it was safe to clean. At the same time, the other
worker had to carry on with routine piecing on the other mule.

Some writers have argued that mule spinning was a mechanised
industry in which the technology itself subordinated the workers.[45] It
seems, however, that in fact technology posed real problems of co-
ordination which were solved by continuing the earlier division of labour
with the spinner having a large measure of autonomy. The spinners, tied
to a particular mill by the promotion structure, were concerned to reduce
employers' discretion in the labour market, yet this did not take the form
of establishing craft control. And many of the spinners' campaigns for
higher wages alone were simply a form of wage bargaining. Their union
was probably the biggest in Victorian Britain to enforce 100 % membership, and they were the most dispute-prone workers in the country.[46]
Leaving aside the numerous industry-wide disputes, mainly over wages,
extensively chronicled elsewhere,[47] there were a number of mill-wide
disputes in Preston, as is shown by Table 4.16. The number of disputes

fell from a high point in the 1890s. About half were over bad spinning. These occurred when there was a large number of breakages in the yarn as it was being spun, which forced the spinner to stop the mule in order to mend them. This caused a drop in piece-rate earnings and spinners consequently demanded compensation. The main problem was that there was no objective way of telling whether the spinners were exaggerating the extent of breakages, and so employers often denied that they had occurred. In 1901 an agreement was reached between the union and employers: if complaints were made then an official test would be held, with representatives of both sides visiting the mill and examining how many breakages took place in a specified time. This made little impact, however, since the spinners claimed that on the day of the test the employers often improved conditions temporarily by slowing the speed of the mules or improving the cotton. In 1912 the Spinners' Union broke off the agreement but, after negotiations, a revised procedure was introduced.[48]

4.4   The undermining of the cotton crafts

The situation in Preston was that there were two groups of workers whose strategic position in the labour market gave them considerable importance: some of these, such as the overlookers, tapesizers and beamers, became increasingly receptive to mutualist struggles as they slowly gained control over the processes of skill transmission; others, such as spinners, were at the forefront of economistic struggles and by 1914 commanded very high wages. Both these groups came under attack in the inter-war period as the cotton industry went into long-term decline.

The initial problem facing the cotton employers was the loss of their traditional markets, particularly in the Far East. Those Preston firms especially dependent on these markets saw massive downturns, with the exports of Calvert's for instance falling from 716 million yards of cloth in 1913 to 186 million yards in 1928.[49] The cotton firms proved unable to cope with this crisis by improving productivity. The reason for this was that as firms lost their markets so they attempted to muscle in on those markets which remained, hence intensifying competition in an industry previously characterised by intense market specialisation. In this competitive environment large firms, which were in a better position to invest and hence improve productivity, were always likely to be up against smaller mills, often in rural areas, which could cut wages and intensify work, thereby negating the potential advantages of the larger firms. Therefore many of the larger firms decided to invest money in improving their marketing facilities, especially in the still expanding home market: this offered a better prospect of competing with smaller rivals, since the potential cheapness of production in these smaller firms would be offset by their reliance on distributors' charging a considerable price, and many of the expanding markets were geared to high-quality production where the larger firms retained dominance. John Hawkins and Son Ltd and Horrockses remained buoyant by buying a chain of retail stores in Britain.[50]

Hence most firms made no concerted attempt to raise productivity, and still attempted to survive by looking for market advantages. The employers' main concern with respect to their workers was, in Marxist terms, to increase absolute rather than relative surplus value, by cutting wages and intensifying work, and this led to a string of major industrial disputes in the late 1920s and early 1930s. Even here it was difficult for the employers to present a united front since, during an industrial stoppage, many firms recognised the advantages of conceding union demands and starting work to supply a market which the stopped firms had left high and dry.[51] As a result the labour force in the cotton industry was in no sense de-skilled at this time, and indeed the partially successful attempt by the employers to intensify work after the 'more looms' conflicts of the early 1930s actually placed a higher premium on finding skilled labour. Yet the cotton employers were determined to reduce wages wherever possible and this brought them into conflict with the elite groups discussed above, and in this battle they could draw upon state institutions to provide them with a lever to undermine the prior importance of the elite groups in recruiting skilled labour.

One of the most important, and most neglected, changes in early-twentieth-century Britain was in the nature of the labour market. In 1908 it was most unlikely that any worker seeking or being placed in a job would have any contact with a state agency. By the 1930s, however, the state's role in the labour market was of massive importance: Labour Exchanges helped fill vacancies; National Health Insurance forced workers to take particular types of work to qualify for benefit; and Employment Bureaux gave advice to youngsters. This intervention by the state had a profound effect on the capacities of particular groups of workers, but there was no general pattern: some workers were seriously undermined, whilst others used the state to develop new types of capacities for action.

The most significant changes were linked to the opening of Labour Exchanges (Preston's was opened in 1910) which for the first time allowed employers in search of labour to bypass the elite male workers whom they had used in the past to recruit workers. This became particularly important in the period of labour shortages during World War I, and in 1915 the employers became much more interested in using the Labour Exchange. In 1915 the Cotton Employers' Association (the North Lancashire Master Cotton Spinners' and Manufacturers' Association) arranged a scheme with the Labour exchange whereby reliable male labour could be tracked down by the Labour Exchange keeping records on all boys so that if they continually left work 'on flimsy pretences' this could be noted for future employers. All workers who left work had to register at the Labour Exchange, and in 1916 the Employers' Association formally asked all its members to notify all vacancies through the Labour Exchange, and asked the manager to help stop their female workforce leaving the cotton industry to go into the munitions industry where better wages could be earned. He duly agreed.[52]

The National Health Insurance Acts of 1911 and 1920 were also of key importance, since workers had to 'sign on' as unemployed at Labour Exchanges in order to qualify for unemployment benefit. By doing this, however, they were also liable to be placed in other forms of work.[53] In order to qualify for benefit the worker had to show that he or she was 'genuinely seeking work', which entailed the collection of signatures from works managers stating that there were no vacancies. The works managers were able to use this access to labour to bypass the overlookers and help cement their growing authority in the workplace.[54] Furthermore the Insurance legislation entailed all workers having a card which they took to their employer when they began work. This again undermined the overlooker's ability to hire and fire, since whenever he dismissed a weaver she or he had to go to the works office to collect her or his card, which allowed the manager to overrule the decision if he wanted. The informal arrangement whereby overlookers had given women time off to cope with domestic commitments became more difficult to continue since regular National Insurance contributions were essential, and these could be achieved only through regular attendance at work.

The development of Employment Bureaux was also of vital importance. Previously learner weavers had been taken on by tacklers on the personal recommendation of parents or friends. The Employment Bureaux however provided alternative means of getting work for youngsters which bypassed the tackler. A survey of 1934–6 in Burnley showed that only 34 % of boys got jobs through the recommendation of parents or friends, whilst Employment Bureaux found work for 24 %, and

38 % stated that they found work by applying directly at the factory. An even smaller proportion of girls, 28 %, found work through family and friends.[55]

These changes undermined the foundations on which the craft autonomy of the overlookers rested. No longer were employers forced to rely on the overlookers to secure a skilled weaving workforce. The onset of mass unemployment in the cotton industry had the effect also of making the supply of labour less of a problem for employers. After a short post-war boom, unemployment rose to 42 % among cotton workers by 1921, and fluctuated between 7 % and 20 % until 1930 when it increased dramatically once more to 41 %, gradually falling to 11 % by 1937.[56]

These changes allowed the employers to mount a campaign against the controls exercised by overlookers, so steadily undermining the capacities for collective action which were of considerable importance in the pre-war period. In 1915 the management of Victoria Mill decided to prevent its overlookers employing members of their own families, a decision which provoked a strike by overlookers and an eventual capitulation by the firm.[57] The application for a wage rise in 1917 led to more concerted action by employers, however. The Cotton Employers' Association formed a sub-committee to examine the overlookers' duties which reported in damning terms that

the overlookers generally considered themselves on the side of the operatives instead of being on the side of the employers, that they did not encourage young weavers or assist them in their difficulties, that they hurried off at the close of day without seeing the workers off the premises and that everything was in order for the following day and that they were too nice in their discrimination of duties.[58]

This led to a climate of considerable hostility and resulted in a series of conflicts in the early 1920s. In 1920 the manager of one Preston Mill attempted to sack an overlooker since 'they had [had] trouble with him for eighteen months; the complaints against him being laziness, sitting on his bench reading newspapers and smoking in the lavatory'.[59] The Employers' Association supported the firm and issued a statement to the effect that they would

reserve to themselves the right to engage or discharge loom overlookers employed by them . . . in future the employers intend to exercise that right without binding themselves to seek the consent of the loom overlookers' association.[60]

Although the union was never totally undermined a series of disputes forced it to recognise managerial authority, and by the later 1920s its controls over recruitment were greatly reduced. The tapers and beamers also were severely weakened.[61]

Whilst the capacities of the overlookers and of members of the cotton crafts were reduced, those of the weavers were improved by these changes, at least in the immediate post-war period. Before 1914 women's solidarity was undermined by the pivotal role of working-class men in the supervision and marketing of labour; the decline of these groups helped a stronger female shopfloor solidarity develop. Before 1914 the Weavers' Union was largely staffed by male weavers: the meeting of mill representatives which met monthly to report on mill disputes and trade matters had only men representatives, and there were no women members of the union committee. The almost complete ending of male weaving labour after World War I, when many men entered the army, changed this. It was during the inter-war period that many symbols of female shopfloor life reached their peak. The most famous of these were 'footings', a party held on the occasion of a weaver's marriage: all the weavers would pay 3*d* a week for ten weeks, then buy some beer and food, and would bribe the overlooker to stay while they celebrated.[62] Other interviewees who began weaving in this period testified to the new solidarity. One woman noted that the women weavers 'were all friendly and helping one another', whilst another noted that when she first started at the mill 'I thought it was wonderful. I enjoyed it and I was with the crowd. Whatever your job, you got the comradeship of your own type.' Another recorded that 'you made friends in the mill. There would be dances at some of the local schools and you would go on a Saturday.' Social evenings organised by workers were frequently reported in the local press. The militancy of weavers was apparent in the industry-wide disputes of the late 1920s and early 1930s, and also in a number of wildcat strikes, usually staged by women in support of other women.[63]

This shopfloor solidarity was at its height in the late 1920s when unemployment was relatively low and the market for weaving labour relatively tight. State legislation in the late 1920s, allied with the higher unemployment of the 1930s, tended to undermine this solidarity, however. Throughout the 1930s women weavers were liable to be sent to different mills during periods of unemployment. This situation was compounded by legislation: women who wanted to claim unemployment benefit had to be prepared to take on domestic service or other forms of work which women weavers had usually looked down upon. This had the effect of driving women out of the labour market altogether, as they were not prepared to do this sort of work, and hence undermined the solidarities which had developed in the preceding decade.

4.5   *The spinners: the weaknesses of a factory elite*

The spinners' factory skills gave them considerable capacities for economistic struggles in the period before World War I. This changed, however, following labour shortages in wartime. Many low-paid piecers were willing recruits to the army, and by 1916 it was reported that less than one spinner in ten had a full complement of assistants.[64] These labour shortages threatened to close down the spinning mules; the employers' response was to attempt to introduce female labour into the mule rooms. The opposition of the spinners to this proposal appears in some respects paradoxical since employers gave assurances that they would be used only as piecers, and that the alternative was unemployment for many spinners. The spinners' opposition to female labour is understandable when their lack of craft control is borne in mind. They knew full well that they could not stop piecers being promoted to spinners and therefore, as the *Cotton Factory Times* stated, 'the only sure way to prevent the employment of females as spinners is to prevent the employment of females as piecers'.[65] So whilst other crafts were prepared to tolerate the use of female labour during the war, the Preston spinners were not.

A great price was paid for this refusal, however. In order to keep the mules going newer working methods had to be agreed, undermining the traditional work team structure. The growth of 'joining' was particularly important here: instead of the usual work team of a spinner and two piecers, joining involved having two joiner minders, and a piecer if available. Although the Spinners' Union initially refused to countenance this method, since, it was claimed, neither of the two joiners could earn a full 'man's wage', during the war the union was forced to accept these arrangements as a means of countering the proposals for female labour, since they meant only two workers were required per mule rather than three. This agreement was not reversed after the war. In 1893 there were thirty-four joiners out of about 850 spinners, but by 1935 there were 130 out of 508, over a quarter.[66] This system intensified to a further degree the internal labour market characteristic of spinning. Few mills were composed entirely of joiners, but in each mill there would be a certain number of mules staffed in this way. The promotion structure was such that a boy would start as a creeler, become a piecer on an old set of mules, then become a junior joiner minder, then a senior joiner and finally, if he was lucky, a full spinner. These joiner spinners were more easily supervised by overlookers.

The procedure for cleaning was also changed. Before 1914 members of the work team had done it themselves, and since it involved loss of earnings because of the need to stop the mule, they successfully campaigned to get extra money to compensate. As with bad spinning this 'cleaning time' allowance provoked considerable conflict since employers claimed that spinners were doing the cleaning in less time than they were being paid for. In 1919 Cliff Mill began to use cleaning gangs, a group of workers who specialised in cleaning all the mules in a mill. The union opposed this system (although the spinners at Cliff Mill welcomed the change) and in 1920 it was ended, but it began to reappear in several Preston mills in the late 1920s.[67] Specialist tubers also began to appear: these would work on perhaps three pairs of mules and be responsible for all the doffing needed.

These developments intensified the internal labour market. The cleaning and tubing gangs were composed of promoted piecers, waiting to become spinners. The dependence on management for promotion was hence increased but, more to the point for understanding the capacities of spinners for collective action, their previous role as co-ordinators of various tasks was lost with the emergence of these specialist workers. The Unemployment and National Health Insurance Cards of the piecers were also held by management and, for the first time in 1932, a wage agreement meant that piecers were given an extra 2s paid by management, over and above the wages paid by the spinner, and a further 2s were added in 1936. And, finally, the power of spinners to define spinning as bad was severely curtailed by the general introduction of counters on spinning mules which counted the number of times the threads broke.

These changes weakened the capacities of the spinners to pursue economistic campaigns, since their indispensability to the employers arising from their co-ordinating duties was severely eroded. As a result they could easily be dismissed. The Spinners' Union recognised this and set about attempting to organise the piecers in earnest. Before the war the spinners had been relatively unconcerned about whether the piecers became unionised, and if they wanted to join the union they had to pay their own subscription. After 1918, however, all spinners were told to subtract the piecers' union dues from their wages, and the piecers were encouraged to hold their own general meetings. Attendance hardly ever reached double figures, however.[68] By the middle of the 1920s it was apparent that the piecers had not been won over.

The capacities of spinners for collective action declined, just as the state of the cotton industry worsened. They could easily be dismissed and there were plenty of piecers ready to take their place. Their capacities for economistic struggles were also greatly reduced and there was a dramatic decline in mill disputes – between 1934 and 1938 there was only one.[69] Whereas before 1914 the spinners could use their autonomy at the point of production to gain compensation for what they deemed bad spinning this was no longer the case in the 1930s; indeed the counters could identify any spinners with a high proportion of breakages, allowing management to blame spinners for bad spinning. In one case the management told spinners that 'they must report any mules making faulty yarn, otherwise it may lead to instant dismissal'.[70]

4.6   *Engineering, craft and service work*

I have concentrated almost exclusively on cotton workers hitherto which, although justified for the period before 1914, overlooks the fact that by the inter-war years the majority of the workforce were otherwise employed, as Appendix A shows. Let me redress the balance in the rest of the chapter by examining how different occupational groups fared after the problems of the 1880s. In the 1890s the only secure forms of male employment were in transport, and otherwise the craft sector pre-dominated. Some craft groups were strong enough to pursue spasmodic mutualist struggles, notably the bakers who, in 1892, responded to the employers' intransigence over the issue of abolishing nightwork by establishing a co-operative bakery, which however lasted only a few years. Generally the overstocked labour market served to weaken these sectors.

Things began to change in the late 1880s, owing to three main developments. Firstly Preston docks were opened in 1892, providing about 500 dockers' jobs by 1911 and helping to consolidate Preston's key position in the transport sector, especially with the expansion of railway facilities to cater for the extra trade. (The number of railway workers rose from 754 in 1891 to 1,792 in 1901.) By 1908 1,700 vessels a year used the docks and Preston became a centre of the wood pulp trade, second only to London, importing 18 % of the British total by 1913.[71] The docks provided work for a large section of the casual workforce: the dockers were casual labourers, but they formed a distinctive occupational community in West Preston near the docks, and became a considerable force in the local trade union movement.

Secondly, in 1897, the Kilmarnock firm of Dick, Kerr and Co. moved into Preston, taking over the old Carriage Works and re-equipping them to produce electric trams and electricity generating equipment, employing several thousand by 1914. This development was of considerable moment for Preston's development, for it established the town as a centre for new types of engineering, and in 1907 Atkinson Vehicles Ltd also built a factory. The failure of Preston as a textile engineering town in the late nineteenth century left some residues which encouraged the growth of new types of engineering whilst those towns, notably Oldham, which had become dominant in textile engineering were passed by. In the early twentieth century wage rates for engineering labourers in Preston, at about 17s a week, were amongst the lowest in Britain. Hunt argues that before 1914 regions of cheap labour did not attract capital because productivity was higher in the regions where wages were higher.[72] Preston however was in the fortunate position of having a pool of cheap labour, existing engineering premises, and some skilled craft workers. These new firms were able to start production in a town where the craft control of engineers had been weakened by recession; indeed the Amalgamated Society of Engineers was weak until 1914, while the Workers' Union, which specialised in recruiting semi-skilled workers, became extremely strong.[73]

This situation changed during World War I, however, when Preston's modern works became a major munitions centre. In Preston, despite its failure to develop a strong craft engineering tradition, the craft unions were able to re-establish themselves, probably as the skilled tool fitters and maintenance workers needed for production. The period immediately after the war was one of intense sectional conflict between the formerly strong general unions and the revived craft ones. In 1919 the craft foundry unions went on strike for wage rises, but the semi-skilled workers organised by the Workers' Union refused to come out, and it was alleged that its members performed work which had previously been the prerogative of the craft workers. Eventually these accusations were dropped and the Workers' Union joined the strike.[74] A similar conflict arose during the major engineering dispute of 1922, when the Engineering Employers' Federation demanded that the Amalgamated Engineering Union (AEU) (formerly the Amalgamated Society of Engineers) should abandon its demands to regulate overtime and manning arrangements. The Workers' Union and the National Union of General and Municipal Workers (NUGMW) were locked out as well, and responded by stating that 'they would resist autocratic actions from whichever source it sprang – whether from employers or other unions'. In the end the Workers' Union and the NUGMW settled on their own terms and the AEU moved that they should be expelled from the Trades Council. The engineers' new-found influence was revealed by their success in this.[75] Although weak for much of the 1920s the union recovered in the 1930s and relations with the general unions also improved. Preston's engineering industry remained reasonably buoyant

Table 4.17. *Number of workers in selected craft trades in Preston,*
1901–51

		1901	1911	1921	1931	1951
Tailors	Male	521	496	338	245	94
	Female	126		283	222	112
Shoemakers/repairers	Male	676	599	454	290	644
	Female	98	82		18	764
Cabinet makers	Male	444	326.		257	161
	Female	30	23		4	4
Watchmakers	Male	86		52	46	36
	Female	1			1	1

Source: Censuses.

in the inter-war period, certainly more so than was the case for the
traditional engineering firms of other parts of Lancashire, and Preston
became a major centre for the rearmament which occurred in the late
1930s.

The printers provided another example of crafts able to find new
strength in a changed industry.[76] Preston had a relatively important
provincial printing industry, and numbers employed grew from 323 in
1901 to 454 by 1951. As was common the printers' handicraft, all-round
skills were challenged in the 1890s by the linotype machine, and the use
of these machines provoked conflicts in 1894–5 as several printers lost
their jobs. A series of agreements enabled union members to gain jobs on
the new machines but employers drove a hard bargain, often by
threatening to use female labour, which provoked considerable
concern.[77]

Since craft printers could no longer rely on the indispensability of their
skills they were forced to organise and develop stronger labour market
controls. After 1900 all shops had to organise 'chapels'. Members were
compelled to attend union meetings or face fines. Furthermore overseers
were recruited and held accountable to the union, so giving the union
effective control over the shop, and machinemen who could have taken
the new printing jobs were unionised. Also of great importance was the
way in which the printers regained their ability to transmit the new
forms of skill through apprenticeship. Alternative means of skill
acquisition, such as that provided by the Harris Technical College, were
successfully opposed.[78]

Outside these two sectors craft workers were in more obvious decline,
as Table 4.17 shows. The general craft sectors such as shoemaking and

tailoring declined: the number of male tailors fell by over five times between 1901 and 1951, while the number of cabinet makers and watchmakers more than halved. Changes in the building trade are more difficult to evaluate: employment remained steady but the size of firms fell (in 1898 there were twenty-five bricklayers for each bricklaying firm, but by 1951 this had fallen to seven). The craft sector was considerably changed over the period 1901–51. Some groups had regained a measure of craft indispensability, and both the Typographical Association and the AEU could enforce a pre-entry closed shop, despite high levels of unemployment. These developments are witness to a point discussed recently by several writers: craft forms of working need not be displaced in 'modern' industry.[79] It should however be emphasised that these were not handicraft craft workers, but instead worked in industries now characterised by a complex division of labour. The demise of the capacities of key groups of cotton workers was offset by the increasing strength and organisation among elite workers in engineering and printing in the 1930s.

Appendix A gives details about the development of the service sector in Preston. Public services became very important following the location of the Lancashire County Council headquarters in Preston in 1888, and thenceforth there was a considerable expansion of employment in white-collar occupations. Before 1914 most of this increasing employment went to men rather than women. The percentage of men in government and commercial occupations (Census Orders 1 and 5) rose from 4.35 % in 1891 to 5.78 % in 1911, while the percentage of women so employed rose from 0.11 % to 0.37 %. This went somewhat against the national trend which showed that women were gaining entry to such employment before 1914, and indicates that in a town where male employment was weak there may have been more efforts by men to enter these occupations.[80]

The period around World War I proved decisive, however, for the entry of women into much clerical work, and this trend henceforth continued. Between 1921 and 1951 the number of men employed in the service sector rose by 12.4 %, but the number of women rose by 82.4 %. By 1951 more women worked as clerks and domestics than worked in textiles. In some respects, since these sectors were expanding, this would have appeared to strengthen women's position in the labour market, but this form of work did not offer a long-term job for women as textiles did: Preston, like most local authorities, operated a marriage bar, and in the inter-war years most clerical jobs were for young women only.

In fact women made very few inroads into high-level service jobs in this period. Women's increasing employment in services was occasionally at the expense of men. In retailing the number of male workers fell while the number of women rose. In most office work women moved into new occupations. In the higher professions men's presence was strong, however. In 1931 19 % of teachers were male, but in 1951 30 % were. It was therefore in the most proletarianised occupations that women's employment increased.

The development of public employment did have some impact by creating a small but important group of workers in 'sheltered' occupations, less prone to unemployment in the 1930s. The number of workers in the 'amenities' – gas, water and electricity – rose from 189 in 1911 to 1,073 by 1951. Throughout the nineteenth century unemployment had threatened nearly all workers. The generally casual nature of the labour market meant that a decline in employment brought with it a threat of wage reductions or underemployment among most workers. Yet certain groups of workers were isolated from the immediate effects of unemployment in the inter-war years. Massive unemployment in the 1930s, at levels of over 15 %, did not therefore carry over to affect all workers through greater pressure on the labour market. Certain sectors were protected by craft structures, others by state employment. Unemployment hence divided rather than united different occupational groups in the inter-war years.

4.7   Conclusions

The nature of working-class capacities is related to the transmission of skills, and the structure of the labour market, linked to household relations, was of great importance in this respect. In this context there were two main groups of workers which lost out as a result of changes which occurred after 1900. The first were those who before 1914 had been pivotal organisers of the labour market, but who after 1914 were undermined by employers determined to cut wage costs and to undermine craft control and who could use state institutions to find labour. The second group comprised the pool of the new long-term unemployed. This expanded rapidly in the early 1920s with the decline of cotton spinning and engineering, fell a little in the late 1920s and then grew in the 1930s when unemployment was usually over 15 %. Before 1914 unemployment was probably not long term, since the affected workers would have been able to compete with other workers in the casual labour market: and in certain sectors, notably the cotton industry where short-time working was important, there was still relatively little long-term unemployment. Nonetheless it was a new feature of the 1930s, and the disorganised state of the long-term unemployed deprived them of capacities to organise effectively.

In contrast with these two groups most other workers increased their capacities in this period. Some casual workers gained forms of labour market protection through the state (public sector transport and utility workers), while some craft workers were able to gain relatively strong positions in the new engineering and printing industries (though the former were still subject to short-term unemployment, at least before the boost to engineering brought about by rearmament during the late 1930s). Capacities based on gender were also changing. Generally women's employment was steadily diversifying from its traditional reliance on cotton, yet mainly into sectors strongly segregated from male employment. Women textile workers held their strongest position in the late 1920s when, no longer subject to the overlookers' patriarchal controls, yet still a skilled and prized workforce, they exercised a new confidence. This was however undermined by mass unemployment in weaving in the 1930s, although the labour market for weaving labour still remained tight with employers complaining of labour shortages since many women left the labour market altogether (largely because of government disincentives), and because very few young people entered the industry.

These changes did not, as we shall see, go uncontested. Those groups which were being undermined used the political process in an attempt to fight back, while those groups which gained measures of security often owed this to wider political mobilisations based around political campaigns and (local) state action. Such changes are therefore an essential backdrop to political confrontations within Preston, and must also be related to the changing character of neighbourhood capacities, and these will be discussed in the next chapter.

5

Urban structure and associational practices

In this chapter I shall examine class capacities based on the neighbourhood, and I shall argue that these changed considerably, with the changes falling into three main periods. Before the 1890s the working-class neighbourhood was not a good basis for collective action since it was continually undermined by middle-class and elite initiative in the form of religious provision. Between the 1890s and World War I this began to change and a wide range of popular neighbourhood institutions developed, but most of these were pre-existing ones taken over by local residents. The inter-war years saw the full flourishing of the working-class neighbourhood based on a range of distinctively working-class institutions, from Labour clubs to the Co-op. In order to understand these changes, however, it is necessary to examine the broader context of Preston's social geography and to appreciate the relationship between the neighbourhoods and their wider environment.

5.1 *Preston's urban structure, 1890–1940*

There is still considerable uncertainty concerning the spatial structure of the English nineteenth-century city. There is general agreement that a well-defined elite of large employers, upper professionals and financiers lived well apart from the rest of the town's populace, but the extent of residential segregation between other members of the middle class and the working class, and within the working class itself, remains unclear. It is easy to be influenced by the exceptional example of London, where the contemporary Charles Booth established beyond reasonable doubt that there was very considerable segregation. Lawton and Pooley argue that by 1871 skilled and unskilled workers in Liverpool were living in separate quarters, but Liverpool may not be typical because of its peculiar ethnic ties. Even less information is available about smaller industrial towns such as Preston, though some research on Wigan, St Helens and Wakefield suggests considerable segregation here too.[1]

Against these observations must be set a number of more recent interpretations, which stress that many towns remained distinctly pre-industrial well into the Victorian period, particularly in seeing a continued mixing of most occupations in most neighbourhoods. Ward has argued that in Leeds in 1871 there was little residential segregation (indeed that there was less than in 1841) with all but the top elite living close to each other. The rise of the 'modern city', he argued, was caused by the growth of corporate capitalism towards the end of the nineteenth century.[2] Recently greater stress has been put on the survival and adaptation of the occupational community where all workers attached to a particular enterprise would live close to their work, regardless of their precise status. Neighbourhoods were vertically integrated with managers and supervisors living close to their workers. This argument has been used in particular by Joyce who has stressed the importance of the factory colony within even large towns as a factor behind employers' domination of such towns.[3]

Bristow's exhaustive analysis of the 1851 Census for Preston has given clear support to this revisionist interpretation. In particular he stresses the lack of residential segregation between skilled and unskilled workers and the continued salience of 'occupational communities'.[4] I have not been able to carry out exhaustive research on this issue but my analysis of three neighbourhoods discussed in Chapter 4 can be used to throw some light on this topic (see Appendix B). There was a complete absence of employers and upper professionals from the three working-class areas, but a number of small employers did live there. There was also a very low level of residential segregation within the working class. The highest numbers of labourers were in Fishwick which had also the highest number of craft workers. In the cotton areas the overlookers lived near other male cotton workers regardless of their status.[5]

The main variations between the three areas seem best explained by proximity to workplace: thus Marsh Lane, which was very near the railway station, had a high proportion of railway workers;[6] the canal area, with a number of cotton mills nearby, had a very high proportion of male cotton workers. Residence was based around occupation rather than status. Finally the petit-bourgeois sector was of considerable importance throughout Preston, though less so in the Marsh Lane area than elsewhere. The importance of these shopkeepers, publicans and craft workers/dealers lay not simply in their numbers but also in their connections with the working class through their control of credit, as I shall discuss presently.

Preston, even in 1881, was characterised by a mixing of all social groups except for a top elite. This elite was not suburbanised however – even in the late nineteenth century – but continued to reside in the old Georgian heart of Preston, around Winckley Square and Avenham (see Map 1). Winckley Square was only two minutes' walk from the main shopping streets, and immediately to the east lay Fishwick, a major industrial centre and the site of the Horrockses works; it was also known as Preston's 'red light' area.[7] In 1851 Winckley Square had been the main residence of Preston's cotton employers,[8] but by the 1890s most of these had left and the Square was inhabited by the traditional 'pre-industrial' elite of professionals and gentlemen. In 1890 fourteen doctors, five clerics, three solicitors, three gentlewomen, two gentlemen, an architect, a civil engineer, a coal agent and a contractor lived in the Square; only a draper's residence struck a slightly more plebeian note.[9]

The continued presence of a central urban elite, taken by Sjoberg to be evidence of a pre-industrial town, had a number of consequences for class relations in Preston. Most importantly, whereas a suburban elite need have no great interest in their city except for employment, the residents of Preston still relied on their town as a place of recreation and of day-to-day living. In Preston this problem was intense since many of the streets neighbouring on the area inhabited by the elite, especially Fishergate, were places of popular gathering. Fishergate was known as the 'monkey rack': it was a place where youngsters courted and, in the later part of the century, it was also known for its violent football disturbances. Their central location forced the residents into a much more active concern with the safety of these areas than would have been the case if they had been suburbanites. Davidoff argues that suburbanis-ation caused members of the middle class to become more concerned in charity work, since their lack of direct involvement in urban life allowed them to develop a certain detachment and practise a tokenistic charity.[10]

This point has great importance in explaining the activities of members of this elite and their concern to forestall working-class mobilisation in Preston. The ownership of land in Preston was rea-sonably fragmented, since the Earl of Derby, who had owned a large part of Preston in the early nineteenth century, had sold off much of his stock after 'retiring' from Preston following his political failures of the 1830s. So the sort of estate development possible in some towns carried out by large landowners, which could fragment working-class settle-ment, could not occur, and instead religion was of immense importance in this respect.[11] Several writers on Victorian religion, notably McLeod,[12] have argued that religious practices were very strongly class specific. The Anglican church appealed to the upper class and some of the 'deferential'

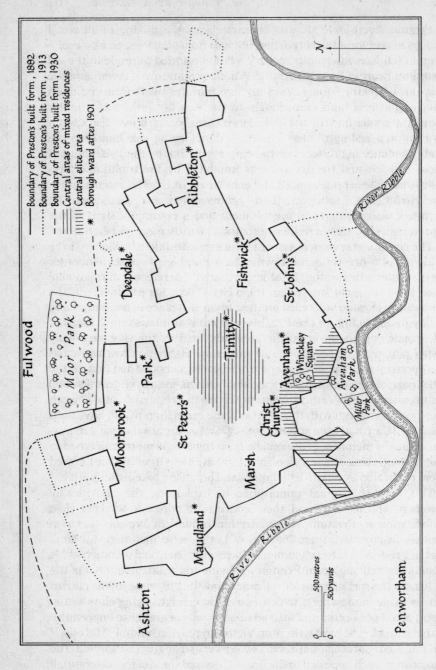

Map 1 Changes in Preston's urban form, 1890–1940

Legend:
— Boundary of Preston's built form, 1882
····· Boundary of Preston's built form, 1913
--- Boundary of Preston's built form, 1930
▨ Central areas of mixed residences
▥ Central elite area
✴ Borough ward after 1901

N

Fulwood

Moor Park

Ashton *

Maudland *

Moorbrook *

Deepdale *

Ribbleton *

St Peters' *

Park *

Trinity *

Fishwick *

Marsh

Christ Church *

Avenham *

Winckley Square

St John's *

Avenham Park

Miller Park

River Ribble

River Ribble

Penwortham

0 500 metres
0 500 yards

working class, while Nonconformity was based on independent craft workers and the lower middle class. McLeod's argument works best for London, however, where there was greater residential segregation, and suburbanisation was well advanced. In other towns most forms of religious provision were sponsored by the urban elite, and were directed towards colonising the working class.

What is meant by this? The concern with central urban space felt by Preston's resident elite led to a particular form of religious provision based on intervening in working-class neighbourhoods to 'open up' the otherwise private worlds they contained. The Anglican church had two churches more or less reserved for the elite themselves to worship at: the old parish church of St John's, and St George's nearby, which had been much patronised by the early cotton employers when they were trying to establish their independence from the old Preston elite (see Map 2). Both were in the heart of Preston near Winckley Square and Avenham. St George's, alone of Preston's churches, had no day or Sunday schools attached to it: a sure sign of exclusive status, since most of its clientele would have sent their children to 'public' (fee-paying) schools.[13]

The other churches were all placed in the midst of the undifferentiated plebeian neighbourhoods. They were primarily concerned not with incorporating the working-class residents but with intimidating them by their very imposing physical presence, with pacifying these potentially dangerous areas. One of the first churches to be built, St Mary's, in Fishwick, was situated in the old hand-loom weaving quarters. One church member recalled that

some seventy years ago [i.e. in the 1820s] that part of Preston . . . called 'New Preston' had a very bad reputation, respectably dressed people could rarely walk through it without being subjected to insult and not infrequently to injury . . . The general characteristics of its inhabitants were an immense capacity for bad language, a great power of alcohol, and a great and supreme contempt for all that was decent and reputable.[14]

As a result, St Mary's was opened. Similar impulses lay behind the foundation of other churches. St Saviour's near Avenham was one of the last to be opened, in the 1860s, and was done so as a response to the feeling that the 'neighbourhood was one of the poorest and lowest in the town, nests of slums and dens of vice abounding on every hand'.[15]

These churches attempted to undermine the neighbourhood as a basis for popular collective action. Their construction usually altered the physical layout of the area. In place of the meandering side streets and yards characteristic of old Preston, the churches were often built in conjunction with a number of new roads, and houses were arranged

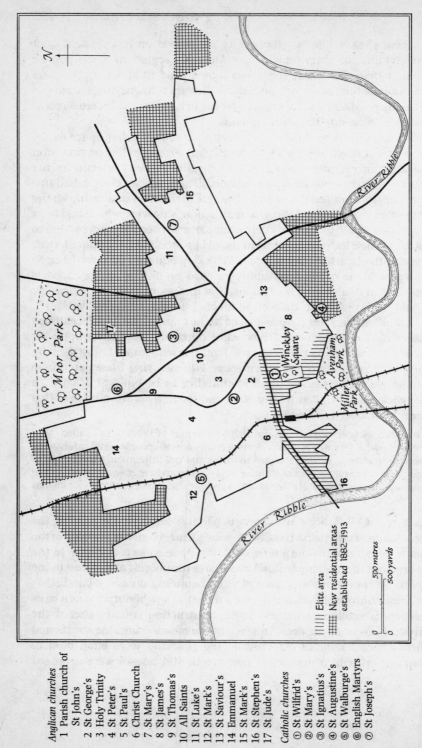

Anglican churches

1 Parish church of St John's
2 St George's
3 Holy Trinity
4 St Peter's
5 St Paul's
6 Christ Church
7 St Mary's
8 St James's
9 St Thomas's
10 All Saints
11 St Luke's
12 St Mark's
13 St Saviour's
14 Emmanuel
15 St Mark's
16 St Stephen's
17 St Jude's

Catholic churches

① St Wilfrid's
② St Mary's
③ St Ignatius's
④ St Augustine's
⑤ St Walburge's
⑥ English Martyrs
⑦ St Joseph's

Elite area

New residential areas established 1882–1913

River Ribble

Moor Park

River Ribble

Winckley Square

Avenham Park

Miller Park

500 metres
500 yards

Map 2 Location of churches in Preston, 1883

Table 5.1. *Preston's Anglican churches and pew rents, 1898*

	Date of foundation	Sittings	Free sittings	Percentage free
Parish church of St John's		1,500	250	16.7
St George's	1726	800	70	8.8
Holy Trinity	1815	1,250	1,250	100.0
St Peter's	1824	1,200	660	55.0
St Paul's	1825	1,200	700	58.3
Christ Church	1836	1,050	450	42.9
St Mary's	1838	1,400	700	50.0
St James's	1841	800	240	30.0
St Thomas's	1839	800	300	37.5
All Saints	1850	1,400	466	33.3
St Luke's	1859	800	650	81.2
St Mark's	1863	992	482	48.6
St Saviour's	1868	730	389	53.3
Emmanuel	1870	967	607	62.7
St Matthew's	1883	674	350	51.9
St Stephen's	1888	393	393	100.0
St Jude's	1890	800	450	56.3
St Andrew's, Ashton	1836	600	200	33.3
St Mary Magdalene, Ribbleton	1889	197	197	100.0
Total		17,553	8,804	50.2

Percentage of seats free: 1913 = 52.8 %

1948 = 63.4 %

Source: Barratt's Directory of Preston, various editions.

around the church in the form of a square. These would be relatively high-quality houses, and some middle-class people would live here.[16]

The churches furthermore ran a system whereby the best and most conspicuous pews at the front of the church could be rented. In this way, every Sunday, upper- and middle-class patrons could visit the church and display themselves to local residents. Pew renting helped to reinforce the hold of the elite over these neighbourhoods. Table 5.1 shows that 50 % of pews were rented in 1898, leaving only 8,000 free sittings for the rest of the population. Although this system was falling into disfavour elsewhere in Britain, since workers refused to attend church under such degrading conditions, in Preston the system was not seriously challenged before 1914.[17]

Each church had its set of wealthy patrons who monopolised most of the lay offices. In the 1880s Christ Church had four wardens: two solicitors, one shareholder and agent, and one 'crier of the Court of the Quarter Sessions'. In 1886 five of the six sidesmen (a fairly lowly office) can be identified. One was a cotton employer, one an assistant manager of livery stables, one a gentleman, one an assistant borough rate collector, and one a landscape gardener.[18] All this despite the fact that the church was in one of the most plebeian neighbourhoods in Preston, next to the railway station.

The churches' most important activity was education. Preston was the largest town in Britain without a School Board, and hence without rate-funded education. All education was based on the voluntary schools provided by the churches, and considerable discretion was exercised by the voluntary school manager and Sunday school superintendent, who were drawn mainly from elite circles. Alderman Joseph Isherwood, a corn merchant, for instance, was superintendent at St Paul's Sunday school. Many middle-class women, such as Edith Rigby, later to become Preston's best known suffragette, were teachers at these schools, the function of which was seen to be the civilisation of the masses. Cartmell wrote:

Our doors are open to all, bad as well as good; consequently the teachers cannot, in a few hours on Sunday, always counteract the home and street influence of the week and they have not always parental authority to appeal to . . . There is drunkenness, low dancing and singing rooms, Sabbath desecration and other kindred vices to work against and if it were not for the sustaining faith and love many earnest minded teachers would give up the work in despair.[19]

The urban residential elite was forced into attempts to pacify the working-class residents, mainly through the church. What was the reaction of the working class to this? There has been a considerable debate concerning the importance of religion in working-class life. The traditional view, echoed by Pelling and Inglis, was that the working class was largely indifferent to it. This interpretation relied heavily on the results of the 1851 religious census which showed low levels of attendance at church.[20] Recently this interpretation has been criticised for two main reasons. There is some evidence that the 1850s were a very low point in the churches' popularity and participation increased in later Victorian times. Other writers have stressed that a concentration on formal attendance ignores the wider role of the church in social life.[21] However, these writers tend to exaggerate the extent of church-based social life – at least in Preston – for the period before 1900. Christ Church, for instance, had only a cricket club (which played four times a year) in the 1870s.[22] Most activities were firmly moralising ones. Some churches

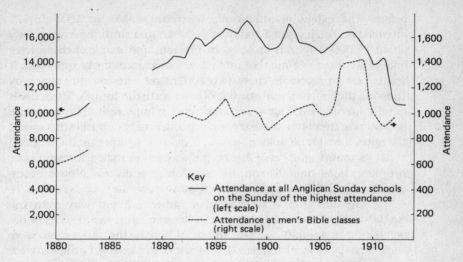

Figure 1 Attendance at Anglican Sunday schools in Preston, 1880–1913 (no data available for 1883–9/91). Sources: *Barratt's Directory of Preston,* 1898; Church service registers

developed Temperance Societies from the later 1870s, and there were a few Mutual Improvement Societies, but there is little evidence of mass participation in church social life. As I shall argue presently, the 'golden age' of church social life began only in the 1890s.

Involvement in church life was weak. Preston held the honour of having one of the lowest proportions of church attendance of all urban areas in 1851 (about 20 %). For the later period, a number of church records can be used to gauge attendance. In five parishes where records survive only 6 % of the eligible population were Easter communicants in 1891. This compares with 8.4 % for England as a whole.[23] However, as only about half the population were nominally Anglicans this figure should be doubled to give 12 % of eligible Anglicans taking part in Easter Communion, a figure probably close to the national average. It also seems true that Easter was not the period of the greatest popular support; figures from St Saviour's indicate that Whit saw more communicants. Furthermore not all attenders were necessarily communicants. At St James's in 1883 there were fifty communicants but the service register recorded that 650 attended.[24] This however probably indicates casual attendance at a ceremony of specific importance rather than a general interest. It does appear that apathy was the norm.

A different picture can be drawn for Sunday school attendance, however (see Figure 1). Peaks occurred in the period 1895–1908, not before. The extent of attendance was remarkable. In 1901 15,375 attended on the highest Sunday of the year, and since there were only about 18,000 Anglican children in Preston, and many of these were babies, we must assume that attendance was more or less universal. It seems best to reconcile these two conflicting sorts of attendance by stressing the instrumental attitude of workers to the church. The schools taught literacy and were for this reason important for promotion prospects in the cotton industry, among other things. Outside this sphere the church had little hold, however. It did not incorporate the working class; its main significance lay in the way it forestalled working-class neighbourhood organisation. By establishing a distinct physical presence it served to intimidate rather than incorporate.

The Catholic church worked in a rather different way from the Anglican. It was extremely strong in Preston, with about 35 % of the population nominally supporting it. Whereas the Anglicans were controlled by a local industrial/professional elite, the Catholics were dominated by a rural elite. There were few major Catholic employers in Preston, and although there were some Catholic professionals, the bulk of support came from the Catholic gentry of the nearby Fylde, an area notorious for its recusancy after the Reformation.[25] Preston, as the old market town of the Fylde, had always been at the centre of much Catholic attention, and the formation of the Preston Catholic Charitable Society in 1731 was to be of great moment. Ostensibly it gave doles to the poor, but it also proved to be the central meeting point of leading Catholic patrons. The Catholic clergy had to say masses for its subscribers, and its existence gave an unusually strong lay control over the local Catholics.

The Society was self-electing, with all members having to be approved by existing ones. Before 1817 no member of the clergy could be a member of the Society, although the significance of the clergy grew thereafter with the weakening and repeal of the anti-Catholic laws, and in 1833 the rector of St Wilfrid's was made the permanent chairman. The influence of the lay members remained strong, however, and the Society functioned as the voice of Catholic opinion. Page noted that 'no great Catholic movement took place in Preston that did not have its rise in and was not forwarded by the First Catholic Charitable Society'.[26]

This early Catholic presence entailed a number of consequences. The church remained predominantly English, and there was no close connection with Irish immigrants as was found elsewhere. In 1834 only 500 of the estimated 8,000 Catholics in Preston were Irish. As Anderson showed, since much migration into Preston was short range large numbers of English Catholics from the Fylde would have continued to move to the town. It was noted in a history of St Walburge's church written shortly before World War I that 'the congregation, nearly all English, are generally attracted to their church and clergy'. Anderson pointed out that in 1851 10 % of Preston's population was Irish born, which suggests that they were a minority of the Catholic population.[27] I examined St Ignatius's marriage registers for the years 1888–90 for some evidence of Irish participation in Preston's life. Only 14.8 % of the brides and grooms had definitely Irish names, whilst another 24 % had names which might have been Irish.[28] Seven of the brides of the fifteen grooms with definite Irish names also had definite Irish names, which indicates some clustering of the Irish, but also suggests that Irish and English Catholics did mix together. There is little evidence of Irish ghettoes or of discrimination in employment. The Catholic church in Preston did not rely on Irish ethnic ties. In 1893 only a handful of the twenty-eight priests were Irish.

The Catholic church was much less concerned with sanitising urban space than was the Anglican. Whereas the Anglican churches were located in the heart of the working-class areas, the Catholic ones were situated either in the midst of middle-class areas, or on the outskirts of town. St Wilfrid's, the oldest Catholic church, was opened in 1793 in Winckley Square, and St Augustine's, opened in 1840, stood only a short distance away in Avenham, near the slopes leading down to the Ribble. The other Catholic churches were all located on the edges of Preston. The most famous was St Walburge's. When it was built in the early 1850s, it was placed on high ground overlooking the town, and on the historic site of St Mary Magdalene's hospital which had stood there in medieval times. It was a 'show' church, with the second highest spire in Britain, and was financed by the local gentry, especially the Talbots, who also helped to build the schools associated with the church. Only 200 of the 1,300 seats were free. Other Catholic churches had similar features.[29]

The primary concern of the Catholic establishment was towards the middle class, particularly in respect of Catholic educational facilities. The Jesuit Stonyhurst College, a few kilometres from Preston, was second only to Ampleforth as a Catholic public school, and another Catholic college opened in 1860 in Winckley Square. There were also private schools for girls, and all the churches had their own day schools attached to them.

The other major Catholic activity was to build up a range of charitable institutions, which helped to secure the dependence of the Catholic 'flock' on the Catholic elite. St Joseph's orphanage was built in 1872 from funds donated by a Catholic gentlewoman, Maria Holland, and it provided for orphan girls. St Joseph's Institute for the Sick Poor was built in 1877 from the funds of the same woman and could look after twenty-five Catholic patients at one time.[30] The most distinctive institutions, however, were the Catholic Guilds, thought to be unique to Preston. Elsewhere Catholics used the Ancient Order of Hibernians as their Friendly Society, which emphasised Irish connections. In Preston the Irish connection was weak, however, and therefore the Catholic Guilds stronger. They paid sickness benefit and death grants, and organised medical attendance, in return for a subscription. First founded at St Wilfrid's chapel in 1839, they soon spread to all the churches. In 1907 they had 7,239 members, out of about 32,000 Catholics in Preston. Most of these were children, however, there being only 1,500 members of the male Guild, out of about 10,000 eligible.[31]

This discussion shows that it would be unwise to exaggerate the cohesion of the Catholics, at least before 1900. They could not rely on ethnic loyalty and, outside education, the Catholic church does not appear to have made a dramatic impact. The Nonconformists were relatively weak in Preston: they represented only about 10 % of the population, a proportion well below that of other cotton towns. This was partly due to the character of migration to Preston (from Catholic rural areas rather than Nonconformist ones). By far the strongest were the Wesleyan Methodists, who in character were the closest of the Nonconformist sects to the Anglican church. They had 1,666 members in their two Preston circuits in 1890. The Methodists were the only sect to enjoy the active participation of cotton employers down to 1890, and they supported voluntary rather than rate-funded educational provision. Of the fifteen lay preachers on the Wesley Circuit who can be identified there were four merchants, three professionals, four small businessmen, two gentlemen, one boot and shoe employer and one white-collar worker. Of the eleven known lay preachers on the Lune Street Circuit there were five professionals, three white-collar workers, two employers and one overlooker. Like the Anglicans this sect was concerned to bolster the hold of a local elite over the urban environment.[32]

5.2 The emergence of the working-class neighbourhood

I have argued that the presence of a residential elite in the heart of Preston was linked to a concern on the part of the elite to undermine working-class capacities for collective action in order to secure central urban space for its own needs and purposes. The elite was less concerned to win over the working class than to forestall its mobilisation. This situation however changed with the steady suburbanisation of the middle class from the later Victorian period. Many parts of Avenham remained exclusive until 1914, but by the inter-war years it was clear that there had been dramatic changes. In 1932 only three doctors lived in Winckley Square; but there were now nine accountants' offices, four land agents' offices, three building society offices, four solicitors' offices and two estate agents' offices. The Ministry of Pensions, the Inland Revenue, the Inspectorate of Factories, the Post Office and the Ministry of Health all had offices there, however. In Great Avenham Street there had been seventeen gentlemen in 1913 but there were only three by 1932 and a number of white-collar workers had moved in. In Latham Street the number of gentlemen fell over the same period from ten to three. Only in Ribblesdale Place and West Cliff, overlooking the Ribble and on the fringe of the old elite area, did they persist. There were still fifteen gentlemen in West Cliff in 1932 (nineteen in 1913), and two Justices of the Peace lived on the street. Even so there were also now a number of offices.

The main areas of new development were the suburbs of Fulwood and Penwortham, both situated close to Preston. Fulwood had been developed from the 1850s, but its population began to expand rapidly after 1890, from 4,112 in 1891 to 6,578 in 1921 and 12,900 in 1948, whilst the population of Preston itself was stable. Fulwood was the most select of the suburbs, the older areas centred on Watling Street Road being highly exclusive, and several Justices of the Peace lived there in the inter-war years. The growth of relatively cheap semi-detached housing in the inter-war years led to an influx of lower-middle-class residents also. In 1931 58 % of the male workforce of Fulwood was in public administration and defence, professional occupations, and clerical, commercial or financial occupations. Seventy percent of the female workforce was in personal service, the professions or the clerical sector. In 1931 only 4 % of the male and 8 % of the female workforce were employed in textiles.

Penwortham, south of the Ribble, also grew after 1890. Its population rose from 1,049 in 1801 to 1,691 in 1891, but by 1921 had reached 3,500 and by 1939 10,912. Penwortham was never as exclusive as Fulwood but certain streets, such as Cop Lane, had large numbers of professional people. It was more of a clerks' suburb than was Fulwood. The other major growth area was Ashton on Ribble to the west of Preston. This had originally been patronised by some of the leading cotton-mill owners after they moved from central Preston. William Galloway, who was connected to Horrockses, lived there at one time, as did the Eccles family who owned a large firm, while the Calverts helped fund Ashton Park. By 1914 many professional people had moved here, especially to the exclusive streets of Pedder's Lane and Egerton Road.[33]

By the inter-war years Preston had virtually no local employers resident in the town. (There was one exception. Astley Bell, after his wife's death in the 1920s, lived out the rest of his life in Preston's Park Hotel, in Avenham.) This was a fairly common development at this time though in some towns local employers continued to remain resident well into the inter-war period.[34] The consequences for the middle class of the employers' move out of town were of extreme importance. Firstly, relations between members of the lower- and upper-middle classes changed. In Victorian Preston the top elite had lived apart from everyone else: now they were likely to live in the same areas as other professionals, small employers, and the growing numbers of white-collar workers. The older central areas became more distinctly working-class as the non-manual workers moved out, while relations between lower-middle- class and upper-middle-class people became closer.

Secondly, the politics of Preston's old middle class underwent a dramatic shift. So long as middle-class people lived centrally they fought a battle to ensure their security in the central areas of Preston. Much of this was linked to an attempt to construct a distinct 'public realm', and Preston was the first town to have public parks, for instance.[35] As they moved out such issues ceased to concern them: they no longer needed central Preston for residence and recreation. A new problem arose however. Formerly, close residence had been important for the maintenance of business contacts. In the Preston strike and lock-out of 1853–4 the close proximity of cotton employers to each other in Winckley Square helped them plan a strategy; such contacts became less possible as employers moved apart. So there was a burgeoning of occupational and professional associations to compensate for this, and these marked a shift from a public setting for interaction to a private, hidden one. The Freemasons also became much more important. They had a long history, dating back to the eighteenth century, but before 1850 theirs was a relatively proletarian society. It went into decline after this date but was revived as a middle-class society and in the 1930s it had sixty members 'belonging almost entirely to the professional ranks of society'.[36] One of Elizabeth Roberts's respondents recalled that his father, on moving from Avenham to Penwortham, became an active mason, and that promotion in the banks of Preston (where he himself worked) was also dependent on membership. Another respondent recorded how tennis clubs became a major centre of suburban life in the inter-war years.[37]

The middle classes' social life in the inter-war years was less concerned with religion than it had been previously and involved the formation of new institutions to bind themselves together rather than being directed outwards to other social groups. These included the Rotary Club, the Toc H movement, and the Young Men's, and Young Women's, Christian Associations, the YMCA and YWCA. Preston's Rotary Club was formed in 1921 and was originally designed to enhance business contacts.[38] It became preoccupied with giving 'service' to the community, primarily by encouraging loyalty in workers. The concern with controlling central urban space was far less pressing now; the main interest of employers was in reliable workers, since their only point of contact with workers was in the production process.[39]

The Preston professional class thus moved from a public to a private sphere. They lost interest in seeing that Preston was a town where they and their property were physically safe. This tendency to withdraw from Preston's social life was increased by the fact that neither Fulwood nor Penwortham were under the jurisdiction of Preston Town Council. Fulwood had its own District Council, and even provided some of its own amenities, notably its water supply. Penwortham was under County Council jurisdiction. This had the effect of making the members of Preston's professional class unconcerned with urban politics, except insofar as they had a business vote and hence wished for low rates. For employers without a direct personal stake in the town, the main importance of urban amenities was in securing an efficient labour force and in providing adequate facilities for their businesses.

The older working-class areas changed in character also. Even before the slum-clearance schemes of the 1930s their population was falling.[40] New working-class housing, based on a grid pattern, was laid out particularly to the north and east of Preston; a number of large firms of developers were mainly responsible for this. It is possible to determine the occupations of the residents of these streets (see Table 5.2). In 1913 four neighbouring streets in Deepdale had large numbers of the upper levels of manual workers, with few labourers and petit-bourgeois elements. Considerable numbers of white-collar workers were also present. Hence as these newer estates developed from the 1880s it seems sensible to argue that a certain amount of intra-class segregation took place. These new estates saw much less residential turnover than was common elsewhere. Twenty-six percent of those resident in 1907 in four streets built in the 1880s had lived in the same houses in 1901. This level of stability rose dramatically in the inter-war years, so that 67 % of the residents in these streets in 1932 had lived in the same houses in 1926.[41]

Table 5.2. *Listed occupations of heads of household of four streets in
Deepdale, Preston, 1913 (percentages; N=93)*

Spinners	5	} Cotton workers = 25	} Manual workers 63	
Overlookers	5			
Weavers	4			
Other cotton workers	10			
Metal workers	6			
Building craft workers	6			
Other craft workers	4			
Labourers	6			
Other manual workers	15			
White-collar workers				9
Foremen				3
Small businessmen/petits bourgeois				3
'Mr'				10
'Mrs'				11
'Miss'				1

Source: Barratt's Directory of Preston, 1913.

The inter-war years therefore saw the development of stable neighbourhoods, in these areas at least.

The impact of council housing was also considerable. Preston's first
council houses were built in 1919, and two estates with about 500
houses were built under the Addison Act. By 1930 1,274 houses had been
built under the 1925 Act and 1,466 under the Small Dwellings Act. These
houses were mainly to the east of Preston, around Ribbleton. The early
estates were designed for the lower-middle class and upper working
class, the idea being that those below them would filter up through the
housing market by taking the houses thus vacated. All the early estates
were geared to these groups (see Table 5.3), and only in the 1930s was
working-class housing intended for lower-income groups provided.

These observations indicate that in two respects the neighbourhood
was becoming more important as a potential basis for working-class
action in the inter-war years. Firstly, homogeneous working-class areas,
with few white-collar or petit-bourgeois residents, developed both in the
old centre of Preston (where labourers were already congregating) and
in the outer grid estates (where there were more skilled workers).
Secondly, there was far more residential stability in these years, and
long-term relationships between regular neighbours were more firmly
based.

Table 5.3. *Listed occupations of heads of household of Holme Slack estate, Preston, 1927 (percentages; N=201)*

Cotton workers	7 ⎫		
Craft workers	14 ⎬	Manual working class	38
Unskilled workers	14 ⎬		
Other manual workers	3 ⎭		
Clerks	17 ⎫		
Travellers	3 ⎬	Non-manual working class	30
Schoolmasters	3 ⎬		
Other white-collar workers	6 ⎭		
Managers	3 ⎫		
Policemen	2 ⎬	Supervisory/managerial	8
Other managers/supervisors	3 ⎭		
		Professionals	2
		Retailers	4
		Employers/small businessmen	3
		'Mr'	9
		'Mrs'	5
		'Miss'	1

Source: Barratt's Directory of Preston, 1927.

These social changes had considerable implications for associational life based on the inner working-class neighbourhoods. From the 1890s to World War I, as the old urban elite became less concerned with church institutions, these were steadily taken over by the working class and became the sites of neighbourhood-based capacities leading to political mobilisation.

There can be little doubt that the popularity of the Anglican church was increasing in these years. Figure 2 shows that there was a considerable increase in the number attending Communion. In Britain as a whole the number of Easter communicants rose by 20.8 % between 1900 and 1930. This reflected the lowering of the age of participation,[42] and yet was below the increase in the number of people aged over 15 in the population, which rose 26.8 %. In Preston, however, the number of Easter communicants in the five churches examined in Figure 2 rose by 65.4 %, while the number of over-15s in Preston rose by 20 %. There were two periods of dramatic increase: between 1900 and 1910, and from 1920 to 1925, but the overall peak was reached as late as 1935. Four of the five churches were inner-city ones (see Map 2), and lay in the heart of working-class areas (St Mark's being a more suburban church). There are no figures available on Sunday school attendance, but

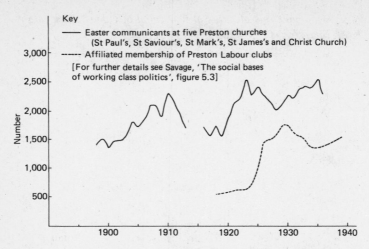

Figure 2   Easter communicants, 1898–1936, and Labour club membership, 1918–39, in Preston (no data available for 1913–16). Sources: *Barratt's Directory of Preston*, 1913; Church service registers; ARTLC

contemporary opinion frequently referred to the declining attendances after 1918, and there are falling rolls in the one church for which I found records, St Jude's. Here attendance fell from 532 in 1908 to below 200 in the 1930s.[43] It seems that whereas in the 1890s all nominal Anglicans had sent their children to Sunday school, but few worshipped there, after 1918 there were two distinct blocs: those who had no contact at all, and those who attended and probably also sent their children.

These changes took place just as the town's elite were dissociating themselves from church life. In 1927 the vicar of St Mary's complained that the clergy of Preston received no help in running their Day Schools and that 'they had lost the support from the local mills which were formerly in the hands of private proprietors, and their burden was now very heavy'.[44] When a cotton employer, William Birtwistle of John Hawkins, attended a church meeting in the same year, the chairman remarked that 'it would be a good thing for the Church if other big employers would show as keen an interest in parochial work'.[45]

The decline of elite involvement was uneven but occasionally it was almost total. In some cases lists of pew renters survive, although there are none for the nineteenth century, and these give an indication of the influential church activists. In St Peter's church forty-four pew holders can be identified for 1926 (though thirty-six cannot, usually because their addresses were omitted from the rent books). Table 5.4 shows that

Table 5.4. *Pew renters at St Peter's church, Preston, 1926 (N=44)*

'Mr' (i.e. gentleman or retired)	3		
'Mrs'	7 (2)		
'Miss'	2		
Professionals	3 (1)	Dentists	2
Merchant	1		
Petits bourgeois	10	Grocers	2
		Confectioners	2
Manual workers	14 (3)	Spinners	3
		Joiners	2
		Drivers	2
White-collar workers	4		

Note: Numbers in parentheses indicate relatives living at the address of a person whose occupation is given in *Barratt's Directory.*
Source: St Peter's Anglican church, Pew book.

the petite bourgeoisie and the working class made up the most numerous category.[46]

At St Paul's church 116 of the 153 seat holders can be identified for 1922 (see Table 5.5). The high number of 'Mr' and 'Mrs' make identification difficult, but nonetheless the predominance of petit-bourgeois, white-collar and skilled manual workers is marked.[47] There were no upper professionals at all; the doctors and solicitors so active in the 1890s had disappeared, and neither were there any large employers. As the elite became less active so the leadership of the church devolved onto the petit-bourgeois and skilled manual groups active in these neighbourhoods. This impression is confirmed by scattered evidence about the occupations of church office-holders. In the late Victorian period these were mostly influential patrons, but after 1900 they were replaced by such people as overlookers, small businessmen and engineers.[48]

The rise of local neighbourhood involvement is interestingly illustrated by the increased support for men's Bible classes (see Figure 1). These were Sunday schools for men, which met every Sunday afternoon to discuss passages from the Bible. They were organised on a 'class' basis with a captain being put in charge of ten or twelve men from a particular area. These classes were more or less autonomous from the church, the teacher having considerable discretion over his class, and often prominent lay speakers would address the meeting.[49] They could thus become important foci of discussion. In 1938 one commentator noted that, since

Table 5.5 *Pew renters at St Paul's church, Preston, 1922 (N=116)*

'Mr'	28 (3)		
'Mrs'	15 (3)		
'Miss'	14		
Professionals (including Town Clerk and Director of Education)	8	Managers	2
Employer	1	Mineral water manufacturer	
Petits bourgeois	19 (4)	Drapers	3
		Butchers	3
		Grocers	2
		Hairdressers	2
Manual workers	21 (3)	Joiners	2
		Overlookers	2
		Engineers	2
White-collar workers	10 (2)	Clerks	4

Note: Numbers in parentheses indicate relatives living at the address of a person whose occupation is given in *Barratt's Directory*.
Source: St Paul's Anglican church, Pew rents.

1914, 'the Bible is the last book alluded to or appealed to for guidance . . . politics, economics, sociology, literature and science have become the principal topics discussed . . . [it] has become very largely a secular debating society'.[50] In fact the importance of these classes for political mobilisation was recognised before 1914. In 1906 Edward Nickson, teacher at St Mary's Bible class, resigned after a furore when he supported a Labour candidate who was a member of his class. Nickson had increased the average attendance of his class from 122 in 1901 to 276 in 1904 (though this fell slightly to 206 in 1906). He was offered a job elsewhere soon afterwards.[51]

The Bible classes reached their zenith in the first decade of the century, when elite involvement had declined, but before the central urban neighbourhoods had lost much of their population, and before strong residential segregation had taken place. These classes were very popular with petit-bourgeois and upper-working-class groups. Cartmell noted that they appealed to those 'who hold good positions in offices, mills etc.'.[52] The lists of St Paul's Bible class have survived, although only forty-five of the 136 people on the books can be traced, but they reveal a strong working-class presence.

The process of the growth of popular interest in the church as elite involvement declined can be illustrated in detail by the case of Christ Church, where good documentation survives. Before 1900 the church's offices were dominated by wealthy patrons. In the late 1880s some of these decided to form a Mutual Improvement Society, to operate on familiar lines to 'civilise' the neighbourhood.[53] The leading proponent was William Bourne, a cotton employer and prospective local councillor. This society arranged debates on various issues of interest and soon attracted a reasonable audience of about sixty. What was novel, however, was the contest of opinion in these meetings. When Mr Ogle spoke on 'strikes, lock-outs and arbitration' and declared that 'labour and capital were as necessary to each other as the wings of a bird', he was immediately rebuffed by a 'working man' who declared that 'labour and capital were fighting for one object: mastership . . . trade unions had done a great deal of good'.[54] The interest of the employers appeared to wane after this and similar incidents, but there was a new popular interest in these church-based institutions. In 1894 a number of young men asked to be allowed to form a club under the auspices of the Mutual Improvement Society. It soon opened with forty-nine members, and had facilities for billiards, chess and draughts.[55] These changes were symptomatic. In 1896 Christ Church became the first church in Preston to set up a Nursing Association, in which the parishioners made contributions to pay for the services of a trained nurse to visit the sick poor. By 1908 five other churches had followed suit.[56] In 1906 the Church Council formed an Entertainments Sub-Committee, and in common with other churches attempted to find new ways of obtaining funds without relying on patrons. In 1906 Christ Church Council asked Preston North End Football Club and their opponents Sheffield United to attend its bazaar.[57]

The importance of popular fund-raising for supporting voluntary schools grew from the 1890s onwards, as the school managers realised that improvements would have to be made in the schools if they were to obviate the need for a School Board. The need to rely on local, popular support caused changes in the management of schools and parents were allowed to elect two parents as school managers. At St Matthew's 400 of the 570 parents voted in these elections. In the National Schools Improvement Fund Bazaar in 1908 £6,000 of the £9,000 raised came from a huge bazaar which included a drinking bar and a sale of work.[58]

Alongside this developing working-class involvement in church life middle-class attachment was weakening. In 1915 the Revd Schonberg and Christ Church Council decided to free many of the seats from rent. Schonberg stated that 'as a national church we are bound to recognise the need of those who [are] in receipt of a weekly wage'. By this time half the congregation were not pew renters.[59]

After World War I other activities were added: Christ Church became the centre of a scout and cub troop. Regular mothers' meetings were held. The church was able to adapt to new leisure pursuits. Even the dancing craze which developed in these inter-war years was frequently developed under church auspices. In 1925 St Paul's formed a Social Club, which met every Tuesday for dancing lessons, and held several dances a year. The interest was such that membership had to be limited to one hundred.[60] Attempts by religious activists to ensure that these activities were linked to religious observance met with little success. In 1932 a resolution that membership cards should be printed with the statement 'we should like every member to attend St Paul's Church at least once a month' was defeated, and replaced by the vague formula that the club 'should promote the Church and social life of the parish'. Many churches also built church institutes, where drink could be served, and a number of sporting leagues, including those in football and billiards, flourished. These institutes became important neighbourhood centres and it was not unknown for trade unions, for instance, to meet in them.[61]

The relationship between local neighbourhoods and the church underwent far-reaching change from the 1890s. Whereas the churches had previously attempted to forestall the development of neighbourhood social life, as they became less able to rely on the support of local notables they were forced to cast around for new sources of finance and organisational help, and many entered into closer relationships with local residents to this end. The peak period of church popularity was probably in the first decade of this century, when the inner urban areas where these churches were located still housed large numbers of skilled workers.

The experience of the Catholic churches was similar, except that because they were located in more suburban areas they were able to continue to expand into the inter-war years. As with the Anglican church, the wealthy patrons who had provided much of the fabric of the church in the Victorian period had retired, and the Catholic Charitable Society, the de facto governing body of Preston Catholicism, took on a more plebeian form. Fifty-eight of its ninety-three members for 1923 can be identified (see Table 5.6). In this year manual and white-collar workers made up a majority, and the Society was, clearly, controlled by an indigenous membership.

Unfortunately there are no records of Catholic attendance at Mass. It is generally thought that the Catholic church was exempt from the general decline in church attendance at least until the 1950s,[62] but this may not have been true of Preston where ethnic ties were weak. The local newspapers give occasional estimates of attendances at annual re-

Table 5.6. *Members of the Preston Catholic Charitable Society, 1923 (N=58)*

'Mr'	7	12 %
Employers	4	7 %
Professionals	11	19 %
Retailers/petits bourgeois	4	7 %
Craft workers	16[a]	28 %
Other manual workers	8	14 %
White-collar workers	8	14 %

[a]Mostly builders. It is not always possible to distinguish workers from self-employed.
Source: Page, *The First Catholic Charitable Society of Preston.*

unions. These were the major social occasions of the year; it might be expected that anyone at all involved with the Catholic church would attend. Although the numbers of those who attended such gatherings increased in the inter-war years they still represented only a quarter of those eligible to attend.[63]

There were also a great many social institutions created in these years, especially the Catholic working men's clubs. The first of these was opened in 1874 in the centre of Preston, and it had 250 members by 1883, though this fell to one hundred by 1910. After this date neighbourhood-based clubs were set up, and by the 1930s there were five of them, all with games facilities and drinking bars. Catholic leagues existed for most sports, with billiards and football being especially popular. In 1907 6,000 people attended the final of the Catholic schools' football competition. Boys' clubs were opened in several areas, with school leavers being encouraged to join and continue their connection with the church.[64]

The Nonconformists were the only group unable to develop a strong cultural presence in these years. This stemmed largely from their ambivalent attitude towards mass entertainment. Wild has shown that in Rochdale, a strong dissenting town, the powerful hold of the chapels over social life evident before 1914 was steadily eroded with the advent of the cinema and dance hall. Nonconformist opposition to drink was particularly significant in this respect. While the Catholics (especially) and the Anglicans came to terms with the need to provide drink-based forms of social life, the Nonconformists did not. The Nonconformists were also weakened by the tenuousness of their neighbourhood base. For the Wesleyans (or the Methodists, as they were known after their reunification with the Primitives in 1930) the church was based on the circuit, with travelling preachers and little autonomy for individual chapels. The other Nonconformist denominations were too small to have more than one church for the whole of Preston. Evidence suggests that it was primarily the self-employed and white-collar workers who were attracted to Nonconformism.[65]

5.3   Working-class organisation and the neighbourhood

I have examined two processes in this chapter: the way in which the changing urban structure of Preston allowed the working-class neighbourhood to become more cohesive in the inter-war years, and the way in which this involved the increased participation of members of the working class in neighbourhood institutions from which they had previously been excluded. The capacities for collective action based on the neighbourhood were therefore increasing in this period. I shall now turn to another vital aspect to this argument: the relationships between popularly controlled institutions and the neighbourhood.

The role of certain trade unions in the workplace and labour market has already been discussed. In the neighbourhood they did not occupy the same position as unions in one-industry towns where they also developed a strong social life. The textile unions were strong, and the Preston Overlookers', Spinners' and Weavers' Unions all had their own premises which were widely used for social purposes. The Overlookers had their own club which served drink and had an extensive social programme, including regular smoking concerts, whist drives, 'knife and fork teas' and benefit concerts. Involvement was to some extent compulsory since members had to pay their subscriptions at the club in the evening and were hence forced to visit it once a week.[66]

The Weavers' Union also had its own Institute, in Walker Street, with some sporting facilities for billiards and dominoes. It was widely used for concerts and gatherings,[67] but it appealed only to a small number of workers, mainly male. The Spinners' Institute was based in Church Street, the central shopping area. Unlike in Bolton, where there was an extensive mill-based social life (each mill had its own shop club and held its own weekly meeting at a local public house), all Preston spinners had to pay subscriptions at the Spinners' Institute. This did have some social facilities, and there was a Ball and Concert Committee and a Tea Party Committee.[68]

The smaller unions were unable to build clubs of their own and still met in pubs or in the offices of other unions. After 1900 however they combined to build a central hall. The Typographical Association had been based in pub premises until 1898, when it moved to the Overlookers' Club, but after a dispute approached other unions to suggest building a United Trades Hall. This was opened in 1904 in Corporation Street, with 2,000 members from the fifteen unions which participated. Subscriptions were paid at the door and unemployed members signed on inside. There was a billiards room, a smoke room, and a 'business' room. There was also a separate Tailors' Club in Anchor Court, with 210 members in 1910.[69]

There was a certain amount of union-based social life, then, but all of it was based centrally rather than in working-class neighbourhoods. Union-minded workers were drawn away from their own streets into a distinctive enclosed world where they would meet other union activists, not their neighbours. In fact the unions congregated in what was effectively Preston's chief shopping areas, near the elite district of Avenham. The union-based social life did change after 1914. Some of the central clubs folded: the United Trades Hall closed down in 1915 because of expense, while the Tailors' Club was closed down in 1920 because it was a 'drinking hive'.[70] More decentralised organisations developed in other unions, the shop clubs for the spinners, for example. The two unions whose clubs continued to flourish were the National Union of Railwaymen and the dockers' union, partly because they were based near the workplace, and in the case of the dockers, at least, near dockers' residences in what was something of an occupational community.

Similar points apply to the Friendly Societies. The capacities for mutualist struggles were weak in Preston, owing to the dominance of the cotton industry and the pivotal importance of the petite bourgeoisie in the plebeian areas. Hence the independent societies, with their mutualist overtones, were weak. The Oddfellows, Forresters, Free Gardeners and Druids had 3,713 members in 1910 out of the 8,635 members of registered affiliated Friendly Societies. Over 4,000 however belonged to the Temperance Societies; the Sons of Temperance had 2,850 members and the Rechabites had 1,760. There were also 733 members in the Orange Order and 2,294 in the Catholic Guilds, neither of which was registered. There were important differences between the two types: the Independent Orders were more likely to be based in local pubs, and to be geared to neighbourhoods, whilst the Temperance Societies rejected pub accommodation and therefore had to build their own premises in the centre of town – in the case of the Rechabites, at Shepherd Street School. In this they were followed by some of the Independent Orders: in Preston the Forresters built their own hall (in 1881), again based near the centre of town.

Both Societies – the Oddfellows and the Rechabites – can be seen as

Table 5.7. *Membership of a Rechabites Tent and an Oddfellows Lodge, Preston, 1882–98*

Occupation (males only)	Rechabites Jubilee Tent 1887–98 (N=170)		Oddfellows Pleasant Retreat Lodge 1882–91 (N=155)	
Cotton workers	99	58.6 %	43	27.7 %
Weavers	56	33.1 %	17	11.0 %
Spinners	9	5.3 %	10	6.5 %
Craftsmen	24	14.2 %	40	25.8 %
Joiners	6		—	
Painters	6		4	
Printers	—		6	
Tailors	—		5	
Sawyers	—		4	
Metal workers	5	3.0 %	9	5.8 %
Labourers/transport workers	7	4.1 %	23	14.8 %
Miscellaneous workers	6	3.6 %	11	7.1 %
Petits bourgeois	14	8.3 %	11	7.1 %
White-collar workers	14	8.3 %	18	11.6 %
Professionals	1		—	

Source: Independent Order of Rechabites, Preston, Jubilee Tent: Candidates' declaration book; Preston Oddfellows Records, Pleasant Retreat Lodge; Register of members.

mutualist, but they could rely little on the capacities of the neighbourhood for their sustenance, and the location of the Temperance Societies in the central areas helped make them amenable to elite involvement. The Temperance Societies, when founded in the early part of the nineteenth century, were composed of craft workers and independent petit-bourgeois elements.[71] By 1890, however, the temperance movement had become more genteel and was supported by all Preston churches and the local elite, and the Preston Temperance Society itself was composed of gentlemen. The Toulmins, a leading Liberal family and proprietors of the *Preston Guardian*, were especially active.

It is possible to compare the membership of a Rechabites Tent and an Oddfellows Lodge (see Table 5.7). The Rechabites were centrally located and enjoyed more elite patronage than did the Oddfellows who remained locally based. One of the most interesting features of Table 5.7 is that the Oddfellows appear to reflect fairly well the working-class population of

Preston as a whole. There were plenty of labourers who belonged, as well as craft workers. The Rechabites show an overwhelming concentration of cotton workers, especially weavers. This may be partly caused by the fact that Rechabites tended to join at an earlier age – late teens or early twenties – than did Oddfellows – there were very few teenage Oddfellows and many did not join till their late twenties. This, however, would explain only a small part of the difference. What is apparent is the overlap with the patterns displayed by the unions discussed earlier. Trades with centrally based unions were well represented in centrally based Friendly Societies. For some of the weavers perhaps, part of the incentive for membership lay in wishing to gain promotion by participating in a 'respectable' organisation.

Before 1890 popularly controlled working-class associations were based mostly in the central urban area of Preston. Key workers, particularly those craft workers who might have laid the ground for mutualist struggles, were drawn away from the neighbourhood to the central areas. Working-class 'respectability' in this period meant dis-associating from working-class areas and setting up in approved public spaces in the heart of Preston.[72] And this very practice further undermined the prospects for collective action based on the capacities offered by the neighbourhood.

This however began to change with a number of developments from the late Victorian period onwards. One of the most important of these was the role of the co-operative movement. The Preston Co-operative Society was originally formed in 1869, after a previous attempt in 1862 had failed. After its fusion with another society in 1873 it grew steadily, with 2,934 members by 1885, 5,992 by 1890, 11,421 by 1900 and about 30,000 by 1919, with the overlookers being especially active, as we have seen. The Co-op was based not in the central retailing area of Preston, but in New Hall Lane in Fishwick, at the heart of the cotton area. While having its central premises in North Road, it made a point of developing branch stores in all the new working-class areas of the town, especially in the north-west of Preston (see Map 3), and adjusted its shopping hours to cater for working women.[73]

The Co-op deliberately tried to weaken the hold of the retailer on working-class neighbourhoods by refusing credit. The pivotal role of petit-bourgeois figures in the working-class economy was undermined, and in Preston this led to serious conflict with the shopkeepers, which reached its peak in 1905 when the shopkeepers set up a Preston Traders' Defence Association which aimed to boycott anyone known to have links with the Co-op. Its main support, according to Laker, was drawn from

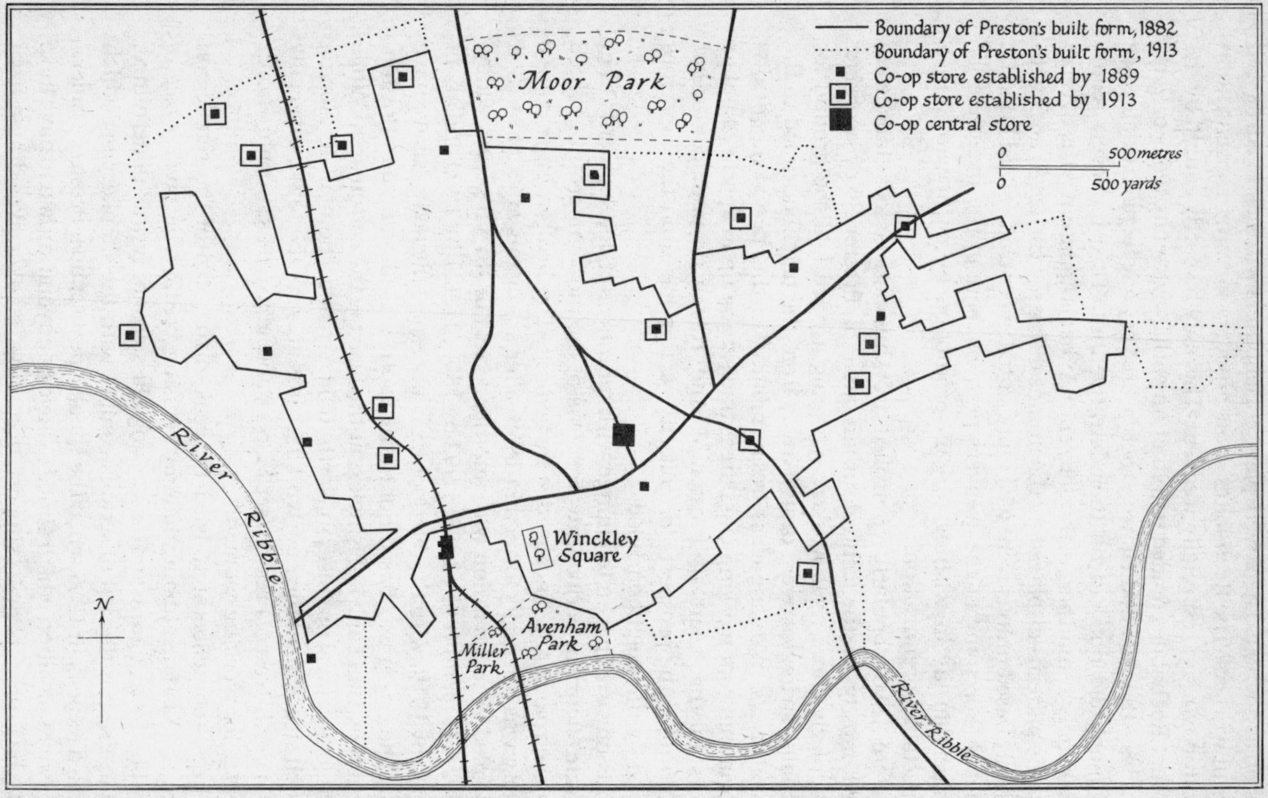

Map 3 Location of Co-operative stores in Preston, 1913

'reputable tradesmen of outer commercial and better working class areas who prided themselves on their skilled status and position within local society'.[74] The boycott however failed.

These changes were symptomatic of the growing rift between the petite bourgeoisie and their immediate neighbourhood, a development linked also to the growing occupational solidarity of the retailing groups. The most powerful of these, such as the Grocers' Association and the Traders' Mutual Association, attempted to control opening hours of shops and holiday periods, and agitated on relevant issues. They helped remove the shopkeepers from the orbit of the neighbourhood and created stronger bonds between retailers. In 1924 the various associations (which by this time included the Bakers' Association, the Butchers' Association, the Confectioners' Association, The Dairymen's Association, the Licensed Victuallers' Association, the Newsagents' Association, and the Pawnbrokers' Association) agreed to form a Chamber of Trade, distinct from the Chamber of Commerce, to agitate on issues which affected them.

The Co-op therefore helped dissolve the link between the working-class neighbourhood and the retailer. This was especially true for members of the affluent working class who did not need to rely on credit, and even, when Co-op membership in Preston became almost universal after 1914, for members of the poorest sections of the working class who had hitherto been reliant on credit and hence more dependent on the retailer. From the 30,000 members of 1919, there were 42,058 in 1925, 55,794 in 1931 and 60,434 in 1935. At this time virtually every household must have had a member. The Co-op developed a lively presence in neighbourhood social life: apart from its considerable educational work, it had its own dance hall and its annual Field Days on Moor Park attracted up to 40,000 people.[75] Particularly before 1914, however, these developments may have had adverse implications for women. In certain respects the old informal retailing networks gave considerable responsibility to women,[76] in terms of using credit fruitfully, and I argued in Chapter 3 that women, as domestic providers, may have been reluctant to see this aspect of their role diminished. The Co-op however was under the strong influence of working-class men, particularly overlookers and other elite cotton workers, and women played little part within it. Even the Women's Co-op Guild which elsewhere became a major base for working-class feminism was weak in Preston, and was confined to 'classes in ambulance work, sick nursing, domestic economy and needlework'.[77] The reaction of the Preston Co-op to the radicalisation of the Women's Co-op Guild in 1905 was to suspend the local branch for insubordination, and it was readmitted only on the basis of its avoidance of controversial discussion.

These twin developments – the formalisation of neighbourhood ties, combined with the decline of women's overall control of neighbourhood contacts – can be seen in other fields. The insurance societies for instance grew rapidly in the inter-war years, based on a collector system whereby collectors (usually male) visited homes once a week to collect subscriptions. These collectors were not appointed by the firm but were elected by subscribers, and so local unemployed people might be employed. These collectors became of vital importance in cementing new forms of 'survival network'. One collector, interviewed by Elizabeth Roberts, remembered that his subscribers

treated you as friends when you got to know them properly. One lady I found in tears. I asked her what was the matter and she said, 'I've just got this [£40 demand] from the Income Tax' . . . I knew the circumstances, I knew how much she had coming in . . . I said, 'This is no good, it's not yours' . . . I said, 'Just tear it up and put it on the fire'.[78]

The collector would give advice on the income tax, the Means Test, and even on whether particular employers were good or bad. Clothing clubs were of similar importance, though these were usually run by women. By the inter-war years a welter of organisations created formal neighbourhood links, which, while giving support for residents, also marked the intrusion of men into a formerly entirely female activity.

The rise of neighbourhood clubs was also of vital importance. These developed late in Preston. 'Working men's clubs' originated as a result of middle-class initiatives in the 1860s to attract working men away from the pub. Nationally this middle-class patronage was thrown off in the 1880s and by 1890 89 % of their income was generated by the clubs themselves. By 1903 the Club and Institute Union, as this movement was called, had 900 affiliated clubs and 321,000 members. There were also a large number of unaffiliated clubs, particularly in London.[79] In Preston the first working men's club was the Forresters, based on the Friendly Society and situated in central Preston. The first neighbourhood club was the Ribbleton Working Men's Club, located in the new working-class suburb to the east of Preston. It was built around 1900 and enlarged in 1907, at which time it had 200 members, and it ran a variety of sporting activities.[80]

After this date all new clubs were Labour clubs, formed by the Labour party. The first was at Acregate Lane, opened in 1904, and it was followed by another at Emmanuel Street shortly afterwards. Originally they were thought of as providing 'rational recreation' and drinking was not encouraged, but after the election defeat of 1910 the Labour party felt that it had to reduce the hold of the licensed victuallers by providing its own drinking facilities. By the inter-war years there were six Labour clubs, and a seventh was opened in 1937. All were situated in the newer working-class estates around Preston (see Map 4), and the influence of the publicans waned as that of the clubs grew. In 1906 Preston had 408 pubs and beerhouses: one for every 277 people. By 1913 this fell to one for every 368 people, in 1921 one for 390, in 1931 one for 440, and by 1939 one for every 464 people, by which time there were only 252 licensed public houses.[81]

The Labour clubs' membership is shown in Figure 2. It is not certain that this reveals the full membership since it is based on returns of members given to the Labour party which might have excluded some members.[82] We can assume perhaps that the official returns testify at least to the prosperity of the clubs, so that funds are proportional to the number of affiliated members; on this basis it can be suggested that the best times for these clubs were in the late 1920s.

The political role of these clubs will be examined in a later chapter: for the moment I want simply to examine their role in the neighbourhood. They became important social centres. Tom Shaw, Preston's Labour Member of Parliament, remarked that 'a club of this kind should be a centre where men could discuss their affairs, exchange ideas and enjoy well earned recreation'.[83] The clubs had bowling greens, billiards, lecture programmes, savings banks, and regular treats for local residents, such as free teas for local children once a year, and day trips.[84] Women could join the clubs, but the extent of their participation is not clear, and it seems that they were responsible more for the 'servicing' aspects of club administration, such as making teas.

5.4 Conclusions

The types of working-class capacity based on the neighbourhood underwent fundamental change between 1890 and 1940. In the early years it was difficult to use the neighbourhood as a basis of collective action, partly because of its shifting and heterogeneous nature, and partly because of the activities of the church in forestalling popular mobilisation. Most working-class institutions were based on the town centre. Informal neighbourhood contacts based on women's networks were mediated mainly through petit-bourgeois figures: shopkeepers, pawnbrokers and publicans. Working-class organisations became increasingly focused on the neighbourhood, however, reflecting changes

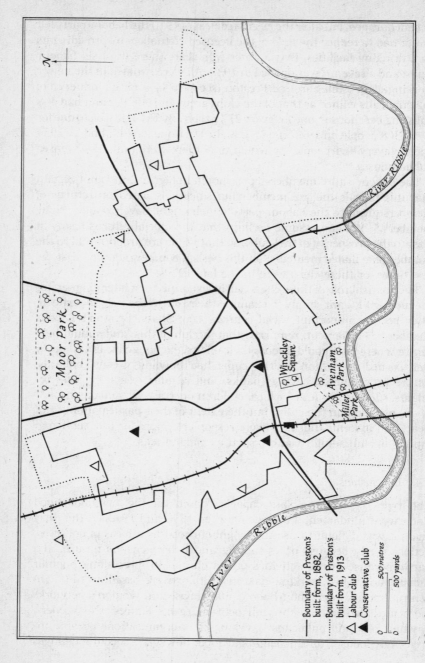

Map 4 Location of political clubs in Preston, 1918–39

Boundary of Preston's
built form, 1882
Boundary of Preston's
built form, 1913
△ Labour club
▲ Conservative club

Moor Park

Winckley Square

Avenham Park

Miller Park

River Ribble

River Ribble

500 metres
500 yards

N

in the social geography of Preston, notably the opening up of newer working-class estates and the growing stability of the population in these areas. A process also took place whereby women's neighbourhood networks became more institutionally structured; this led to some male involvement in these hitherto female areas of life. These popularly controlled institutions had to compete with newly popularised older institutions, especially the church, which experienced something of a revival in these years also.

The neighbourhood therefore became a more salient base of collective action, yet the continued vitality of the church meant that this was not necessarily to the advantage of the Labour movement. Furthermore, women's capacities, which were improved in the workplace (at least for cotton weavers), were somewhat undermined in the neighbourhood. This had the effect of loosening women's identification with household and neighbourhood, which had made them prone to economistic struggles, pushing them instead into a reliance on work-based capacities (for those of them who were in paid work). This, as I indicated in Chapter 3, would be more likely to produce statist struggles.

In the last two chapters I examined economic and social change in Preston and, while the potential political implications have been hinted at, my task in the next two chapters will be to elucidate the course of political change, and to analyse how political actors seized upon the prospects opened up by the changing character of capacities for collective action in given political contexts.

6

The emergence of independent Labour politics, 1880–1914

After the enfranchisement of some urban voters in 1832 the towns became, for a few years, the citadels of the Liberal party. Today, in the 1980s, political alignments are also polarised along an urban–rural axis, with the Labour party deriving most of its support from urban areas. The late Victorian period was to some extent distinctive in being a period when political alignment had only a weak urban–rural dimension.[1] The enfranchisement of numbers of rural labourers in 1884 helped the Liberals in the countryside, whilst the Conservatives made steady gains in the towns, particularly in Lancashire. Preston, along with its neighbour Blackburn, presented the most marked case of an urban working-class seat supporting the Conservatives in this period, as Table 6.1 shows.

This Tory hegemony almost certainly rested upon working-class votes. Although considerable sections of the male working class, and all women, were not enfranchised until 1918, the majority of voters were workers. About 60 % of adult males in Preston had the vote, a figure close to the average for county boroughs (see Table 6.2). In 1911 there were 19,729 voters in Preston, and the Census shows that even a loose definition of 'middle-class' occupations would account for no more than about 8,000 of these voters.[2] Even if we assume that all these 'middle-class' men voted Tory, this still leaves a considerable number of workers who must also have cast their vote to the Conservatives; but in fact many sections of the middle class voted Liberal. Contemporaries were in little doubt that Toryism was based on the working-class vote: the *Preston Herald* stated firmly in 1886 that 'they all knew perfectly well that there were more Conservative trade unionists than Liberal'.[3]

Preston, as an extreme case of urban Conservatism, throws interesting light on the general issue of working-class Conservatism. One possible explanation can be dismissed easily: Preston's Conservatism was not

Table 6.1. *Percentage of electorate voting Conservative and number of parliamentary seats in selected Lancashire towns and major urban centres, 1885*

	Percentage	Seats
Preston	55.2	2
Blackburn	53.9	2
Bolton	48.5	2
Oldham	45.9	2
Burnley	43.6	1
Manchester	45.2	6
Sheffield	42.8	5
Liverpool	40.3	8
Leeds	36.7	6
Birmingham	33.6	7
Bristol	32.9	4
English constituencies	41.4 (in contested seats)	

Source: F.W.S. Craig (ed.), *British Parliamentary Election Results 1885–1918*, London: Macmillan, 1974.

Table 6.2. *Extent of adult male enfranchisement in Lancashire boroughs, 1911 (percentages)*

Blackburn	62.6
Oldham	59.3
Burnley	59.1
Preston	57.9
Bolton	57.7
England and Wales (all seats)	65.6
English and Welsh county boroughs	59.9

Source: Craig (ed.), *British Parliamentary Election Results, 1885–1918*.

based on Conservative traditions. Indeed throughout the early nineteenth century it was something of a radical stronghold, with the famous radical agitator 'Orator' Hunt winning the parliamentary seat in 1830, and the Liberals also doing well until the middle of the century.[4] More generally Clarke has argued that in Lancashire, at least, the Tories relied on 'status' politics, with voting based on ethnic and religious ties, so that the Tories did well where the Anglican church was strong. As I demonstrated in Chapter 5, however, religion was not a potent force in this period, and was becoming much more prominent from around 1900 when Tory hegemony was in fact under attack. Phillips confirms that sectarianism was weak in Preston, and that 'politics and religion were not as rigidly aligned as in the other Northern towns'. Other writers emphasise the centrality of ethnic cleavages between Irish and English workers: once again however Preston does not fit this model, since the existence of large numbers of English Catholics meant that the Irish were better integrated than elsewhere, and that the Catholic church was not an exclusively Irish church. There is little evidence of Catholics being confined to particular jobs or neighbourhoods by the end of the century.[5]

Patrick Joyce has emphasised deference to a mill-owning elite as the mainspring of Conservative dominance in mid-Victorian Lancashire. His argument is weakened, however, because it does not tally with the periodisation of Lancashire's history. The main period of employers' paternalism and political activity was from 1840 to the 1870s, yet through much of this period the Liberals remained strong, and the real period of Tory power, in electoral terms, was from 1880 to 1900, the period when – according to Joyce – employer paternalism was breaking down. In the case of Preston Joyce's theory certainly has little to commend it. By the 1880s most of the politically active employers were Liberals, such as J.R. Smith, Joseph Eccles (both Liberal councillors), Levi Fish and J. Tullis. The leading Tory magnates, led by Edward Hermon, the proprietor of Horrockses and Tory M.P. in the 1870s, had retired from active participation in public life by then. While several employers retained Tory leanings and might sign election nomination forms, they were not otherwise politically involved.[6]

A much better starting point for explaining working-class Conservatism is to consider the character of practical politics and the capacities for collective action. In Preston these were overwhelmingly economistic. The strength of the Conservatives lay in their ability to tap these active struggles in order to secure a strong electoral base. I have already indicated the type of capacities tending to produce such a form of practical politics in Preston: the predominance of factory skills, the pattern of gender relations, and a neighbourhood structure where petit-bourgeois elements were of major significance. It was however the decline in Preston's local economy that was of vital importance both in helping these struggles to reach the formal political agenda, and in allowing the Conservative party to latch onto them.

6.1   *The politics of urban regeneration*

So long as capitalist employment remains reasonably plentiful workers who engage in economistic struggles can take as given the existence of a labour market and attempt to warren their way into it and to secure niches and gain measures of security. In these cases economistic struggles are frequently unrelated to the formal political arena. When employment declines, and the central concern of workers is to find new forms of wage labour (and hence of capitalist investment), more concerted action is necessary, usually to persuade capital (in some guise or other) to invest. In Preston the struggles to deal with the decline in employment discussed in Chapter 4 were overwhelmingly economistic in the sense that few attempts took place to establish co-operative production or to force direct state employment to undermine the capitalist labour market. These economistic struggles surfaced frequently in the 1880s and were primarily fought over the issue of how regeneration could best occur. This was the basis of Tory hegemony.

This is best seen by discussing the conflict which developed in the 1880s over the development of Preston docks. The Ribble Navigation Company had been set up in 1837 to improve the Ribble and increase Preston's water-borne trade.[7] It had, however, proved ineffective, and traffic fell steadily, so that it seemed likely to fail completely by the 1880s. At this point, however, W.E.M. Tomlinson, a leading local landowner and President of the Conservative working men's club, formed a committee of ratepayers to press for action by the Corporation of Preston. As a result of this campaign the Corporation, which already owned one-third of the shares in the Company, bought it outright, and proposed to build a dock and deepen the Ribble. Originally it was estimated that a 6*d* rate for a few years would suffice and that the scheme would soon become profitable. This did not occur: the opening of a satisfactory channel proved difficult, and expenditure rose. By 1886 about 15 % of the Corporation's expenditure went on the scheme, a figure which had risen to about 30 % by the middle of the 1890s. By 1893 of the total Preston rate of 7*s*, 2*s* 1*d* went on the Ribble and Preston had become one of the highest rated towns in the country.[8]

The significance of the scehme was that its rationale was to attract trade to Preston. The Corporation was to provide the conditions under which private firms would invest, and the employees of the docks would not be those of the Corporation, but would be employed by private shipping companies. This was therefore an economistic solution to Preston's economic difficulties which was concerned to use the (local) state to prime the pumps for capitalist investment, rather than to demand that the local authority provide work as of right. The scheme ran into opposition, however, primarily from the leading cotton employers of the town. These stood to gain little by the development of the Ribble, since all their trading arrangements were carried out through Liverpool and Manchester. In the late 1880s they formed the Preston Property Owners' and Ratepayers' Association to oppose the Ribble's development. This was different in character from most similar associations which tended to be dominated by small landlords.[9]

It was the working class and petite bourgeoisie which became the chief supporters of the scheme. The Trades Council backed it consistently, while the Spinners' Union Secretary, Thomas Banks, emphasised that 'we are in a retrograding condition with only one hope left and that is the development of our river . . . our hope, our prayer, is that it may prove to be a success upon a great scale'.[10] In 1888 the growing opposition to the scheme forced the Corporation to hold a ballot of all ratepayers and property owners, and the result showed massive popular support: but while the middle-class property owners gave the scheme a bare majority (1,501 to 1,256), the ratepayers, with their more working-class complexion, voted emphatically in favour by 11,608 to 3,579.[11]

These tensions came to a head in the 1888 municipal elections. Preston Corporation had applied to parliament for a further extension of borrowing powers. In opposition, four leading employers decided to contest the municipal election as the 'Party of Caution'. They proposed to abandon the attempt to dredge a fresh channel in the Ribble, and to make do with a minimal scheme. In five of the six wards the 'Party of Caution' opposed Ribble supporters, a remarkable political rupture in a town where municipal elections were usually uncontested.

In response an ad hoc working-class campaign developed to support the Corporation's proposals. A 'Party of Action' was formed when 'the working men supporters of the Corporation scheme . . . banded themselves together, irrespective of belief, in all parts of the town'. 'Working Men's Committees' were set up.[12] They were met by a determined use of 'influence' by the employers. Eccles had on his election platform a number of people who 'were in some position of authority in one or other of the great mills in Fishwick owned and worked by the members of the Party of Caution'. The *Preston Herald* revealed the use of the 'screw' in several firms where employees known to be favourable to the Ribble development were interviewed by managers. Supervisors who were known to favour the 'Party of Caution' were given time off to 'canvass' other workers.[13]

Yet all this proved ineffective. The 'Party of Caution' candidates were all decisively defeated, in many cases by some of the largest majorities known. The *Preston Herald* declared that 'it had been a working man's victory. The Party of Action was almost entirely composed of working men . . . The victory . . . was undoubtedly due to the complete confidence of the heads of working class households in Preston in the Ribble scheme.' Anti-employer sentiments were also well reported. One speaker at a victory meeting spoke of 'the objects the working men of the town had in doing their best to support the Corporation in their endeavour to make the Ribble navigable and to lend their help to protect the town and its representatives from unscrupulous attacks being made upon it by a combination of capitalists'.[14]

On the practical issue of finding fresh forms of employment Preston's working class was active and easily overcame the opposition presented by the town's leading employers. The Ribble Navigation incident fits in badly with the image of those who see the Victorian city as dominated by a power elite of employers and other notables. While theorists have emphasised that an indication of power cannot be provided simply by looking at whose decision holds sway (because of the ability of those in power to keep certain issues 'off the agenda'), it must be recognised that it is difficult to keep some issues of basic importance to the people – what I have termed practical politics – off the agenda indefinitely.[15] The Ribble scheme was not an isolated incident: another conflict developed as a result of urban change in the early 1890s. The expense of the Ribble scheme had the effect of diverting money from other branches of the municipal budget, particularly health services. Between 1884 and 1891 the proportion of borough expenditure on sanitation-related items fell from 36 % to 21 %, and in absolute terms rose by only 13 %. Preston's health was notoriously bad and in 1891 a death rate of 26.6 per thousand was recorded, higher than that prevailing in nearly all other comparable towns.[16] This problem was accentuated by the general weakness of mutualist health care in Preston, which might have been able to compensate in some way for the poor public provision.

An outcry was provoked, and a distinctly working-class campaign developed. The retiring borough councillors were held responsible for the problems and the Conservative party, which had originally planned to support their re-election, was forced to reconsider after a fervent campaign. In a specially convened meeting of the Conservative party one of the leaders noted that 'the vast number of working men were determined to fight for the best candidate', and the retiring candidates were 'de-selected'. A 'True Conservative' wrote to the local paper stating that 'as a Conservative I am heartily tired of the unbusinesslike work of the town council . . . and I hope my fellow working men, be they Liberal or Conservative, will as far as lies in their power . . . make a change'.[17] The striking result was that this did not force the working men to run some of their own number as candidates but they approached the very candidates – the cotton employers – who had been so decisively defeated three years previously. Four employers were 'approached and importuned to stand by a number of working men'. They were all known for their concern to keep rate expenditure down, Simpson, for instance, having stated that 'our town used to be one of the lowest rated in the country and if you see fit to elect me I will do all I can to restore it to such a desirable position'.[18] All the other candidates were linked to the Ratepayers' Association. Their main attributes were that they declared they would run affairs 'efficiently'.

These candidates now basked in the popularity bestowed upon them. Instead of the 'screw' they had tried to apply in 1888 they relied on working-class organisation to elect them. Hamilton 'placed himself unreservedly in the hands of the working men's committee'. On the eve of the election the *Lancashire Daily Post* noted that the 'new candidates . . . appeal distinctively to the working men's votes . . . the Conservative working men have revolted and they ask all their fellow workers who share their anxiety to see their town improved to vote for [them]'.[19] The candidates duly swept home.

These elections were interesting in that in both cases formal party politics were suspended. They allow the practical politics to be revealed in an unusually clear way, and what they revealed was an economistic working-class politics. There was a concern to attract (capitalist) employment through local authority provision, yet in the vital issue of health care the main concern was to get efficient administration within an existing budget.

Conservative support was built on this bedrock: it did not rely on deferential workers or people who for some reason were acting irrationally against their interests. Rather it relied on workers pursuing their interests in a particular economistic way. The process by which the Tories tapped this rich vein was slow, but by the 1880s had reached a peak, whereby over 50 % of the electorate regularly voted Conservative (see Table 6.1). The key figure in this respect was W.E.M. Tomlinson, who proved remarkably perceptive to the practical concerns of Preston's working class, at least in the 1880s. Throughout the mid-Victorian period working-class attachment to the Conservative party had been undermined by the patrician structure of the local Conservatives, who remained dominated by the residential, mainly professional elite based in Winckley Square. This group, as I indicated in Chapter 5, was deeply concerned to retain its control over Preston's central space, a fact which led to their constant attempts to undermine independent working-class Conservatism. Confrontation began in 1867 when working-class Conservatives built their own Conservative club. Within a few years, however, middle-class Conservatives began to frequent it and started to 'screw up' the subscription to the point where the working class could no longer afford to join. (This club later fell into disuse.) In the late 1870s two clubs were built, to cater for the different classes. The 'gentlemen and middle classes' built their club in Guildhall Street in 1878, scarcely a minute's walk from Winckley Square. This club charged a high subscription (one guinea), and became extremely exclusive, with facilities for reading, dining, playing cards and smoking.[20] The working-class Conservatives approached Tomlinson asking for a loan to build their own club. Tomlinson was primarily a landowner, owning many of the newly developed housing estates to the north of Preston (he was largely responsible for developing the Deepdale area), but was also a major shareholder in the local railway company, the Lancashire and Yorkshire. He agreed to provide a loan and the club, the Conservative working men's club, was built, and it had 700 members by 1882.

These two clubs were frequently in conflict, no more so than in the early 1880s. The prime cause was the fact that the middle-class Guildhall Street club controlled the Parliamentary Committee which could choose the prospective parliamentary candidate – it could nominate twenty-five of the thirty members of this committee. In 1882 the sitting Tory MP, Sir John Holker, resigned, and the Parliamentary Committee chose Robert Raikes as his replacement, well aware that the national Tory leadership wanted him to return to parliament because of his parliamentary experience. This angered local Conservative working men. A placard appeared appealing

To all independent Conservative electors of Preston and all who value liberty and political freedom. Fellow electors – the time has come when we as Conservative working men must assert our independence as free electors and return Mr W.E.M. Tomlinson to the House of Commons. Of late years it has been the custom of a small clique in Guildhall St to dictate to Conservative electors in the borough as to who shall be the candidate.[21]

Tomlinson, as we have seen, led the campaign to develop the Ribble in the late 1870s. Eventually it was agreed that the Conservative working men's club could have ten of the thirty seats on the Parliamentary Committee and that Tomlinson would be strongly considered when the next vacancy arose. The Conservatives easily won the 1882 by-election (see Appendix C). Nine months later however Raikes resigned his Preston seat in order to represent the safer and more prestigious seat of Cambridge University. The Parliamentary Committee decided by twenty-one to six not to support Tomlinson as the new candidate, and instead nominated R.W. Hanbury, another outsider, a former MP for Staffordshire. This incensed members of the working men's club, and their Executive Committee, together with a few members of the Guildhall Street Club, asked Tomlinson to stand as an independent Conservative. Hanbury's nomination papers were signed by eight employers, five professional men, six small businessmen and a gentleman. Tomlinson's were signed by four employers, three workers, and one gentleman, together with four who cannot be identified (and are therefore probably working class). The class dimension to the difference was apparent.

In his skilful campaign Tomlinson linked his candidature to working-class economism. He did not stress his wealth for its sake, but for the way in which it could help the 'working man'. He declared himself the 'candidate of the working man', whilst one of his supporters, Dr Holden, emphasised that 'he looked upon Mr Tomlinson as a champion for the working man'.[22] Tomlinson argued his case on the basis of his local interests as a landowner, such that it was in his interests to see a prosperous Preston. His leading champion, Clarkson, outlined his qualifications:

His large properties in the town; his varied and commercial interests; his goodwill towards the working man, and his supposd abilities as a barrister and a local man to push through the new bill which the Corporation will seek to pass in order to legalise the purchase of all navigation rights on the Ribble.[23]

Tomlinson himself stressed that

It was his first duty to look after local interests . . . 'I desire to place myself more especially before you on the grounds of my intimate connection with the town, the extensive interest I have in its welfare.'[24]

And, most revealingly of all,

It was of importance to all classes, but of special importance to the working class, that they should have in the town a local man.[25]

Tomlinson therefore campaigned precisely on the sorts of economistic issues which were so close to the hearts of Preston's working class, and won a resounding victory. Even assuming that all the Liberals voted for Tomlinson (no Liberal stood), over one-third of the Tory vote went to Tomlinson. The Guildhall Street club learnt its lesson well, and democratised its party to the extent of having a 'Conservative 300' elected by all party members to make all decisions. Even in Liverpool, the only other town with mass working-class involvement in the Conservative party, where indeed there were 8,000 members of the Conservative working men's clubs in the 1890s, working-class Conservatives had no executive power.[26] In Preston, however, many people were able to use the power base of the working men's club to launch a political career. This was particularly true of petit-bourgeois figures, so important in working-class neighbourhoods. John Green, for instance, who had worked in a cotton mill before becoming a watchmaker and jeweller, had become active in 1892 when 'working men of St John's Ward had invited him to come forward as a candidate for a seat on the Board of Guardians' (the public body responsible for relief of the poor) and he later became a Conservative councillor.[27]

The Conservatives' hold on practical politics lay partly, as we have seen, in the economic decline of Preston. Tomlinson was keen to emphasise how local rentiers, like himself, were also vitally concerned with urban regeneration.[28] Toryism made no bones about accepting the reality of class, simply emphasising that working-class interests were served by local employers able to provide employment. This ready acceptance of class was manifested in many ways: Tomlinson stressed that 'the working classes of this country were more indebted to the Conservatives than the Liberals'. A 'Conservative Working Man' wrote that 'the success of trade depends primarily on the enterprise of our capitalists, the inventive ability and great commercial acumen of our great trade managers, and last but by no means least the faithful honest labour . . . of the millions who make up our working class'.[29] Working-class Conservatism was not based on the denial of the salience of class, and it placed no great emphasis on appealing to people as members of ethnic groups or religious blocs. In fact, in Preston, the Conservatives did not attempt to play down class divisions but merely harnessed them to their own ends.

The Liberals' weakness was due to their reluctance to come to terms with these same forces. One small indicator of this was the structure of their 'Reform club'. Unlike the Conservatives who had separate clubs for their middle- and working-class members, the Reform club was technically

open to everyone, with subscriptions ranging between 10s and one
guinea according to income. Only those paying the guinea subscription,
however, were allowed access to the basement billiards room! The
Liberals remained essentially populist, being unable to make any specific
appeals to members of the working class as such, and this allowed
leading Liberals to present themselves as leaders of a popular coalition
which did not in fact exist. The resulting elitism was consistently
attacked by Conservatives. In 1885 the *Preston Herald* noted 'what scant
sympathy there is at all times at the Headquarters of Preston Liberalism
for everybody below the social level of a manufacturer or tradesman'. In
1891 Liberal employers who had been asked to stand as candidates on
the sanitary issue were held to believe that 'working men who are not
rated directly . . . should be thankful enough to pay their rents and leave
the management of the town's business exclusively to their landlords, to
millowners and to large capitalists'.[30]

By the 1890s no Liberals dared put themselves forwards as Liberal
candidates in municipal elections, and sought refuge under other
banners, such as 'Young Preston' or, occasionally, 'Radical'. At the
parliamentary level the Liberals had attempted to put forward 'Labour'
candidates in the 1880s, but this backfired because of the hostility of the
Tory trade unionists. By 1892 they were reduced to putting up Catholic
landowners in the hope of milking a Catholic vote, but when this failed
they withdrew, and left the seat uncontested after 1892.

The strongly organised trade unions threw their weight behind the
Conservative cause throughout the 1890s. Occasionally some hint of
political independence appeared: particularly in 1891 in the municipal
election in which the sanitation issue reached its height. In this year the
Joint Trades Council and Friendly Society Council nominated a candidate, George Oakey. He was a typical working-class Conservative, who
had signed Tomlinson's nomination papers nine years previously, and
advocated that Corporation land should be let at nominal rent to private
firms, while also supporting fair wages for Corporation employees, and
sanitary improvements. Even in this case, however, the unions put little
effort in to secure their candidate's election: in later years the secretary of
the Trades Council recalled that Oakey won 'not on the account of the
very great assistance rendered by the [Trades] Council, but simply and
solely because of the aid given by the Friendly Societies and the
personality of Mr Oakey'.[31]

The unions' other independent venture was in 1893 when the Tory
secretary of the Weavers' Union, Luke Park, stood as municipal

candidate, having failed to win a Conservative nomination. He stated that 'he should always see to the labour interest in the [Town] Council if returned but in all other matters he would expect to be allowed a free hand. He would be stripped of every creed and be purely a workingman's representative.'[32] Only a handful of trade unionists turned out to help in his campaign. His candidature testified to the recognition of an independent working-class economic interest throughout these years and to its weak propensity to find independent political representation. The Tories had the working-class vote well under their control.

6.2   The emergence of independent Labour politics

This situation changed from the turn of the century. The initial challenge from about 1893 came from the newly formed Independent Labour party (ILP), which until 1900 was the leading opposition to the Conservative party in Preston. Its challenge failed, however, which testified to the fact that organisation and commitment alone were not enough to undermine Tory hegemony.

The Preston ILP claimed to have 300 members by 1894, although this dropped to about one hundred after the middle of the 1890s. The ILP nominated municipal candidates in 1893 and 1896 but they were all decisively beaten. The ILP tried to change the issues of local politics, away from economistic concerns to ones more concerned to develop state services, such as demolishing slums, providing playgrounds and municipalising amenities. The problem was that the capacities for this form of struggle did not exist, and concern over such issues provoked a backlash from working-class Tories. The Tories characterised the ILP candidates as 'champion[s] of "Nationalisation" and "Municipalisation"', and in 1896 one Conservative was asked to oppose an ILP candidate by 'working men, both Liberal and Conservative', and apparently 'many trade unionists voted for Mr Willian [the Tory]', who won a clear victory. The failure of the ILP in the 1890s shows clearly enough how activism is fruitless unless tied to practical struggles.[33] There were however a number of developments which were soon to put independent Labour politics on the agenda.

The success of the Conservatives lay largely in their ability to present policies able to link up with working-class economism. Their ability to do this was under threat, however, from the late 1890s, for a number of reasons. Some of these were related to national developments. The Conservatives had been in power at a period when trade unions were under strong legal attack and the Conservative administration appeared unsympathetic to trade unions, particularly in the aftermath of the Taff Vale judgement in 1901 whereby trade unions were held to be liable to pay the legal damages caused by industrial disputes. It is impossible to overestimate the importance of this single issue. It turned trade unions, which had previously been hostile to Labour representation, around to an attitude of much greater enthusiasm. Even as late as 1899, by which time nearly every working-class town in Britain had seen some move towards independent Labour politics, usually in the form of local candidates, there was little sign of a stirring in Preston.[34] In this year there was an attempt to establish a 'Municipal Workers' Committee' to sponsor independent working-class candidates, yet it made little headway with the Trades Council. In 1900 the Committee stated that 'it was their earnest desire to see the two workers' organisations [the Trades Council and the Municipal Workers' Committee] co-operating in the interests of the workers whom they were supposed to serve . . . it was help rather than hindrance which they expected from the Trades Council'. Only seven unions (out of about fifty) supported it, yet in the same year the Trades Council gave full support to a 'Patriotic Ball' in support of the Boer War organised by the Conservative working men's club.[35] The Municipal Workers' Committee faded away soon afterwards. Yet only two years later trade union enthusiasm for independent politics ran high, and the Preston Labour party was formed in 1902. This was in the wake of a meeting arranged by a national Labour Representation Committee (LRC) organiser. He declared: 'Last night Mr Hodge and myself attended the Preston Conference and I think it will be safe to say that a more unanimous and successful Conference it was hardly possible for anyone to attend.' Hodge added 'I do not think that there can be any question as to the success of this movement.'[36]

The main organisations had been won over to independent Labour politics by 1903. This did not, however, as I shall discuss below, imply any change in their economistic concerns, but simply a strategic recognition that these might be more easily advanced outside the Conservative party. Nonetheless the working-class electors of Preston did prove more resistant to breaking with Conservatism than did the trade union leaders. In 1903 Tomlinson died. His popularity had declined steadily, partly because of rumours (which he had always denied) that he gave funds to the strike-breaking Free Labour Union. The ensuing by-election gave the fledgling Labour party its first chance to test the waters. It was opposed, however, by the owner of Dick, Kerr and Co. which had recently opened in Preston, signalling the long-awaited upturn in the local economy. Kerr campaigned in true Tory style, emphasising his local interests and the value of these for the working class. He claimed to be a 'Labour candidate and he thought his qualifications were quite equal to those of his opponent', and declared 'Lancashire labour was the best labour in the world'. The Labour party did not campaign on policy issues and had no differences with the Conservatives on that score, but merely on whether the working classes should be represented directly. Billington, secretary of the Spinners' Union, chose this moment to resign from the Conservative party, stressing that 'the only way for working men to secure a redress of the grievances under which they labour at the present day was to send men from their own ranks'.[37]

Despite Labour efforts, and the national political context in which Labour was beginning to make impressive inroads, notably in its by-election victories in Woolwich and nearby Clitheroe, the working-class Conservative vote held up well. One Labour activist declared afterwards that 'he was ashamed of the trade unionists of Preston . . . they have not acted in accordance with their promises . . . the result is a disgrace to the trade unionists of Preston', while Billington, having only just joined the Labour party himself, felt sufficiently affronted to lament that 'the voters were an utterly hopeless quality and he had done with them'.[38]

The actual breakthrough of the Labour party occurred between 1904 and 1906. In these years it won its first Town Council seats (three), and in alliance with the Liberals overturned forty-seven years of Tory hegemony by winning the parliamentary seat in 1906. There were three major factors behind this development. Firstly the Conservative party became steadily less able to articulate economistic politics. Secondly, as employers became more directly politically active the trade unions also felt they needed direct intervention. Finally the 'labour interest' was changing in character, and the growth of municipal employment was raising new issues encouraging direct Labour representation.

The first point related primarily to the 'capture' of the Tory party by tariff reformers, who advocated the placing of tariff barriers around the empire in order to stop unemployment being caused in trades undercut by foreign competition. While such a policy was perhaps attractive in the Midlands where the metal industry had been suffering from American competition, and where tariff reform's leading advocate, Joseph Chamberlain, found his power base, in Lancashire such a step signalled a dramatic shift away from free trade, long held to be vital to the prosperity of the cotton industry. Cotton employers were concerned that this would lead to tariffs being raised against their own goods, and many left the Tory party. In Preston Frank Calvert, a former chairman of the Conservatives, formed a Free Trade League. This single issue of free trade was unquestionably the main issue at the general election of 1906 in Preston, and many trade unionists deserted the Tory party because of its change of policy. The spinners, hitherto the bastion of working-class Conservatism, held a special meeting and condemned the proposal. In the election the *Preston Guardian* noted 'the unwonted spectacle of the leading capitalists of the town speaking for the Labour candidate, contributing to his election funds and lending him their motor cars'.[39] The Conservatives had in one fell swoop lost their credibility as the party of the economic interest of the workers.

Clearly the shifting character of national politics explains to a large extent the rise of Labour as a viable political force in Preston. There were however some more local processes which were involved. One of these was the changing politics of the cotton employers. After their momentous victory in the 1854 cotton dispute the cotton employers had never been particularly well organised in Preston until the conflict over the Ribble development came to a head in the late 1880s. The Cotton Employers' Association became much stronger in the 1890s, largely to provide a voice for employers over relevant parliamentary legislation, notably the Workmen's Compensation Bill of 1895, which they strongly opposed. By 1900 the Employers' Association had become far stronger and was active on a variety of fronts: enquiring into the charges imposed by the Preston Gas Company, and in particular questioning rate assessments. This activity culminated in a meeting of a municipal sub-committee of the Employers' Association in 1903, whose duty was to encourage members to stand in municipal elections to represent the interests of the trade. The Association paid all election expenses and, while not averse to gaining the backing of either Tory or Liberal parties, its candidates stood primarily as 'cotton' candidates. This mobilisation demonstrated the weakness of the employers' hold in the local Conservative party.[40]

The main concern of the employers was over rates, and was provoked by further plans to raise expenditure on the Ribble. In 1904 Preston Corporation had to apply for further borrowing power to finance the dredging of the Ribble, and approached the Employers' Association for its support. This was not forthcoming, however, and the Association resolved 'expressly and emphatically [to] repudiate any share in the responsibility for the proposed expenditure on the Ribble and is not prepared to support the Corporation in the meditated application . . . for further borrowing powers'.[41] The Association's municipal candidates supported this view.

The independent politics of capital were found to provoke a reaction from labour: a feeling that since capital was engaging in sectional interest, labour also had to gain direct representation. The first Labour party breakthroughs and the mobilisation of the unions were linked to the recognition of the employers' more aggressive political profile. J.R. Smith stood as the Employers' Association unofficial municipal candidate in 1903, and the Labour party opposed him, putting up the official of the Beamers', Twisters' and Drawers' Union, Swarbrick, whose union was not recognised at Smith's mill. The candidature was justified in terms of the need to represent labour directly even though capital's interests were still held to be identical with labour's. Wooley (President of the Preston Weavers' Union) stated that 'Smith said the interests of employers and workmen were identical. He [Wooley] believed they were, but if they had a few Labour men in the Town Council to look after labour interests a little more it would be a little better.' Swarbrick was defeated but became the first Labour councillor at a by-election shortly afterwards. In 1905, however, the Employers' Association candidate was indeed defeated by a Labour one, a factor which was so degrading to the employers that no more could be found to suffer the potential humiliation of losing to one of their workers.[42]

A further development led trade unions to become concerned with direct labour representation: the question of municipal workers. The later Victorian period was one of considerable expansion of municipal employment, and although Preston had not been notable for its enterprise in this direction (the docks apart), its municipal employment increased from the 1890s. The main driving force behind this expansion was a new political party, the Progressive party which, while concerned to reduce expenditure on the Ribble, wanted to see a much bigger role for the municipality in provision of services, particularly in sanitary provision, tram services and electricity production. The Progressives also demanded the provision of public washhouses, paving of streets, establishment of recreation grounds, municipalisation of telephones, and even the building of council houses.[43]

The party originated as the latest in a long line of attempts by local Liberal notables to find a niche in local politics. It was novel in that it marked an end to attempts to appeal to existing interest groups (the 'labour' interest, or the Catholic interest, both of which were spoken for), with a new emphasis on disrupting the old polity by creating a new political agenda. It articulated non-economistic demands, and changed the main agenda of local politics from questions of how to attract waged employment to how to provide state services. It was able to feed on certain of the capacities of the residents of the newer, outer, estates who needed transport and new amenities. Its status as a suburban party seems reasonably clear. The leading activists were employers or professionals living on the outskirts of Preston, including E.J. Andrew, an Ashton architect, T. Parkinson, a biscuit manufacturer who lived on Moor Park near Fulwood, W. Johnson, a theatre proprietor from Ribbleton, and Henry Cartmell, a solicitor from St Anne's. They were labelled the Ashton Party, with one Tory claiming that they 'were a clique that met in Fishergate but which had its origins in Ashton among a few people who thought they knew more than anyone else . . . the scratch my back society'.[44]

In Chapter 5 I drew attention to the growth of new working-class estates away from the older inner-city areas where petit-bourgeois figures held sway. It is difficult to determine precisely whether it was these people who were attracted to the new Progressive politics, for Preston's wards covered both inner- and outer-city areas. They did however do particularly well in the two wards with specific suburban bases: Park ward to the north was a large, growing area composed of newer working-class housing, and the Progressives won here in 1899 and 1901 on the two occasions when they stood candidates. They also won Maudland comfortably, the seat which contained Ashton.

The Progressive tide flowed between 1898 and 1899, when Tory dominance was halted, but thereafter the Conservatives reacted by taking on board many of the Progressives' specific policies and won back their ground. By 1902 the Progressive assault had been absorbed. There were two long-lasting effects however. Just as the abandonment of free trade helped weaken the Conservatives' links with working-class economism in national politics, so the adoption of 'progressive' politics at municipal level helped the same process here. Secondly, and more importantly, the Progressive phenomenon was a leading factor behind the creation of a larger municipal workforce. In 1899 the Corporation took over the tram system, and between 1893–4 and 1906–7 rate expenditure rose by nearly 50 %, most of which filtered through to local wages.[45]

The problem for the unions was simple: they were suspicious of the Progressives' links with the Ratepayers' Association. This had been revived in the late 1890s after its failures in the Ribble campaign. The Progressives tried to appeal to a ratepayer interest, such as when Rawsthorn in 1899 stressed that 'ratepayers should insist upon greater attention being devoted to questions affecting their welfare'. The Progressive strategy may have appeared contradictory in calling for more state intervention while protecting the ratepayer. In fact their proposals were that profits created by municipal transport and electricity could be used to relieve the ratepayer or improve services. In 1900 the *Preston Guardian* explicitly supported the plans for municipalising public services where profits could be used for 'the benefit of the ratepayer'. This strategy was widely canvassed at this time as a means of alleviating the rates burden which had grown rapidly since the 1880s.[46]

The problem, from the unions' point of view, was that profits earned in municipal enterprise could be gained by paying low wages to municipal workers. The Progressives on several occasions insisted that they would adhere to trade union conditions and rates of pay, but nonetheless there were suspicions about the attitudes of leading Progressives to unions. Parkinson refused to allow trade unions at his biscuit factory, a fact which may explain the difficulty he had in winning a Corporation seat. Hubbertsey, another Progressive, declared in 1907 that the 'trade union was a very needful organisation for the worker, but he thought it should confine itself to its proper sphere'.[47] The fact that many of the Progressives were Liberals, who were generally regarded as anti-union after the example of the Liberal cotton employer J.R. Smith, also contributed to the unions' negative perception of the Progressives.

The Corporation was known to pay low wages to many of its workers and they were poorly unionised. The only way by which wages could be improved was therefore by direct Labour representation on the Town Council, a fact which the Labour party was not slow to recognise. In 1906 W.S. Coates, a Labour candidate, proclaimed that 'the Corporations were large employers of labour and he would use all legitimate means to make the corporate body model employers'.[48]

The issue of municipal work was important also in another way: as the Corporation expanded so did the number and size of the contracts which it placed with private firms. This gave the unions a strong incentive to ensure that the Corporation placed contracts with unionised firms. This agitation for 'fair contracts' was mentioned in virtually all Labour candidates' addresses. Indeed it was a dispute of this sort which led the Trades Council to develop a more active political role. As I showed above the Trades Council in 1900 was still lukewarm about Labour representation, yet later in the year the Corporation placed an 'illegal' contract. The printers' delegate to the Trades Council pressed that 'the Trades Council take immediate steps to secure the return to the town council of those candidates who are only in favour of and will assist in obtaining the recognition of the fair wages clause in all municipal contracts'. In 1900 the Trades Council duly asked all candidates for municipal office whether they supported 'fair contracts'. It was concern over this issue which swung the Trades Council behind independent Labour representation by 1903, when it was stressed by all the Labour candidates.[49]

6.3   Patterns of Labour support, 1900–14

I have argued that the emergence of the Labour party in Preston did not result from any change in the economistic propensities of the local working class: rather it was brought about by the inability of the Conservatives to articulate these struggles, the growing pragmatic realisation that national developments made independent Labour politics more viable, and finally the posing of 'the labour interest' in new and acute ways because of the practices of local employers and the growth of municipal labour. Yet it is important not to neglect entirely the changing character of different occupations with their different capacities for collective action, for it is these considerations which help explain why members of some trades were far more interested in Labour politics than were others. It is the patriarchal nature of economistic politics which is of especial importance in this regard: those trades which were threatened by female labour were to the fore in the local Labour movement, but those whose own patriarchal position was unchallenged were the least enthusiastic.

Patriarchal concerns were apparent in many of the leading activists. Although the party was a consistent supporter of the principle of female suffrage, it still opposed women's position at work. Jeremiah Wooley, secretary of the Weavers' Union, used his position as a Town Councillor to denounce publicly those employers who refused to employ male weavers. On one occasion Wooley denounced employers who engaged 'women in the sheds, leaving the husband to see to the house or walk the street'. Luke Park, the Trades Council and Friendly Society candidate in 1893, mentioned that 'he had laboured for 18 years in the cause of these people to obtain for them adequate wages, which would enable them to keep their wives at home',[50] a point reiterated in 1906 by another Labour candidate who stressed that 'if by an agitation they could bring about the desirability of better wages being paid to the men workers they would be able to dispense with women workers altogether and mothers could then stay at home and look after their own children'.[51]

It was J.T. Macpherson, Preston's Labour MP between 1906 and 1910, who was especially vociferous on this issue. He suggested soon after his election that he might have to 'challenge' the women who worked in the mills:

The mother who went to work at 6.0, if she was as strong as Hercules could not keep up her work in the mill and her work in the home . . . he made bold to say that wages and conditions would have been higher had the labour been confined to the [male] operatives.[52]

These instances show how economistic concerns were closely tied to patriarchal ones. Higher wages were both cause and consequence of women not working. This patriarchal element in Labour politics – frequently underestimated by writers preferring romanticised interpretations of Labour history – was also revealed by the experience of the Women's Labour League. This was formed in 1906, after a national initiative, to encourage female activism. It soon began to demand statist reforms, with much greater levels of state intervention. Thus in Preston speakers at various meetings called for municipal savings banks, municipal insurance schemes, municipal crematoriums and lantern lectures, municipal restaurants and laundries, state housing, old age pensions, free breakfasts for children and state-funded 'women's cafés'.[53] This attempt to promote statist, non-patriarchal politics was not likely to succeed in a town where all the capacities at this time favoured economistic politics. The rest of the Labour party became hostile to the League, and in 1907 Edith Rigby, the honorary secretary, resigned, saying that

she must join the band of women who were willing to work for the vote. Many of them had been surprised at the little support which had been given the Labour [League] from the Labour sections for really the majority of the members of the committee had come from the ILP while they felt they had not received the support they merited from the trade union movement . . . Many men in the trade union movement had not encouraged their wives to think politically and to study the political situation. They only considered women important when they could persuade them to vote 'the other way' in a municipal election.[54]

Rigby's departure coincided with the break-up of the Women's Labour League as most of the activists joined the Women's Suffrage and Political Union (WSPU). This became a powerful force in Preston, with its own club and over one hundred members by 1910. The Trades Council frequently cold-shouldered the WSPU (while continuing to pay lip service to women's suffrage). In 1907 the Trades Council refused to give financial support, and did not support a suffragist request to urge the Parliamentary Labour party to move an amendment 'to the Address next session regretting the omission from the King's Speech of any mention of the claims of women to the franchise'. One result of this was that the WSPU, which nationally came to back the Labour party because of its support for women's franchise, was locally antagonistic. In 1912 one speaker complained that 'there is not a single solitary protest from the

Labour Party against the sweating of women. The Labour Party only represented the men.'[55]

The ILP which, like the Women's Labour League, also supported statist demands was frequently in conflict with the local Labour party. The ILP affiliated to the LRC in 1903 but had little voice and left in 1906 when the local party refused to countenance secular state-funded education. The LRC insisted that Macpherson's candidature in 1906 'was in no way connected with the Socialist movement', and Macpherson was extremely hostile to the ILP, at one time accusing its members of sending him abusive postcards. After leaving the LRC the ILP stood its own candidates for the Council. In general it demanded state secular education, unemployment relief and the payment of MPs, but the candidates did not poll well, and although membership rose to 250 by 1908 the ILP's influence remained small.[56]

This economism should not however be seen simply as an example of 'moderate' Labour politics. On wage issues the Labour movement could be extremely militant. The fact that very few demands were made upon the state should not hide the fact that the Labour movement was keenly concerned with issues such as the minimum wages paid to workers. In 1913–14 a campaign was launched demanding a 25s minimum wage. It was the raising of wages which was to lead to improvements in the quality of life. So when an ILP speaker demanded the 'endowment of motherhood' Labour activists subjected the idea to 'considerable criticism and the opinion was often expressed that many of the evils to which [the speaker] alluded could be eradicated simply by raising wages'. Similarly at a meeting only a week before the launch of the minimum wage campaign Labour activists opposed the Corporation's plan to borrow money for public works. However, militant struggles over wage issues did not imply any struggles over state intervention.[57]

The main pillars of the Labour party were those trades whose capacities for economistic struggle were strong, but which were threatened by female labour. The Weavers' Union led the way in this respect, for although it had been a bastion of Toryism in the 1890s its politics changed fast. In 1893 some union activists even opposed Luke Park's candidature for the Council, and Wooley and Park were both Conservatives. By 1902, however, the 'cotton people', mostly weavers, gave overwhelming support to the formation of the LRC.[58] This occurred over the same period as that which witnessed far-reaching changes in the career patterns of male weavers because of the practices of elite factory crafts, and it was the ensuing concern for the position of these male workers which fed into support for the Labour party. Weavers' officials were convinced that the number of female weavers could be reduced if the wages paid to their male relatives were increased and it was for this reason that they were so concerned about Corporation workers' wages.

Another union which gave strong support to the Labour party was the Typographical Association. This also was under pressure at this time, due to the introduction of new machinery and threats by some employers to use female workers. The Typographical Association was active in the Municipal Workers' Committee and in 1900 it passed a motion that 'it was thought advisable that the Trades Council should take a more active role in municipal matters'. The union overwhelmingly supported the formation of the LRC in 1900, well before other unions. The printers' interest in these issues lay in the realisation that if all municipal printing had to be done in union shops, this would provide a considerable boost to the union. They were to the fore in campaigning over 'fair contracts'.[59]

There were some unions however which were far less enthusiastic about Labour politics. The overlookers were notable in this respect. They did not join the LRC till 1905, and evidently left it shortly afterwards before rejoining in 1920. Many overlookers were active in the United Trades Unionist league set up in 1908. This was a body of trade union members who opposed Labour representation and were pledged to 'combat socialism' and which had Conservative connections. This League had 300 members (more than the ILP) by 1908.[60]

The overlookers' reluctance to get involved in Labour politics can be clearly linked to their patriarchal position in the weaving sheds. Their authority was increasing down to 1914, and unlike the weavers they were not under pressure to engage in wider formal political action to shore up their workplace autonomy. Furthermore, these elite cotton workers had succeeded in turning their occupation into a craft, and this helped them pursue mutualist struggles. Indeed, one group of overlookers built their own houses with bricks from a derelict mill. They were also active in the Co-op, which was still a Conservative body. In 1900 a local ILP member reported that the ILP had been unable to win a seat on the Co-op Board, adding that 'this is a very slow, old Conservative town, and anything like a move goes down badly with our Co-Operators'.[61] In the 1903 by-election leading Co-operators supported Kerr, the Tory. After this the Co-op became more independent and its president between 1909 and 1913 was Joshua Wallwork, secretary of the Tapesizers' Union and a Labour party supporter. Nonetheless the Co-op's mutualism kept it distinct from the rest of the Labour party. It was especially important in encouraging owner-occupation (despite one member stating that 'it was a bad thing to make capitalists by enticing people to buy their own houses') and by 1912 was lending £120,000 per annum in housing loans. Wallwork himself indicated that the principles of co-operation were more important than those of trade unionism and in 1912 he opposed wage increases for female shop assistants which would have entailed a fall in the 'divi' (dividend paid to members).[62]

Evidence regarding the politics of other unions is lacking, especially for those in the engineering sector. Outside the craft and engineering sectors unionisation took place slowly, and there is little evidence of unionisation before 1914 in the public amenities or the docks, both of which were still characterised by casual employment. It does seem possible to say that whilst most unions formally aligned themselves with Labour after 1903, those where female labour was a pressing issue were the most active. In any situation of economistic politics there are problems in changing from sectionalism to struggles for the improvement of all workers. In Preston the key factor behind the latter movement was the threat of women's labour. Union officials always felt the best way of reducing female labour in their trades lay in improving the conditions of *all* male workers, especially the low paid, since – as they saw it – the wives of such male workers would be less likely to work.

This interest in the threat provided by female labour is indicative of a weakness in Labour politics at the time, however, since female labour affected only a few groups of men and, as I indicated in Chapter 4, the position of most male workers was improving in this period. It was mainly the weavers and printers who were exposed to the threat of female competition and who were most vociferous. To be sure the trade unions' role in social life reached its zenith in this period, with the opening of the United Trades Hall, so the formal alignments of these unions were of considerable importance for many workers. But generally the Labour propensities of most unions were more pragmatic, based on the provisional recognition that their economic interests were best served by independent politics. This left one problem for the Labour movement, which became more severe. One of the major developments of the decade before 1914 was the emergence of the neighbourhood in working-class life and the steady development of capacities for collective action based upon it. The Labour party's reliance on union-based and work-based capacities left it unable to mobilise at the neighbourhood level, however, as I shall now discuss.

6.4   *Neighbourhood capacities and the recovery of Conservatism*

As the Conservative party lost its hold over trade union opinion, it searched around for alternative bases of support, and after 1900 it increasingly found these in the neighbourhood. This transition was manifest in a number of ways. Firstly, local councillors (mostly Tory though it is difficult to identify them all by party) were becoming increasingly likely to live in Preston. In 1883–5 under two-thirds of town councillors lived in Preston, but by 1901–3 nearly three-quarters did so. Furthermore it was from the working-class neighbourhoods that these local councillors were drawn. Only 15 % lived in these areas in 1883–5, but by 1901–3 this figure had risen to over 40 %. Conservative organisation developed strongly in the neighbourhoods. The Primrose League, a social organisation appealing especially to women, was the most significant example in this respect. Although weak in the 1880s it grew considerably and by 1912 had 1,830 members who were organised on a neighbourhood basis. Each ward had two districts which held regular socials and meetings. The Labour party, by contrast, had virtually no ward organisation. In the 1903 by-election the Labour party had no ward committees and was unable to carry out a canvas. By 1904 the Labour party claimed to have ward committees in eight of the twelve wards but these soon faded, and nearly all organisation was based on the unions.[63]

This growing neighbourhood base was symptomatic of the shift in support for the Conservatives. The churches found new popularity in the period after 1900 and as the Conservatives lost their grip on the 'labour interest' they began to play on this religious element in their appeals. Having advertised themselves in the 1890s as the party which catered to working-class demands, they shifted their claims to stress their role as the defenders of the Anglican faith. They became far less concerned with schemes such as the Ribble development, and adopted a ratepayers' perspective, so subordinating producer demands to consumer ones. Particularly important in this respect was the defection of the few remaining employers from the Conservative ranks, which helped throw petit-bourgeois figures into far greater prominence. This new base of support made the Conservatives more conscious of the ratepayer since, as Offer's work indicates, it was the small business people and shopkeepers who paid the highest proportion of their income in rates. The Tories took on a new role as the party of municipal thrift. In 1901 John Foster opposed the municipalisation of electricity and wanted no more money spent on 'open spaces and playgrounds', while in the same year Councillor Hale stressed that the town should spend no more money. In 1906 the Tory, Mallott, was opposed to the use of Corporation contracts to deal with the smoke nuisance, to the building of municipal lodging houses and to the abolition of private slaughterhouses.[64]

The licensed victuallers were a particularly important sector of the petite bourgeoisie to throw their weight behind the Conservatives, and their commitment to Conservatism was of considerable influence in working-class areas. Previously they had supported trade union causes: in 1897 the Preston licensed victuallers had actually granted money to the engineers during a lock-out, and at one point they tried to join the Trades Council. Part of the reason for these close relations was the importance of trade union patronage to publicans, but this declined as the unions opened their own premises. The Trades Council had traditionally met in the Stanley Arms and allowed its delegates to drink during meetings, a practice which came under fire from the growing number of teetotal union delegates. In 1900 there was a heated debate over whether intoxicants should be allowed, with one delegate stating that 'he thought that if the working men of this country would only give the licensed victuallers a little more of the cold shoulder than they did, it would tend to the solution of a great many trade unionist problems'.[65] The proposal to ban alcohol was defeated, but with the opening of the Trades Hall trade union custom was withdrawn from the pubs. So the emergence of union-based social life severed the ties of dependency between these two groups.

The publicans were further encouraged to make their political voice heard by changes in licensing laws and liquor taxes proposed by the Liberal government, which threatened massively to increase the cost of a licence.[66] After 1906 publicans were more politically active than they had been for some time previously. In 1907 they officially supported the Conservative municipal candidate and they continued to support the Conservatives at later elections. It was their influence which led the Labour party to consider building its own club. Following the defeat of the Labour candidate in the January 1910 elections Wooley complained that

licensed victuallers had flaunted their politics to such a degree that whilst not a great believer in clubs it was intended to make it possible for their own people to go and talk and have a glass of beer if necessary in their own premises in different parts of town.[67]

Most important was the attempt of the Conservatives to draw on church support. Throughout the 1890s the Tories played down sectarian issues since they knew that the Catholic voters would support them, because of their stance on voluntary education, so long as extreme Anglicanism did not become prominent. The national Labour organisers were clearly surprised at religious alignments in Preston. In 1903 Hodge, the Labour candidate, referred to the 'religious perversity of the Roman Catholic element . . . only straggling Catholic votes were received'.[68]

Their heavy defeat in the general election of 1906 and the recognition that they had lost the 'labour interest' forced the Tories to use religion as their new basis of support, and the Liberal government's plans to remove rate support from voluntary (i.e. church-run) education under the Birrell Bill provided them with the occasion. The resulting campaign saw the full emergence of the neighbourhood as a political force. (This of course was the period when attendance at Sunday schools reached its peak.) The 1906 municipal elections were the first to be fought on explicitly religious lines, with the Conservatives accusing the Labour party of supporting state secular education even though Labour denied this. All the Labour candidates were defeated, the chairman of the LRC complaining that 'they had the churches, the beer barrels and the toffee stalls against them'. Labour was thrown by the use of these tactics which were to become commonplace. The Preston Labour party's annual report alleged that the defeat 'was entirely due to the raising of the religious cry and the plentiful supply of beer for the men and sweets for the children'.[69]

The Conservatives clearly felt that they were onto a good thing. In the 1907 elections religious education was the main issue and in 'one of the most memorable contests ever waged in the municipal history of Preston', Labour's biggest ever challenge, with five candidates, was completely routed. In its annual report the Preston Labour party lamented its helplessness in the face of the religious issue:

We do not begrudge the Conservative Party their victory, but we do protest against the means taken to obtain that victory . . . we cannot help thinking that the motives which accentuate people who are continually raising the religious cry in these contests is something more than the religious welfare of the children.[70]

The defeat was so demoralising that Labour did not contest the 1908 elections.

The astonishing growth of popular Catholic organisations after 1906 was yet another problem to face the Labour party. The campaign against the Birrell Bill caused the Catholics to abandon their patron-based structure and to develop more popular forms of organisation. The Catholic Parents' League was formed which by 1909 had enrolled 14,000 out of the estimated 16,000 Catholic parents in Preston. This league was organised on a parochial level, and after the defeat of the Bill continued as a social group. In 1908 the Catholics organised a trade union sub-committee which was set up in every parish to campaign against secular education 'as entirely foreign to the real objects and aims of trade unionism'. The Catholics also set about systematically registering Catholic voters for the first time.[71] The development of a cohesive Catholic social life based on the parish again pre-empted Labour organisation in the neighbourhood.

It is clear that Labour's basic weakness before 1914 was its inability to develop organisations to tap neighbourhood capacities. Labour had clearly won the battle for the politics of the workplace, particularly in those trades threatened by female labour. This victory, however, led the Conservatives to find alternative bases of support in the neighbourhood and their reliance on small businesses, publicans and the church proved so effective that Labour polled worse in 1907 than at any previous time. Yet the Conservatives themselves faced problems resulting from their new support base. At one level it forced the Labour party to react by developing its own independent presence through Labour clubs. In the short term however the more serious problem was the danger that relying on religious sentiments could encourage sectarianism, hence splitting the Conservative vote.

The rapid increase in Catholic organisation led to demands that Preston should have a Catholic mayor. Whilst in 1906 and 1907 the Tories won both Catholic and Anglican backing since both sects supported voluntary education, in 1909 the Tories had to take sides. After negotiations about the mayoralty broke down the Conservatives stood in the municipal elections on the basis of retaining the Anglican monopoly of the mayoralty. In one ward there was a straight Catholic versus Protestant contest; in the rest Labour stood against the Conservatives and supported the principle that the mayor should come from any religious faith. There was unprecedented religious fervour: Councillor Miller gravely declared that 'in the present crisis, the like of which he had never known in the municipal history of Preston, every Churchman ought to take a stand and not foresake his principles'. An extreme Protestant backlash ensued, and the Revd Urquhart declared that 'we as Church People could sweep the whole borough of Non-conformity and Roman Catholics as well. He hoped the day would never come when the regalia of the municipality would be carried to a Roman Catholic chapel.'[72]

Although the Protestant candidate defeated the Catholic, elsewhere the Catholic vote swung behind Labour and enabled it to win a seat and poll well. This election marked the end of automatic Catholic identification with the Tories. The Catholics now had their own organisation which was to vacillate between Tory and Labour.

In 1910 the emergence of the neighbourhood as the basis of Toryism was enough to defeat the Labour and Liberal MPs and, against the Lancashire pattern, two Tories were elected. No Labour councillor was elected after 1909, and although they presented a serious challenge in 1912, four Labour candidates were defeated. A Labour activist sadly noted: 'they had met again to celebrate a defeat. They had done it so often in the Labour Party that they had learned to do it properly. It was a difficult matter in a town with the Conservative traditions of Preston.'[73]

In one sense then Labour had established itself by 1914. Nearly all trade unions had accepted the necessity for independent political action, and on this basis Labour made a considerable impact between 1904 and 1906. Labour had become the major, indeed only opposition to the Tories. This development does not square comfortably with Clarke's interpretation of political developments in Lancashire. Although he excepts Preston and Liverpool from his general argument that politics were becoming based more on class than status and that this process was benefiting the Liberals who developed a programme based on the need for social reform, Preston does in fact reveal some interesting points. The Liberals in Preston were enthusiastic 'New Liberals' largely because the weakness of Gladstonian Liberalism in the town encouraged the party to try out any new ideas – hence the early adoption of progressivism, and the Preston Liberals' opposition to the Gladstonian Liberalism of their MP, Harold Cox, who refused to countenance any state social reform, even old age pensions. Yet the Liberals were still totally ineffectual at the municipal level, failing to put up candidates, and by December 1910 it was clear that their only hope lay in national political issues. In Preston at least the Liberals played down any social reform element in this campaign and focused on the constitutional issue of 'the Peers versus the People'. 'New Liberalism' had run its course by 1910, and the working class did not support it.[74]

Labour, however, although the main opposition party, was unable to establish any neighbourhood presence: as I indicated in Chapter 5 social life based on the trade unions was concentrated in the centre of town. The Tories were therefore able to establish a presence in the neighbourhood where they had hitherto been weak. They built up ward committees and relied on popular church-based social life, publicans and local petit-bourgeois figures.[75] Urban Conservatism still found a ready home in Preston.

7

The transformation of the Labour
party, 1914–40

Preston's unusualness was apparent before 1914. After this date it seems
to conform much more to national trends, as Appendix C shows. Even so,
electoral support for Labour in Preston went through distinct phases
which were somewhat out of step with the rest of the country. Firstly,
Labour did extremely well in the immediate post-war period. Elsewhere it
was disorganised and did badly in the 1918 general election, but in
Preston Tom Shaw headed the poll and the Conservatives performed
worse than at any general election (apart from 1906) for over thirty
years, while at the 1919 municipal elections Labour, almost without
effort, became the leading force in municipal politics. Whereas before
1914 Labour had never won more than two seats on the Council at any
one time, in 1919 it won six of the nine seats it contested, winning 52 % of
the vote in these wards. This so intimidated Labour's opponents that in
the following year they did not put up candidates against Labour in
seven seats.

Support for Labour in Preston fell back in the early 1920s, and in 1924
Labour won only one Council seat (see Appendix D). While Labour's loss
of popularity was common throughout the country, in Preston it does
seem to have had distinctive local causes. As we shall see this period
coincided with the culmination of Labour's advocacy of patriarchal
economistic politics, which was popular with many (especially men) in
the post-war drive to remove women from their wartime employment.
After the early 1920s it steadily became less popular, especially with
women voters, and led to a considerable drop in support.

Between 1925 and 1930 support for Labour in Preston climbed again,
to unprecedented heights. Labour won both parliamentary seats in 1929
for the first time, and in 1928 and 1929 won seven of the twelve Council
seats. This brought Labour councillors close to controlling the Town
Council; they were prevented from doing so only by the presence of non-

elected Tory aldermen. The increase in support for Labour was a process happening throughout the country which has generally been ignored by historians concentrating on the industrial conflicts of the early 1920s. In Preston, however, this trend was linked to the creation of a popular statist politics, which in turn was brought about by the Labour party coming to rely increasingly on neighbourhood bases of support (rather than work-based ones), with women becoming far more active in the party.

Finally in the 1930s support for Labour fell back: Labour failed to win a parliamentary seat, and was unable to mount a serious challenge to win the Town Council. Labour's failure in this decade was surprising since in most areas of high unemployment the Labour party recovered quickly from its electoral debacle in 1931.[1] In Preston, however, unemployment divided the working class. This allowed the churches to come to the fore once more in a new paternalist form (catering for the unemployed). The alienation of women from the party because of the policies of the 1929 Labour government was also a major cause of Labour's decline in popularity. Behind the scenes however statist politics were being consolidated as the trade unions, hitherto exclusively economist, increasingly came to seize on state intervention as the means of dealing with unemployment. This led to a redefinition of Labour's statist politics, however: whereas in the late 1920s it was consumer demands for state intervention which were of paramount importance for the local party, by the 1930s it was the demands of public sector workers for safe employment which came to the fore. In this process a particular vision of popular local state intervention was increasingly replaced by one emphasising central state bureaucratic intervention.

7.1   *The culmination of economistic politics: Labour, 1914–24*

In 1914 there were few signs that Labour could emerge as a dominant force in local politics, yet by 1920 this was precisely what had happened. Some writers have indeed seen the war years as a period of dramatic change in working-class consciousness and action.[2] In Preston, however, the emergence of Labour was not due to any transformation in Labour politics: rather it occurred as a response to the problems faced by certain groups of male workers before 1914, notably the threat of female labour, which simply became more general and hence attracted greater support to Labour from male, if not female, workers. Furthermore as the local state increasingly co-opted the local Labour movement into wartime administration Labour politics simply seemed more viable. Yet the state was still seen in negative terms, with a large number of workers actually opposed to many of the forms of wartime intervention.

By 1914 the Conservatives, having regained their political supremacy, had succeeded in establishing the principle that trade unions should be confined to a narrow range of economic functions. As they had lost the support of the unions they were now able to reduce the roles of the unions without fear of damage to their electoral base. The most notable struggles in this field came in the attempts of the trade unions to secure direct representation on the Board of Management at Preston Royal Infirmary, but their claims were continually denied, despite precedents obtaining in other parts of the country.[3] In a similar way since 1904 elections for the Board of Guardians had been arranged between the leading religious denominations such that each of them could nominate candidates in proportion to their numerical strength in the town, thus obviating the need for elections to be contested. The Labour party managed to exact a couple of seats, hence becoming part of this 'compact', but they were given to non-union Labour activists; this further undermined the significance of trade unions outside the workplace.[4]

The war period saw a dramatic change in this policy of pushing the labour interest to the sidelines. Almost all the members of the local Labour party supported the war. In 1914 only three delegates opposed the war effort, and the Trades Council did not affiliate to the pacifist Union of Democratic Control. Tom Shaw, the Labour candidate, was extremely active in promoting the war effort, and when he stated that the only way of getting peace 'was by defeating the military autocracy of Germany', he was given overwhelming support in the Labour party, only four of the fifty or so delegates voting against putting him forward as Labour parliamentary candidate. The local Textile Trades Federation was even prepared to countenance conscription in 1915, when nationally nearly all unions were strongly opposed to it.[5]

The Labour party demanded a full role in wartime administration, and succeeded in getting representation on local relief committees which supervised relief, education and 'after care' (for school leavers). It had members also on the Town Council Belgian Refugees' Committee, on the local Committee for War Savings, and on the Food Control Committee which organised the distribution of food.[6] So despite the fact that it had only one elected councillor the Labour party was able to claim that it had played a vital role in wartime administration, and consequently to emphasise its own viability (in electoral terms). It was precisely on this record of efficient war administration that the Labour party campaigned in 1919. Wooley emphasised that 'the ratepayers need neither fear nor expect any "wildcat" schemes from the Labour members who would demand a pound's worth of value for every pound spent'. In 1920 the Labour party coined the phrase 'economy with efficiency' as their campaign watchword, with speakers emphasising that 'they looked at things from the point of view of efficient service'. The *Lancashire Daily Post* observed that in 1921

the tenor of most of the [Labour] addresses was an indictment of the dominant party for maladministration in the past, for unbusinesslike procedure in saddling future ratepayers with the responsibility of long past expenditure and a refutation of the accusations laid against the Labour Party of having no regard to the rates.[7]

Recently Reid has suggested that it was the experience of wartime state intervention which led to the Labour party adopting far more state-oriented policies.[8] In Preston, however, the growing influence of the state, locally and nationally, did not lead to a re-evaluation of its importance. At most there was a switch to what I have called economistic regulationist struggles. This was despite the fact that the local state seemed to have benefited the Labour party during the war by attempting to co-operate with the unions over introducing new working practices, such as in the informal joint committee on 'the war problems and female labour' which discussed ways of introducing female labour into the workforce, and in the negotiations over dilution in spinning and engineering where, ultimately, the unions' demands were upheld.[9]

Hostility to state intervention was equally apparent in the textile unions' dislike of compulsory state insurance. This was despite the fact that in the war period the Cotton Control Board, which regulated production by closing down certain mills and paying benefit to the unemployed operatives from a levy on working mills, has often been presented as a particularly advanced and progressive form of state intervention.[10] Although the state smiled more favourably on trade unions these unions did not respond by becoming more positive to the state. The practical politics of the Preston working class remained economistic: this made it difficult for the unions to alter their anti-statist stance.

These observations give rise to a question: why should the Labour party in Preston have become more popular after 1918 if it was pursuing much the same sort of politics as it had done before 1914? The answer has only partly to do with national developments. The Labour party nationally performed badly in the 1918 election and gave little sign of real electoral advance until the early 1920s when support in Preston was actually declining. The main reason for Labour's increased support in Preston was that many male workers were deeply concerned with issues of female labour brought about by the widespread employment of women at this time and so were prepared to support the Labour party in its economistic concern to restore pre-war working conditions.[11]

The cotton unions' hostility to female labour had continued throughout the war years. In 1915 their trade paper declared that 'for the sake of both sexes it is essential that women should be saved from exploitation at the expense of their brothers and fathers, and it is their brothers and fathers who must see to their protection'.[12] After it became apparent that female labour would be used, the unions switched their emphasis to ensuring that it would be removed after the war. 'We claim the solemn obligation to all the men who went away will necessitate those women going out again as quickly as possible . . . we must get women back into the home as soon as the war is over'.[13] In Preston the Labour party was based on the Trades and Labour Council. This was dominated by the unions which organised the skilled male workers in the cotton and engineering industry. The relative weakness of ward organisation in Preston, together with the absence of a strong socialist movement, meant that there was little challenge to the authority of the union group in the local Labour movement, and the unions' concern with female labour fed through to Labour politics in the area. In particular this concern was of some importance in the two main issues over which Labour contested the early post-war elections: unemployment and housing.

The local Labour party was extremely active in agitating over the question of the unemployed. However, Labour's definition of unemployment applied mainly to men. There was little sympathy with the position of female workers. The Trades Council had attacked the use of female labour at lower rates of pay by the Bristol Co-op. The Council was also disturbed by proposals to use female labour at the docks and in 1917 ran an extensive campaign against the proprietor of the Empire Theatre who sacked his male musicians and hired female ones. In 1919, when the Lancashire Insurance Committee (a local government agency) dismissed all its male workers and replaced them with women, the Labour party campaigned vigorously against it.[14] Many of the Labour party's campaigns at this period were over attempts to get central government grants for public works schemes and £750,000 was spent on such schemes between 1922 and October 1925.[15] To qualify for these grants all the schemes had to use male, demobilised labour, however. Labour's support at local level of state initiatives over unemployment went along with a concern, especially on behalf of the cotton unions, to remove state legislation on unemployment insurance. The cotton unions wanted to get out of the central state scheme originally introduced in 1911 and extended during the war. Whiteside argues that this was mainly linked to a desire on the part of regularly employed workers not to subsidise unskilled labourers when they were unemployed,[16] but this would not explain the continued hostility of cotton unions to the state unemployment insurance scheme well into the 1920s when it was becoming apparent that all was not well in the cotton trade, and hence that the cotton unions too would be making their fair share of claims on the fund. An important factor which helps to explain the cotton unions' hostility to the state unemployment insurance scheme is the point discussed in Section 4.4 above, namely that this legislation had in many ways undermined the labour market controls of the elite male workers over female labour, and that its abolition, and replacement by a union- and employer-run scheme, seemed to offer greater hope of a restoration of pre-war conditions with a labour market policed by the male workers themselves.

This hostility to women's paid labour had implications for the organisational structure of the Preston Labour party and its stance on wider political issues: it attempted to prevent the independent organis- ation of women in the party. In 1917 the Ministry of Labour approached the Preston Trades Council over the appointment of a local advisory committee to assist in the demobilisation of troops, and asked the Trades Council to nominate a woman to sit on it to represent women's interests. The Trades Council refused, however, and nominated only male representatives. In 1918 the National Executive of the Labour party wrote asking the local party to organise women, to which the Preston Labour party replied that it would hold ward meetings to organise 'both men and women'. In 1919 the Preston Labour party agreed to send delegates to a Labour party Women's Section Conference, but 'the general feeling was that care should be taken not to look on the work of women in the party as distinct from that of men'.[17] Preston did not set up a Women's Section until 1924, well after most other constituencies. In 1922 the Women's National Organiser of the Labour party discussed areas without Women's Sections. Most were either rural areas or areas where Labour was generally weak, but she also referred to 'a very small number, chiefly in urban areas, where there is a feeling that to have a Women's Section with its own officers is to divide the sexes and create a sex war'.[18] Perhaps it would be more accurate to say that it might have given women the means to fight back a little in the continuing 'sex war'!

There is good evidence that the local Labour party was not concerned with women's issues in its political campaigns. It did not develop any campaign to reduce women's burden at home by improving educational provision through the use of nurseries, or by the development of extensive public health services. Indeed the provision of health services was overwhelmingly geared to wage earners: the main hospital scheme remained that run by the Preston Royal Infirmary whereby workers paid 2*d* a week to insure them against the cost of hospital treatment but, for the old and the young, long-term health care was still based on the family. Although local Labour parties elsewhere were becoming increasingly interested in using the local state to improve health, in Preston these concerns were absent. The Preston Labour party continued to support the charitable structure of the Royal Infirmary, and in 1921 noted that 'interest taken by workers in the fund [for the Infirmary] had never been greater, neither had the work carried on by the Institution been more valued or so highly praised'.[19] Although the number of wealthy subscribers had dropped as suburbanisation continued, charitable gifts were still not uncommon and such was the enthusiasm of the local party for these that it even thanked the patrons concerned. In 1922 the party resolved 'to thank Sir Charles Brown for his latest generous gift to the Preston Royal Infirmary and [expressed] its gratification at the improvement in his health'.[20] Jeremiah Wooley expressed his support of the voluntary principle:

There were some people who were of the opinion that the state should take over the responsibility of maintaining such institutions [as the Infirmary], but he believed that the voluntary system was by far the best because it had real interest and enthusiasm behind it.[21]

In 1925 it was proposed that a Nursing Association should be set up in Preston on voluntary lines, to be financed by charitable contributions. The Executive Committee of the local Labour party proposed to support this and to give money towards it. This provoked a debate, during which one member declared that

he looked at the matter purely from a socialist point of view. These voluntary aid associations were absolutely detrimental to the interests of the working class. The driblets taken from the working man, meagre as was his income, amounted to a good deal in the long run. There were, for instance, flag days for this, that and the other. Our policy is that the municipality and the state should do all that is needful for the interest of the citizens whether men, women or children.[22]

A statist view had finally emerged, but support for the Nursing Association was passed by 'a large majority'.

Perhaps the most blatant example of the party's patriarchal concerns was its stand over maternity and child welfare. During the war it supported proposals for maternity and child welfare clinics, and four were opened. These were voluntary organisations, using unpaid labour of, in the main, middle-class women, but with a grant from Preston Council. Yet after 1918 the Labour party treated these bodies with hostility, partly because of the class characteristics of the staff. The Spinners' Union Secretary, R.C. Handley,

referring to maternity and child welfare[,] paid tribute to the pioneers of the movement and the workers, but declared there were so many people who felt that if they got their names on the memorandum of some of the centres as vice-president of this or that clinic they had achieved all that was required. They simply wanted to be the show people.[23]

While this was true enough the situation at the maternity and child welfare clinics was no different from that at the Royal Infirmary which had earned Labour's praise. It seems that a deep-rooted feeling also existed that there was relatively little need for these institutions. One Labour candidate stated that 'he took quite as much interest in the welfare of mothers and children as his opponent. In fact he got into closer terms with working people, shopkeepers and businessmen and knew more of their requirements.' T.H. Atherton observed that 'the maternity and child welfare committee had brought nothing but bills before the Council', while Jeremiah Wooley felt that the once-weekly provision of a room in the Weavers' Institute was perfectly adequate. There were some individual Labour activists who did campaign for better maternity centres, but the overall tenor of the campaigns was to play them down.[24]

The main exception to the party's hostility to state services was its support for public housing which was vociferous and not without success.[25] Yet the type of housing envisaged by the party was of a certain type. It advocated orthodox three-bedroomed housing, and was opposed to more radical, labour-saving, house designs which were being mooted at the time, such as houses without individual kitchens. The success of such designs depended on some form of communal kitchen, but the Preston Labour party did not support the idea of such 'national kitchens', and was apparently unconcerned when the neighbourhood kitchens set up during World War I were closed down.[26] Furthermore the Labour party was keen to see publicly built housing sold off. In 1923 W.E. Morris, the Labour Chairman of the Housing Committee, stated that 'the Labour group wanted the Corporation to set aside a portion of the [building] scheme for the erection of houses which could be sold to occupiers. They wished to encourage people who wanted to own their own home.'[27]

The policies of the Preston Labour party were, then, linked to its

170   *Transformation of the Labour party*

Table 7.1. *Supporters of Labour representation in the Preston Spinners' Union, 1892–1927*

	For	Against	Percentage for	Percentage of all members for
1892[a]	215	193	52.7	32.9
1913[b]	174	50	77.7	21.7
1927[c]	585	95	86.0	86.0

[a]Ballot on the principle of labour representation.
[b]Ballot on whether to have a political levy.
[c] Actual figures of those *contracting in* to pay the political levy (figures for Preston Province).
Source: Preston Spinners' Union, Annual Report 1927; White, *Trade Union Militancy*; CFT, 1892.

concern about female labour. On the one hand it advocated measures likely to lead to nuclear family life, especially in the provision of public housing. In the sphere of education and health, where public provision might have eased women's domestic work and made it easier for them to obtain paid labour, there was little action. Furthermore, just as in the pre-war period, the most active groups in the Preston Labour party were those which were most affected by the issue of female labour. Foremost amongst these was the Amalgamated Engineering Union, which was not very active before 1914, but became the Preston Labour party's most powerful supporter after 1918. In 1921 four of the sixteen executive members of the Trades and Labour Council were from the AEU. In 1922, following the engineering dispute (discussed in Section 4.6 above), the AEU was influential enough to secure the expulsion of the Workers' Union and the NUGMW after the disagreements between these unions during the lock-out. This was despite the fact that the Workers' Union had a much longer history of activity in the Labour party.[28]

The spinners were another case in point, their commitment to the Labour party reflecting their growing concern over female labour. Table 7.1 gives details of members supporting the Labour movement at different times, and shows that still in 1913 less than a quarter were sufficiently committed to vote to establish a political fund. This is consistent with the argument that it was the members of those trades who were particularly threatened with female labour who were the keenest Labour supporters at this time, since at this time spinners still held a pivotal role in the patriarchal labour market. By 1927 however

86 % of the spinners contracted in to pay the political levy, and it could have been the fights over female labour they waged in the war years which were of key importance here.

The Labour party was then a conservative force in post-war Preston: its main concern was to establish pre-war structures of gender relations and male security in paid employment. Such policies, while they appealed to many male workers, brought with them problems. In the long term, capacities for such economistic politics were in decline, as our discussion of the cotton industry showed, and the weakness of the neighbourhood base remained. The short-term problem was that women found the Labour party unattractive and switched their vote to the Conservatives.

7.2   The undermining of economistic Labourism, 1920–30

Before 1914 there was a considerable number of feminists in Preston, mostly aligned against the Labour party, and this antagonism was to continue after the war. The main feminist group became the Women's Citizen Association (WCA) which began to play an active role in local politics. It would be wrong to portray this body as concerned merely with the interests of women as mothers, for it was able to develop a far-ranging feminist political programme which also argued for women's rights in paid employment, and in so doing clearly came up against a Labour movement concerned to undermine them. Hence, as well as campaigning on 'women as mothers' issues, the WCA also opposed the marriage bar on women council employees, and demanded full 'technical and industrial' education for girls so that they would not be disadvantaged in the labour market. The WCA even went so far as to challenge sex segregation in employment. In 1924 one of their speakers declared that 'what they really wanted was that the whole level of women's earnings even in those occupations that were exclusively women's should be raised and that on the whole women should have the same chance as men of doing higher paid and more skilled classes of work'.[29]

Not surprisingly this concern was not to the liking of the Labour party. Initially the WCA attempted to be non-political and approached all the main political parties, emphasising the 'non-party and non-sectarian character of the Association', in the hope that they might agree to allow the WCA candidates a free run in local elections. The Labour party, however, refused this request, and the WCA steadily moved more closely into an alliance with the Conservatives in order to get support for its candidates. From 1920 leading women members began to stand as municipal candidates, always in opposition to Labour ones, stressing the need for women to be fully represented. In 1920 Alice Pimblett stood under the auspices of the Municipal Representation Association, stressing that 'she felt it very necessary that women should be directly represented on the Council. The Town Council was not a political affair but it was directly connected with peoples' homes and many points came up which called for the understanding of women – such as education, housing, maternity, child welfare etc.'[30]

These were the very issues about which the Labour party was ambivalent. Pimblett won the seat despite Labour opposition. In 1921 the increasing confidence of the WCA was revealed in the candidature of Evelyn Lees. The local newspaper reported that 'something almost unique in connection with local elections was the meeting in support of the candidature of Mrs Hubert Lees. The majority of the audience consisted of women, the speeches with one exception were by women, and the policies of women in local councils were the burden of the speeches.'[31] The Conservatives began to co-operate with the WCA, recognising the political gains to be made. Their Women's Unionist Association saw its membership rise from 300 in 1919 to 1,700 in 1922. Some of the Association's demands were taken on board by the Tories. Thus in 1921 a Conservative speaker supported equal guardianship of children, with maintenance of children to be deducted from the man's wages by the employer and given to the mother.[32]

By the time of the elections in 1923 this alliance had reached the stage that the three female candidates, all WCA members, stood with Conservative support against Labour candidates. The Labour party made no attempt to put forward women candidates of its own. The local newspaper noted that 'there is no blinking the fact that the Conservative Party – small blame to them – is organising the women's element in the electorate very effectively judging by the nature of the attendances at their meetings'.[33] The Conservative parliamentary candidate in 1922 emphasised that if the Tories were to win 'in his opinion it was the women of England to whom they had very largely to look'. Many of the Labour candidates were disparaging about the WCA members' maternity and child welfare work during this election campaign.[34] One Labour speaker criticised the Conservatives: 'The Tory Party in Preston was like a former King of Dahomey who formed a corps of Amazons, in that they sent in the women to fight.'[35]

In the ensuing elections two of the three women were successful, and their mobilisation of the 'women's vote' can be seen by the fact that the

Labour vote dropped by more than 6 % from its 1919 level in those wards where women were standing in 1923, as against only 2 % in those wards where male Tories opposed them. It is noteworthy that Labour did rather better at the parliamentary level, retaining its seat throughout the 1920s, than at the municipal level, where in the middle years of the 1920s it suffered a considerable loss of support, in 1924 winning only one of the twelve seats. It appears that the 'women's vote' did exist, and that it increasingly went to the Conservatives, but that it was more manifest in local politics, where the franchise did not exclude women aged under thirty from voting, and where 'women's issues', notably in provision of local services, seemed very important.

The Labour party had by the middle years of the 1920s lost a considerable amount of popular support. Its neighbourhood base remained weak. The Labour party blamed its failure in 1920 on its lack of ward committees, but little action was taken to remedy this until 1923 when an organisational sub-committee was formed. This made a far-reaching decision to mobilise more actively in the neighbourhoods, forming ward committees, and to carry on more active political work at the Labour clubs. More generally 'the social side of the people of the Party should be catered for to a greater extent than at present'. Lectures were held in the wards and systematic canvassing was begun, apparently for the first time.[36]

In the late 1920s the Labour party became much more active in providing social facilities. In 1924, for the first time, a Labour gala was held, with a fair and 'field day'. This was organised by the Labour clubs, which provided the volunteer workers and stalls, and 7,000 people attended. It was decided to make it an annual event and in 1925 12,000 attended. There were also frequent ward socials and picnics, hiking clubs and Labour choirs were formed and whist drives and Labour balls took place.[37]

The increase in ward organisation was closely linked to the development of Women's Sections from 1924. It was agreed to form a Women's Section in 1923, though it was to be 'subject to the authority of the [organisational] sub-committee as to policy and finance'. The Women's Sections were formed on a ward basis, sometimes connected to particular Labour clubs. In 1925 they organised a Women's Week with meetings held in Labour clubs, and as a result of good publicity 'strong and virile [sic] Women's Sections have been formed, 7 branches having a membership of nearly 500', which was to rise to 635 by 1928. In 1929 the Women's Sections were officially 'complimented on their activities' by the Labour party.[38] Little is known about the type of women who joined these Women's Sections, but there seems little doubt that they were women who had not previously been active in formal politics, since the Women's Sections made great play of the need to hold 'speaking classes' and to give tuition on how to canvass, take charge of committee rooms and take on official posts. There is some evidence that many of the women were cotton workers, since emphasis was placed on having meetings at times when those employed in the cotton industry could attend. In 1930 the Women's Central Council of the Preston Labour party decided not to take part in a pageant because of a shortfall in income which was caused by the 'black outlook in the cotton trade', implying that many members were cotton workers.[39] It may well be that the undermining of patriarchal relations in the cotton industry in these years provided women with greater capacities for political action, and these were developed within the Labour party.

The rise of ward organisation and women's involvement was linked up with wider changes in the Labour party's finance, organisation and policy. Labour had relied primarily on trade union support for its election funds in the immediate post-war period. Records of contributors to the 1924 election fund show that 56 % of the £245 raised came from local trade unions, 29 % from Labour clubs, and 16 % from individual contributors. By 1928, however, the £168 raised for the 'Bid for Victory' came from different sources: only 22 % from the unions, 34 % from individuals, 24 % from the Women's Sections, 16 % from neighbourhood activities, and 4 % from the ILP and Individual Members' Section. So by this time the Women's Sections provided as much extraordinary finance as did the unions.[40]

The organisation of the Labour party was also radically changed, so that by 1930 non-union members had much more voice. In 1918 the LRC and Trades Council formally amalgamated to become the Trades and Labour Council, structurally based on the old Trades Council. The sovereign body was the monthly meeting at which delegates would be accepted in proportion to the number of members registered for each affiliated organisation. This gave great power to the large unions. If individuals were not union members they could join the party only by belonging to a Labour club, the ILP or the Individual Members' Section. With this type of structure it was difficult for members of the middle classes to join the Labour party, since they would be most unlikely to be attracted by the proletarian atmosphere of the Labour clubs and so would have to make the effort of joining the party through the ILP or Individual Members' Section. The ILP had about 300 members, mainly craft workers, while there were only about fifty Individual Members.[41]

The Labour party Executive annually elected by delegates was therefore dominated by union officials and representatives. In 1921 twelve of the sixteen members were union delegates. The four non-union members were two women (elected as Labour Association representatives), one Labour club representative, and one member of the ILP.[42] It is easy to understand how the economistic concerns of the leading unions were so easily translated into political action! Nonetheless the interest shown by many unions in formal labour politics was, if anything, reduced after the middle years of the 1920s, partly because of the growth in national machinery for wage bargaining, but also because the craft unions, as we have seen, were quite successful in re-establishing craft structures in the 1930s, which made them less interested in formal politics.

The hold of the unions over the Preston Labour party was steadily eroded throughout the 1920s. The creation of a Women's Section in 1924 led to their representation at meetings. The ward committees were denied representation for a long time: in fact it was not until 1938 that they could send delegates to Executive Committee meetings. Nonetheless they began to exercise considerable informal power, particularly over the choice of municipal candidates. In the early 1920s the choice of candidates was decided by the Executive Committee after constituent bodies, mostly unions, had proposed names. In 1919, of the nine candidates selected six were proposed by the unions, two by the ILP and one by the Labour Association. In 1923 the Transport and General Workers' Union (TGWU) 'forwarded the name of Mr John Bamber as candidate for the vacancy in Maudland ward'.[43] This procedure increased the chances that candidates less well known in their wards would be selected and may have been a further factor behind the poor performance of Labour in the middle years of the 1920s. In 1924 the Executive Committee decided that all ward committees should be consulted before candidates were chosen, that voters' lists should be supplied to all Labour clubs and ward committees, and that the Ward Secretary should be consulted over the choice of chairman for election meetings. By 1926 it was evidently expected that wards should nominate their own candidates, for Fishwick and Ashton were criticised for being slow to do so. By 1930 the TGWU was complaining that it was unable to get any of its nominees selected as candidates.[44]

The Executive Committee retained greater control over the choice of parliamentary candidates, which proved to be one of the most controversial issues in internal Labour politics. Throughout the 1920s

Labour fielded only one candidate for the two-member seat, allowing the Liberals to put up their candidate. Such a procedure was felt to win the votes of a few Liberals for the Labour candidate which would otherwise have been used against Labour. The ILP, however, was furious at this arrangement, and tried persistently to get the party to stand two candidates, but was stopped chiefly because the United Textile Factory Workers' Association (UTFWA) (the Lancashire-wide organisation of all textile unions which campaigned mainly on political issues and sponsored a number of 'textile' Labour MPs, including Shaw) threatened to stop financing Shaw if it did so. While it was felt that Preston was a reasonably safe bet for one Labour MP, if two were put up they might both lose as the Liberals could retaliate and stand two candidates themselves. The UTFWA did not want its money wasted, especially since the other Labour candidate would most likely not have been one sponsored by the UTFWA.[45] The threat to close the purse strings was effective, and it needed the sitting Liberal MP to defect to Labour in 1929 for the arrangement to break down. But by then the hold of the unions over the parliamentary candidature was not being repeated at the municipal level.

Membership was based on ward organisation after the introduction of a stamp scheme in 1924, whereby members could pay their subscriptions weekly to a visiting collector. This had the effect of building up regular contacts between party members at their homes. It is difficult to ascertain how many paid in this way, but by 1938 there were 1,357 Individual Members.[46]

The structure of the Executive Committee of the Preston Labour party also underwent major changes, partly because of the effects of the Trades Disputes Act of 1927. This Act prevented trade unions from using any money other than that from the political levy to finance political activity. Since the Labour party was based on the Trades Council the Act would have forced the party to use money from the political levy even for purely 'industrial' purposes carried on in association with the Trades and Labour Council. The party therefore split its Executive Committee into two sections: an industrial and a political one, of eight members each. Although this change was purely formal in that the two sections continued to meet together, it had the effect of allowing eight places on the Executive Committee to be filled by non-union representatives. As a result the number of women and ward representatives increased. In 1928 three women were elected onto the political side of the Executive Committee; there were four Labour Association representatives, two Labour Club representatives, one from the ILP and one from the Individual Members' Section.[47]

These changes had a considerable impact on the type of policies pursued by the Preston Labour party. It now relied far less on the unions and on work-based capacities, and far more on the neighbourhood. Put bluntly, popular statist politics, emphasising that consumers' needs could be met only by local state intervention, emerged in the years after 1925. The Women's Sections were of great importance in this respect. Whilst they were not initially active in policy matters, they became far more so once established, and were to the fore in arguing the case for greater provision of public services. In 1927 the Labour party had no policy of supporting state-funded nursery schools and took little interest in the matter. In 1928, however, the Women's Sections organised a conference on nursery schools and the demand for nursery schools began to be raised shortly afterwards by local Labour candidates. The Women's Sections also supported open-air (nursery) schools and cheap slipper baths (and the provision of public baths was to become a major theme among local candidates). In 1931 the Women's Sections held a conference on the 'socialisation of medical services' and supported the provision of municipal lodging houses for working women and of public washhouses, again a demand taken up by Labour candidates.[48]

Another issue raised was over education. The conservatism of the Labour movement on this issue has been remarked upon above, and indeed throughout the early 1920s the topic was largely ignored by Labour candidates. From the middle years of the 1920s, however, a far more active concern with state-provided education developed, again with women candidates to the fore. There were demands for a greater number of free places for children at secondary school, smaller classes, and the provision of allowances to 'bright' children to allow them to stay on at school. In 1926 the Labour party put the education issue at the front of its campaign, demanding the building of more secondary schools, greater facilities for technical education, and more free places at school, and these were demands which were to recur for the rest of the decade.[49]

The increase in its neighbourhood base led the Labour party to campaign more actively on the provision of urban amenities for working-class areas. As we have seen, before 1914 the Labour party considered municipal enterprise from the point of view of the worker and was opposed to attempts to use profits of municipal business to benefit the ratepayer or subsidise other services. The Corporation was seen as an employer whose business must be carried out on proper lines. This approach was continued in some quarters, notably the Tramway Department, which Jeremiah Wooley, the Chairman of the Transport Committee, regarded as a personal fief which could be run only on sound 'business lines'. In 1929 a major issue of the local election campaign was the refusal of the Labour party to reduce tram fares, with several of its Conservative opponents supporting lower fares, if necessary subsidised from the rates.[50] Generally, however, the Labour party became less concerned with the producers of urban services and more concerned with the consumers. In 1931 the National Federation of Building Trades Operatives complained of the use of non-union bricklayers by the Corporation. The Labour party seemed relatively uninterested in this, however, and simply noted that the 1927 Trades Disputes Act prevented discrimination in favour of union labour. The great concern for Corporation workers so apparent before 1914 faded after the war, partly owing to the unionisation of these workers, a point to be discussed further below.[51]

From the middle years of the 1920s the Preston Labour party became an enthusiastic supporter of municipal enterprise to benefit householders. In 1925, following the municipalisation of the electricity supply, the Labour party advocated its provision in all homes. There was also a greater emphasis placed on municipal housing built for low rent, which contrasted with the party's previous advocacy of building council houses to sell. As recently as 1923 the party had refused to set up a Tenants' Defence League, but its concern with tenants' issues increased thereafter. The party successfully campaigned for lower council rents (a clear sign of statist concerns). The West End Labour Club, for instance, protested about the rents charged for houses on the Swansea Road site, which gives an indication of how tenants used the neighbourhood bases of the Labour party.[52]

In the later 1920s, then, the Labour party, based on the Women's Sections and neighbourhood organisation, took a much more positive view of the local authority and its potential to intervene in economic and social affairs. There was also a loosening of the patriarchal stresses of the party, largely under the influence of the Women's Sections. In 1927 a (male) Labour candidate, speaking of the need for nursery schools for the children of working mothers, was asked

by a woman as to why they should have such schools, and why married women should work instead of their husbands having better wages. The candidate agreed but said his experience showed that in towns where women were not able to work there was not the same pleasure of life for working people.[53]

A rare occasion here of qualified support for married women being able to work! Indeed the Labour party came to support the provision of family allowances in 1930, and took no objection to the Women's Sections co-operating with the WCA on 'women's issues'.[54] However, there were still many labour activists 'formed' in an earlier period who remained opposed to female labour. On the issue of whether women corporation workers should have to resign on marriage, the Labour position did not go as far as condemnation, arguing that each case should be decided 'on merit', that is to say, on whether the female wage was important for the overall household income.

7.3   The appeal of statist Labourism

There was then a far-reaching shift in the Preston Labour party's organisation, policy and personnel in the later 1920s. This tapping of female and neighbourhood bases of support, which led to consumer-oriented statist politics, also generated unprecedented levels of electoral support. The popularity of Labour in this period, so often interpreted as simply a sympathy vote for the miners' defeat in the 1926 General Strike, should be linked to these wide-ranging changes in the character of Labour politics. The local party was well aware of the significance of growing female support in this period. The Labour revival in the local elections of 1925 was attributed by Councillor Ellison to 'the splendid efforts of the party workers and particularly of the women'. In the 1929 general election most of the canvassers were women, and 'Councillor Morris says that a very considerable proportion of young married women of Preston – those of 21 upward who have been enfranchised – have thrown in their political lot with Labour'.[55]

The role of neighbourhood organisation was also vital. Figure 2 shows that membership of the Labour clubs correlated exceptionally well with the overall Labour vote, both reaching a peak in 1929. There were other indications at ward level about how far neighbourhood organisation was essential to sustaining the Labour vote. Fishwick ward, although a working-class area, was never won by Labour in the 1920s, yet with the introduction of the stamp scheme it became the site of a strong ward committee, its stamp scheme being more extensive than that of any other ward. In the 1930s, perhaps as a result, Fishwick became the safest Labour ward in Preston.[56]

The reverse trend was found in nearby Ribbleton, Preston's safest Labour seat in the 1920s, which possessed the most extensive Labour organisation in Acregate Lane Labour Club and Ribbleton Working Men's Club. Yet the Labour vote fell here dramatically from 1929, and remained weak in the 1930s. This drop may well be attributable to a dispute over candidates in 1929 when the wish of the ward committee to have Henry Butler as its candidate was overruled by the Executive

Committee, with the result that, against the swing, Labour's vote fell from 56 % to 44 %, and it lost the seat.[57] Labour's ward organisation in Ribbleton fell apart, and it had very few members in the 1930s. These instances show that Labour's electoral fortunes did depend by this time on ward organisation.

The 1929 parliamentary elections were the high point of this upturn in Labour fortunes. Shaw won 29.5 % of the vote (in a seat where electors had two votes so in fact well over 50 % of individuals voted for him), a proportion not exceeded even in the Labour landslide of 1945. Shaw's victory also saw the emergence of an unprecedented number of 'plumpers', voters who would not use their second vote to support the Liberal candidate. Before 1929 the highest proportion of Labour plumpers had been in 1906 (18 %), but this number fell to 16 % in 1918, 13 % in 1922 and 12 % in 1924. In 1929, however, no less than 33 % were plumpers, which reveals the dramatic growth in the numbers of committed Labour voters in these years (since these were voters who could not bring themselves to use their second vote for a non-Labour candidate).

This triumph was repeated two months later when the Liberal candidate elected in Shaw's wake was offered a post in the Labour government. He accepted, and after the local Liberal party expressed disquiet, resigned and stood again as Labour candidate. In the first straight Labour–Conservative fight since 1903 Jowitt won 55 % of the vote, and for the first time Preston was represented by two Labour MPs. 10,000 people gathered to hear the result, which was recorded by the *Lancashire Daily Post*:

When the result was announced by Councillor Ellison there was a burst of cheering which continued for so long it was almost deafening. Men and women cheered themselves hoarse. They sang, they laughed and some of them cried. There has never been such a display of political enthusiasm in Preston, not even when Mr Tom Shaw has been returned.[58]

The next morning, when Jowitt took the train to London, a crowd of 3,000–4,000 gathered at Preston station to see him off.

This was very impressive. But what happened to popular Labour politics in the 1930s, when support for Labour in Preston fell back?

7.4   Unemployment and Labour politics

The popular politics of the later 1920s were based mainly on neighbourhood and female support, but were also dependent on (relatively) full employment. This was important in a number of respects. The struggles to remove women from the labour market which were manifested in Labour policy in the early 1920s diminished as male employment improved, creating a more tolerant approach to the issue of female involvement in the party. Similarly the involvement of women in the party was probably facilitated by their position in fairly secure employment in cotton weaving. Finally unemployment was the main issue over which the crafts mobilised, since it was one which could not be dealt with by mutualism. The sudden growth in unemployment from 1929, especially in cotton and engineering, led to an unemployment rate of 20 % by 1930s and this brought issues of employment to the top of the political agenda.

The fading away of women's activity in Preston was especially significant. Membership of the Women's Section fell from 635 in 1929 to 421 in 1931 and 287 by 1933, before stabilising at around 250. Much of this decline was caused by the alienation of women from the party because of the Labour government's policies. The 1930 reform of the National Insurance Act (the Anomalies Act) meant that women workers could get benefit only if there were no vacancies in domestic service. Unemployed cotton weavers had to be prepared to take on servants' jobs, which had always been regarded as being 'below them'. The Women's Sections however failed to take a clear stand on this issue. In 1930

a well attended meeting of the Women's Sections of the Preston Labour Party . . . unnanimously decided to send a resolution to Miss Margaret Bondfield, Minister of Labour, against the decision that Lancashire mill girls must enter domestic service or lose unemployment benefit . . . it was stated that without training the girls were unfitted for domestic service'.[59]

This fell short of condemning the proposal altogether, and became simply a complaint about the lack of training facilities. The same ambiguity surfaced again in 1932 when the Women's Sections investigated the centre provided to train domestic servants. They deplored

the fact that girls must go to domestic service. If they have to go instead of being unemployed we want them trained properly. No one could tell me these girls were being properly trained at the end of a session at the present domestic centre.[60]

The loyalty of leading Labour activists to the party prevented them from openly denouncing the Labour government's decision, but by not doing so they helped alienate less committed women. By the 1930s the Women's Sections began to fight shy of political campaigns and tended to become a 'support' organisation for the party, organising such things as fetes and baking competitions.[61]

There was another way in which the central Labour party helped undermine the campaigning style of the Women's Sections. In the late 1920s different women's organisations had started to campaign together on issues of joint concern. The Women's Peace Campaign was run by the Women's Sections of the Labour party, the Women's Total Abstinence Union, the Women Liberals, the Women's International league for Peace and Freedom and the WCA. This aimed at 'a united women's movement for peace which might seek to further their objects by bringing before the candidates and the electorate the question of education and its effects on peace'.[62] In 1928 the Women's Sections were given permission to invite non-Labour party speakers to give talks, and WCA members appear to have spoken on Labour platforms. It seems that some Labour party members might even have joined the WCA. In any event, Dr Marion Phillips, the central Labour party's Chief Women's Officer, wrote to the Women's Sections 'deprecating Labour women being members of non-party organisations of a general political character, as all our energies should be put into the task of making our organisation stronger'.[63] This order to put party before women's interests prevented the Women's Sections from keeping links with other women's organisations and made it more difficult for them to appeal to all women. The Labour party thereby lost its status as a party able to appeal distinctly to women.

Another group severely hit by unemployment in Preston was that of young people. The undermining of craft controls in weaving meant that there were fewer patrimonies where son followed father, though in engineering, where unions regained some strength in the 1930s, these may have been more common. It was generally easy enough for children to find 'blind-alley' employment, until they were eighteen years old or so, but there were few long-term jobs. The alienation of young people from the party was related to the feeling that the party represented only those in work. In the late 1920s there had been a reasonably strong League of Youth, with 130 members in 1926, and equal numbers of males and females on the committee. After facing suspension for consorting with the 'Young Workers' Unity Committee' in 1927, it declined in numbers, and it became apparent that the interest of 'youth' was being lost. In 1931 the Chairman of the party spoke of 'the necessity of something being done to bring within the Party the younger people and said advantage should be taken of the widespread movement for rambles and "hiking"'.[64] The formation of these had little effect however. In 1933 a delegate was still able to emphasise that 'it was the young people we had to get hold of'. In 1937 the Labour candidate defeated at the 1936 by-election noted that 'one effect of centring the [election and political] work in the clubs was that the parents would not allow their sons and daughters to work within the party' (because children under eighteen years were not allowed to enter licensed premises).[65]

There are some indications that unemployed youngsters actively campaigned against Labour. In 1934 W.H. Francis, one of the earliest activists in the Labour movement, was not selected as a Labour candidate. He had been unhappy with the growth in Labour's neighbourhood-based organisation, especially that centred on the Labour clubs. He said that

he had been turned down by the local executive . . . because he was a teetotaller and local preacher. He was not a member of the club because he could not consistently take part in the movement. He felt he could not participate in club life during the week and then go into the pulpit on Sunday.[66]

Francis stood as an independent candidate and emphasised that the only support he was getting was from 'unemployed lads'. He polled respectably but did not win.

From the middle years of the 1920s the Tories were left as the party of municipal thrift, largely because of the continued impact of petit-bourgeois figures on the Conservative party. Such anti-state, economistic policies were now out of step with the practical politics of Preston's working class, however, and the Tories were left very much on the defensive. Yet unemployment allowed them to seize the initiative again. It stimulated the churches to resume an importance in the neighbourhood, as suppliers of patronage to the needy. The Conservative party still relied on the churches to gain electoral support and in the 1930s they became very important in providing facilities for the unemployed and tended to gain influence in the neighbourhood as a result. Leading middle-class patrons also involved themselves in initiatives directed at the unemployed. In 1932 a local Tory councillor stated that 'he thought it desirable that they should do something to keep the men's minds alive and to keep men fit for when the labour market improved'.[67] This led to the creation of Unemployed Allotment Holders' Associations, through which the unemployed were given rent-free allotment gardens: there were 240 of these by 1932 and 500 by 1933. They held their own agricultural shows, socials and concerts.[68]

There was also an Unemployed Football League which had by 1933 twenty-four participating teams and 500 unemployed to call on, and 2,000 spectators saw the Preston Unemployed beat the Southport Unemployed five goals to one. A 'listening in' circle was created for the unemployed to listen to the radio. In 1934 a Council for Social Services was set up, composed of churches and local voluntary groups with 'a great desire to do something which might be called applied Christianity and they were imbued with the idea of assisting the unemployed'. A recreation centre was set up for the adult male unemployed and the Unemployed Social Centre, as it was known, attracted one hundred unemployed shortly after opening. Concerts for the unemployed attracted 800 people.[69]

The Labour movement's attempt to integrate the unemployed was much weaker than that of the churches. It was not until 1936 that the Labour party set up an Unemployed Association which was to be a social club for the unemployed and, although this held some social events, it never attracted many people.[70]

Throughout the country, Labour was heavily defeated in 1931, owing to the crisis caused by MacDonald's desertion of the party. In Preston, however, there was no revival in the rest of the decade to compare with that found elsewhere. Cook and Stevenson have shown that by 1935 Labour was as popular nationally as it had been in 1929, yet in Preston the two Labour candidates won only 46 % of the vote compared with 55 % in 1929. Elsewhere high unemployment tended to encourage Labour voting, but this was usually in areas where there were general unions which could mobilise the unemployed in support of Labour. In Preston, which had no dominant general union but a greater number of craft unions, especially in engineering, no such hold over the unemployed could be established. In Lancashire the renewed role of voluntary organisations helped undermine Labour's growth, based as it had been on the neighbourhood.[71]

Important changes again took place in the character of Labour politics in this period. Unemployment, once more a pressing issue, became a major priority. In the 1890s, we saw the use of an economistic strategy whereby the local authority provided conditions conducive to investment by firms. Elements of this approach remained in the 1930s, manifested in the desire of the Labour party to encourage Courtaulds to build a new factory in Preston, and in its support of awarding public contracts to local firms.[72] Generally however greater emphasis was placed upon the need for central state intervention. In 1919 the local Labour party argued that the government should organise commodities 'essential to the well being of the community', that local authorities, with state support, should initiate public works schemes in housing, arterial roads and road repairs, that state-controlled and financed 'National Workshops' for disabled soldiers and sailors should be set up, and that hours of labour should be reduced.[73]

The emphasis placed on central state intervention was new. It would be easy to see this as caused by enthusiasm for central state intervention during the war, were it not for the fact that, as we have seen, the cotton unions, at least, were hostile to state insurance regulation. A major factor behind support for state intervention was in fact the decline in local capital, for long a mainspring of economistic struggles on which major emphasis was placed by the Conservatives. The re-capitalisation of the cotton industry in the immediate post-war period showed that firms were no longer attached exclusively to Preston, and that unemployment could not simply be solved by getting more local employers in. In 1919 the mayor of Preston noted that

the cotton trade was the staple trade of Preston and he regretted, as he felt sure all responsible men regretted, that the cotton mills in this town were changing hands. Capital, however, was a big roller and would roll everything underneath. It was far better that they should have at the head of these mills gentlemen of their own town and council. It was fear of outside capital that he dreaded and he did not like it.[74]

The same sentiments affected the Labour party. The Spinners' Union secretary and Labour mayor, Handley, stated that

under the present system capital refuses to be confined within counties, frontiers or boundaries of any description. In its thirst for an adequate or exorbitant return on its outlay it has extended its activities to the unindustrial areas . . . with the result that the monster is no longer controllable by the recognised rules of the past.[75]

It was in this context that the central state was felt to be so important. This issue faded as unemployment eased a little in the later 1920s, but it came to the fore again in the 1930s. This time even more emphasis was placed on central government intervention, with the 50 % grants system being condemned as inadequate. In the 1930s there was a debate about how far local initiative could ease unemployment. Councillor Rhodes of the AEU emphasised that

no suggestion for local action he had yet heard did more than touch the fringe of the problem or cater for more than one class of worker. Further, he contended, such [local] schemes, though relieving unemployment for the moment, threw the men back when completed. He still insisted that national initiative was the reality required.[76]

On this issue, unlike in the case of the services so strongly campaigned for in the late 1920s, the Labour party advocated central, rather than local, state intervention. This was an example of a shift in statist politics from a welfarist to a labour market character.

Unemployment made another major impact, in changing the relative strength of different trade unions in the Labour party. Before 1914 the cotton unions were dominant, and between 1914 and 1925 the engineering unions also became influential. In 1921, when the AEU was formed from the amalgamation of different craft unions, it became the single most powerful, with over 1,100 of the 10,780 union members in Preston. In the 1930s membership of the Weavers' Union fell from 14,000 to 8,000, and of the Spinners' Union from 690 in 1925 to 240 in 1939. It was particularly the TGWU and the NUGMW which expanded in the 1930s, based on the organisation of municipal workers and of semi- and unskilled workers. By 1938 the TGWU had 8,000 members and the NUGMW 3,000, making up half the total of Preston's union membership (about 20,000).[77] These unions were active in organising municipal workers, and hence had a more positive view of municipal services than did the cotton unions.

In the 1930s in fact the TGWU became the foremost exponent of the extension of local authority services in order to improve employment prospects. Wooley, Chairman of the Transport Committee, was frequently criticised for his persistent antipathy to state enterprise. His refusal to accede to the TGWU's request for a regrading of tram workers led to attempts to expel him from the Labour party, which were only narrowly defeated. It is notable that on Wooley's death in 1935, although the papers referred to him as the 'father of the Labour Party in Preston', the party refused to offer the usual condolences.[78]

The case of the tram workers was one of several where the TGWU and the NUGMW pressed the Labour party to become active in the cause of municipal workers. The NUGMW asked for a charter spelling out the conditions of municipal workers, and pressed for formal promotion procedures. The union was also more generally concerned with the extension of municipal services in order to secure its members' jobs. The NUGMW was active in campaigning for the installation of gas in council houses (though it failed to get the support of the Labour party on this), and made frequent demands for better transport facilities.[79]

In the 1930s the Preston Labour party became a confirmed supporter of the principle of improved services, even at the cost of rate rises. In 1936 Singleton, a Labour candidate, stated that rate increases were not in themselves bad: 'If we have to have these social services and bear the responsibility of public assistance which is steadily increasing, then we have to pay for it. I do not believe in cutting the rates at the expense of the social services or the unemployed.' Williamson, another Labour candidate, also stated that 'he was not afraid of the bogey of high rates on condition that they were well and wisely spent'. The Labour party's main emphases were on a better municipal health service, the provision of public works schemes for the unemployed, slum clearance and the extension of borough boundaries to make middle-class suburbs liable to rates.[80]

By the later 1930s much of the statist philosophy which seems so characteristic of post-war Labour politics had developed, largely from the way in which the Preston party now responded to the demands of the large general unions and, to a lesser extent, of local residents. These politics were adopted not as a result of middle-class entry into the party, for the large numbers of Individual Members were to be found mainly in the working-class wards. The most active middle-class member, Percy Taylor, the former mill owner turned socialist who had been the leading left-winger in the 1920s, became less active in the 1930s. The lack of finance meant that the party had to continue to rely on self-financing middle-class candidates in parliamentary elections, particularly in 1935 and 1936, yet these were not residents of Preston and took no part in local politics after their election campaigns were over. Before World War II these new statist policies never commanded popular assent, and the party was once more reduced to being the chief opposition.

Even in this period of the 'nationalisation' of politics local factors played an important role in facilitating particular sorts of political mobilisation. Before 1914, and especially during its period of economic decline, Preston's social situation, and the highly patriarchal character of its labour market, had been unusual, and this helped produce distinctive political patterns. Yet after World War I socio-economic changes were more the product of national, non-local processes (such as state intervention), and helped produce more common patterns. The apparent uniformity of Labour's electoral advance in many working-class towns, particularly in the 1920s, should be taken as evidence not of the power of national effects, but rather of the significance of commonly found local effects in many different parts of the country. It is these local processes which are of central importance in the analysis of political change.[81] National patterns of electoral change are only aggregates and averages of different local processes; they are statistical artefacts. This point will be demonstrated in the following chapter.

8

Conclusions

The Labour movement in Preston was strongly affected by its local environment. The capacities of various groups of workers to pursue different forms of practical politics had a major impact in forestalling certain forms of mobilisation and promoting others. Yet this process was always complex and mediated by the structures and activists of the political parties themselves, and since these parties were mainly concerned to secure electoral backing to gain strength in parliament, what happened at this national level was frequently of major importance in divorcing the parties from their local capacities. In Preston this process was observed on several occasions. The growing hostility of the state to trade unions at the turn of the century, allied to the Conservative party's adoption of tariff reform, undermined the local party's hegemony which had been based on its programme to advance working-class economistic interests in a stagnant local economy. Similarly the policies of the 1929 Labour government over women's issues and unemployment alienated these groups more generally from the Labour party.

National developments were therefore mainly of negative importance: they served to undermine existing forms of political mobilisation; but, so long as the party's national programme was compatible with local party efforts, the process of putting together a workable electoral bloc depended on local party action working within the capacities present in the area.

This point is demonstrated above all by the weakness of the Liberals in the late Victorian period. In this respect Preston, along with other North Lancashire towns, notably Blackburn, stood out from all other large towns, where the working class generally voted Liberal. The Preston working class's unusual political allegiance was not simply a case of the local social structure determining political forms. The existence of Irish immigrants did not in itself necessarily lead to a backlash producing Conservative support, nor were members of the working class inevitably

188

deferential because of their labour market position. Rather the Preston case shows that Toryism was based on the seedbed of economistic working-class politics preoccupied with the problem of regenerating Preston's local economy. In Preston key sections of workers, notably the spinners, had strong economistic capacities, while craft workers were relatively weak. This in itself did not guarantee Conservative strength, however. The creation of popular Toryism was due largely to the skilful leadership of W.E.M. Tomlinson, in recognising the class base of possible Tory support, and in creating a programme to appeal to it. The role of local party leaders in creating institutional structures and programmes for successful electoral mobilisation is of crucial importance, and parallel instances of it exist: for example Salvidge's construction of an Anglican working-class Toryism in Liverpool.[1]

Yet these party activists were all forced to work within the constraints of the possible. Tomlinson was successful because he could draw on the dominant type of economistic practical politics. Despite considerable effort the Liberals (in the 1880s) and the ILP (in the 1890s) could not counter Tory strength since the capacities for mutualist struggles (which the Liberals supported) or statist ones (advanced by the ILP) remained weak in this period. The early Labour party on the other hand competed directly with the Conservatives in drawing on economistic politics. The outcome of this local conflict was not pre-ordained by the character of the local social structure since both parties were fighting to make use of the same dominant local capacities: in the end the Conservatives lost as much because of national developments in the political arena as because of local factors. Nonetheless it was also apparent that Labour's advance was boosted by certain developments, notably the growth in municipal labour and the conflicts between male and female labour.

However, one cannot talk of simply 'one' set of capacities: there are different groups of workers with different capacities, and these may not overlap with neighbourhood capacities. The Tories, in the electoral contest, were forced to search for alternative bases of support and in the period immediately before World War I were quite successful in recasting the Conservative party along new lines based on neighbourhood capacities, with the urban petite bourgeoisie playing a pivotal role. In making these strategic choices the party was laid open to new demands (mainly, in this case, over keeping rates low). Although party activists can usually make choices about the need to win over certain groups, they are often less aware that this very process will lead to new issues being raised which they would rather not have brought out into the open.

This was clearly revealed by changes within the Labour party. After World War I the party was dominated by well-organised male workers concerned to remove women from employment and to make security of employment their first priority. But when it became apparent that this was failing to win mass support, activists in the party's organisational sub-committee decided to establish neighbourhood organisation. It was probably thought that these neighbourhood structures would be only support groups for the union-dominated party, but by organising support for the party along these new lines statist demands were placed on the agenda of formal political institutions for the first time.

Parties are not simply the idle products of social change. In the battle to gain electoral support they are forced to latch on to various capacities in order to generate support. They may be more or less conscious in this process, but they are normally not aware of how new demands may be raised when they shift their bases of support. Political parties are also constrained by the fact that they have to operate among the capacities and practical struggles which exist outside themselves: while they are crucially important in forming these into a programme they cannot create practical politics themselves, for these arise from people's practical negotiation of their immediate environment. Political parties can help associate political programmes with particular forms of practical struggle, and are often most successful when showing how certain forms of practical politics can be applied to a wide variety of other problems.

These considerations help give better insights into the rise of the Labour party. Two processes need to be examined: the way in which parties operating in the national political arena are able to make various appeals to forms of practical politics, and the shift in character of class capacities and practical politics. Before 1914 it was mainly the first of these which was all-important, with the political parties battling it out to represent existing, though more strident economistic demands. The Labour party came into being largely because the two existing parties proved deficient in this area.

It is now generally agreed that the early Labour party in most areas, and the national parliamentary party, was basically economistic. Thane stresses that in the early Labour party 'for most trade unionists the capacity to strike or to threaten to do so was a more important guarantor of "welfare" for themselves and their families than the social measures from the state. There can be no doubt that most trade unionists would have preferred adequate wages and full employment . . . to dependence upon publicly funded benefits.' Lanagan refers to 'Labourism's' support of a situation where 'possession of a job and secure place in the labour market, depending on various degrees of skill and dexterity, conferred corresponding degrees of status upon its owners'.[2] At the local level the concern of Preston's Labour party for wages and conditions of municipal workers was repeated elsewhere.[3] It is notable that support for state intervention came from areas where non-wage-earners were involved, and here it was recognised that some state provision (in terms of old-age pensions, the feeding of schoolchildren etc.) would not only relieve the burden on the wage-earner, but also, in the case of old-age pensions, help alleviate pressure on the labour market.

The inability of the then existing parties to absorb working-class economistic politics must be elevated to a major place in explaining the early growth of the Labour party. Indeed what is significant about the emergence of the Labour party was the extent to which it was facilitated by the orientation of the existing parties. Before 1900 both the Liberal and Conservative parties were primarily geared to working-class mutualist struggles. The Liberal party in particular represented the 'respectable' working class organised through mutualist societies, such as the Friendly Societies, building societies and Co-ops. The Conservatives, in the main (Preston probably being an exception), competed with the Liberals on this ground. Pugh has shown that the attempt by the Conservatives to win a mass following through such organisations as the Primrose League also drew on mutualist working-class struggles, as evidenced by their support of owner occupation for the working class and the fact that most branches of the League had Friendly Societies attached.[4]

The problem of course was that mutualist politics were becoming steadily less viable with the undermining of craft production and the emergence of considerable unemployment from the 1880s. The Conservatives' advocacy of tariff reform in 1905 attempted to appeal to working-class economistic interests by preventing foreign competition and so securing employment, but they failed to recognise that outside its home base of the Midlands tariff reform seemed unattractive in those industries dependent on exports and hence vulnerable to foreign reciprocation of tariff barriers.[5]

The Liberal party, however, did not become a party stressing working-class economistic demands, but continually tried to strike other popular chords. As is shown by the submissions of Liberals to the 1892 Royal Commission on Labour, one of its main hopes was to develop mutualism in industry, by encouraging co-operation, developing Boards of Arbitration which would undermine the divide between capital and labour, etc. The Liberals' final move, however, was to some form of state intervention, with certain state reforms compensating for their inability to come to terms with the working class's economic demands. By so doing they left economistic interests unrepresented and allowed trade unions to develop a role as full spokesmen for these types of struggles. These developments explain the ease of Labour's rise in the early 1900s: the Labour party moved into a political space which the other parties could not fill. Geographically Labour was generally strongest where economistic trade unions were strong.[6]

If the main stream of the Labour party grew because of the strategic defects of the other parties, the more 'left-wing' organisations did rely far more on places where class capacities were less economistic. The ILP in some areas pursued mutualist politics (in its emphasis upon respectability and temperance), and in others advanced statist issues, as it did in Preston, emphasising the need for municipalisation. Howell emphasises that the ILP did best in medium-sized towns with stable populations, where neighbourhood capacities were most likely to be present. The ILP's two strongholds both had exceptional features: Leicester was a town where the craft boot and shoe workers had been dramatically displaced by new technology in the 1890s, and where the workers had responded with mutualist, co-operative production in the short term, but with statist demands in the longer term, which could best be mobilised by the ILP. Similarly in Merthyr Tydfil (Wales) mutualist struggles took place, as we saw in Chapter 2, and the ILP's doctrine of self-reliance proved congenial here.[7]

To explain the fortunes of the Labour party after 1914 attention should be switched to the dramatically changing character of class capacities and the success of the Labour party, at least in the later 1920s, in seizing upon them. Many historians have been diverted from the study of changes in class capacities by the remarkable industrial conflicts of the period, which culminated in the General Strike. In Preston, at least, these industrial disputes tended to divide the Labour movement, and close examination of Labour's electoral fortunes shows that they were not very important in increasing Labour's popularity in many parts of the country. Shepherd and Halstead show that the period of Labour's greatest growth did not coincide with a period of industrial militancy; Cronin argues that between 1900 and 1905 there were extremely few industrial disputes in Britain – but this was also the period when the number of Labour councillors nationwide increased.[8] On the other hand the period of massive industrial conflict between 1910 and 1914 was one when Labour failed to make any electoral headway.

Problems with attempts to link political change to militancy at work arise also in White's analysis which related specifically to Lancashire. He linked the emergence of the Labour party in Lancashire to worsening industrial relations as employers launched attacks on the cotton workers' wages and working conditions in the context of increasingly severe international competition. It is however clear that in Lancashire the periods of the greatest industrial conflict were not those of Labour's best electoral performance. White makes much of the 1913 ballot held by the cotton trade unions on whether their members supported Labour representation. This appeared to show considerable majorities in favour, but the abstention rates were very high, and for several groups of workers an earlier ballot in 1892 on the principle of Labour representation showed higher majorities in favour.[9]

In the 1920s the national picture is also clear. Many historians have seen the dramatic growth in support for the Labour party between 1925 and 1929 as little more than an appendage to the General Strike and earlier industrial conflicts, and of little significance in the face of Labour's defeats. Cronin's verdict that 'the defeat of the General Strike meant more than a temporary defeat: it also served to complete the process of stabilisation begun in 1920–1' is typical. Yet it was only after 1926 that Labour made massive electoral advances. Between 1921 and 1925 Labour lost a net total of forty-two seats in English and Welsh municipal elections. Between 1926 and 1929 Labour gained a total of 452. These gains were made in a decade when union membership almost halved – from over eight million in 1920 to just over four million by 1929.[10] Cronin's work shows that in the period between 1926 and 1929 there were fewer strikes than in any other between 1889 and the 1970s. Labour's support was clearly not related to industrial issues.

In Preston intense industrial conflict could co-exist with support for the Tories. The spinners, overwhelmingly Tory politically, were among the most dispute-prone workers in Victorian Britain, yet when they shifted their allegiance to Labour in the 1920s their industrial militancy had declined dramatically. As I emphasised in Chapter 1 we must recognise the disconnectedness of various social practices: because militancy exists in one arena we must not infer it in another. Industrial conflict is not a primordial experience which necessarily affects wider political allegiances.

It would be wrong, however, to attribute Labour's growth in popularity to purely political factors, as is appropriate for the period before 1914, although the extension of the franchise was of considerable importance.[11] Reid argues that the workers' wartime experience of seeing the state involved in production gave them the sense that the state could be used to improve their lot: independent politics were thereby encouraged.[12] However, Reid generalises too much from the experience of shipyard workers, for in many other fields wartime state intervention in industry was treated with hostility, mainly because it undermined informal labour market controls which workers (particularly in badly unionised industries) relied on. Similarly, as has been observed on many occasions, the wartime splits and divisions within the Liberal party, which some observers have felt to be an adequate explanation of its demise, were to be found also in the Labour party.[13]

It was not until the middle years of the 1920s that the Labour party was able to mobilise along new lines and secure unprecedented measures of support. The character of Labour politics at the local level changed considerably. In this respect it is important to emphasise the discontinuities in Labour politics in the 1920s, and to see the positive, rather than the negative shifts which were taking place. Recently a number of historians have begun to argue for a discontinuity thesis in respect of the rise of the Labour party. McLean shows that the development of the Labour party on Clydeside owed relatively little to the much-cited industrial conflicts of the years spanning World War I, and rather more to the housing campaigns and the mobilisation of the Catholics in the early 1920s. Whiting argues that in the context of a 'new industrial town', Oxford, the development of the Labour party owed relatively little to earlier craft traditions.[14] The Labour party underwent a fundamental change in character in the early 1920s in many areas: it changed from a party based on certain trade unions to one based on neighbourhood organisation. Howard argues that Labour's ward organisation was weak in this period, but his account is highly selective.[15]

There are considerable grounds for arguing that the process observed in Preston, where neighbourhood-based capacities increased considerably in this period, were to be found in a number of other areas. Pritchard's careful research into the Leicester housing market shows that, just as in Preston, the population was markedly more stable after World War I. In 1908 the average annual rate of turnover was 15 %, but by 1920 this had fallen to about 5 %, of which much was caused not by people moving, but by people dying and being replaced by other residents. Pritchard remarks that 'the situation between the two wars must have represented an absolute minimum residential mobility'.[16] The operation of the Rent Restriction Act, which gave sitting tenants protection against rent increases, must have been the main factor at work here. From the 1930s this stability was undermined, as public housing programmes, allied to slum clearance, led to the removal of people from older urban areas, a tendency exacerbated by the considerable flows of population from some depressed areas to the expanding south and Midlands of England: yet by the later 1920s none of this was under way.

This element is only one side of the story however. In these older urban areas a new network of popularly controlled neighbourhood institutions developed. National statistics indicate that a rapid decline occurred in the number of public houses, but an increase in the numbers of clubs. In the retail sector the petit-bourgeois corner shop was replaced by the Co-op, clothing clubs, and works-based retailing networks. In many areas this provided the Labour party with a new basis for mobilisation.[17]

The transition to neighbourhood-based politics was however uneven. In the interwar years the local Labour movement fell into one of four types. Firstly, in those areas where trade unions had historically been weak, it was necessary for the Labour movement to find alternative sources of support, and so it was overwhelmingly based on neighbourhood organisation. Some indication of these areas is provided by Table 8.1 which shows those constituencies where individual party membership was above 1,000 in 1930. The table lists a number of constituencies which are not frequently mentioned in the literature on the rise of the Labour party. Faversham has rarely appeared to be a Labour stronghold. None of the great industrial storm centres figures on this table: there are no Scottish or Welsh constituencies (except Newport), no Sheffield, Leeds, Manchester. Virtually all the seats listed in the table were Labour deserts before 1914 (the exceptions being Woolwich, Derby, Deptford, Poplar South and Chester-le-Street), and thirty-five of the forty-four had no official Labour candidate before 1914. Yet in the 1920s it was in these constituencies that Labour's vote began to take off. In 1929 thirty-three of the forty-seven MPs from these constituencies were Labour.

These figures indicate that in certain areas of weak trade unionism the Labour party developed as a party based on ward organisation, and it was this type of constituency as well as the heavily industrialised ones that gave Labour strong support in the 1929 election. Many of these constituencies were in the London area and the Home Counties more generally, often in primarily residential areas. Here the Labour party was based on ward organisation which built on neighbourhood capacities.

Secondly, alongside these areas where the Labour party appears to have been based around ward organisation, were those where the Labour party seems to have shifted from a trade union to a ward basis, in the same manner that Preston did. Some of these (e.g. Oldham) are included in Table 8.1. Many of these were in Lancashire, and there

Table 8.1. *Labour party membership and Labour party support, 1900–30*

Constituency	Individual members, 1930	Seat(s) won by which party, 1929	Percentage of vote for Labour, 1929	Labour candidate before 1914	Labour's maximum of vote before 1914
Woolwich (2 seats)	4,355	Lab., Con.	53.7[a]	Yes	61.4[b]
Reading	2,500	Lab.	43.5	No	
Lewisham E.	2,500	Con.	41.7	No	
Greenwich	2,435	Lab.	46.3	No	
Oldham (2 seats)	2,280	Lab.(2)	51.2	Yes	24.6[c]
Salford N.	2,250	Lab.	46.2	No	
Faversham	2,036	Con.	38.9	No	
Derby (2 seats)	2,018	Lab.(2)	57.4	Yes	34.1[d]
Swindon	1,900	Lab.	43.6	No	
Bermondsey W.	1,800	Lab.	60.2	No	
Romford	1,742	Lab.	44.9	No	
Deptford	1,720	Lab.	55.2	Yes	52.2[e]
Ilford	1,700	Con.	20.7	No	
Dartford	1,620	Lab.	50.6	No	
Poplar S.	1,612	Lab.	64.8	No	
Newport	1,605	Lab.	39.5	Yes	16.5[e]
Watford	1,550	Con.	23.8	No	
Darlington	1,500	Lab.	44.0	Yes	48.3[e]
Enfield	1,465	Lab.	43.3	No	
Maldon	1,464	Con.	35.1	No	
North-east Ham	1,359	Lab.	42.1	No	
St Albans	1,335	Con.	27.6	No	
Harrow	1,260	Con.	29.8	No	
Bermondsey Rotherhithe	1,250	Lab.	61.6	No	
Poplar, Bow and Bromley	1,200	Lab.	69.4	Yes	55.6[d]
Salford W.	1,200	Lab.	42.8	No	
Skipton	1,200	Con.	31.8	No	
Wellingborough	1,200	Lab.	42.2	No	
Cambridgeshire	1,091	Con.	31.7	No	
Penryn and Falmouth	1,081	Lib.	28.9	No	
Colchester	1,069	Con.	38.5	No	
Norfolk N.	1,065	Lab.	47.5	No	
Edmonton	1,040	Lab.	59.3	No	
Spelthorne	1,040	Con.	30.7	No	
Hendon	1,038	Con.	23.5	No	
Mitcham	1,038	Con.	30.8	No	
Rossendale	1,035	Lab.	36.0	No	
Bristol S.	1,020	Lab.	56.5	No	
Accrington	1,000	Lab.	52.3	No	
Camberwell N.	1,000	Lab.	58.0	No	
Carlisle	1,000	Lab.	40.4	No	
Plymouth Drake	1,000	Lab.	44.3	No	
Tottenham N.	1,000	Lab.	54.0	No	
Chester-le-Street	1,000	Lab.	69.8	Yes	64.8[f]

were several double-constituency seats where individual membership of the Labour party was high (Bolton, 1,200; Preston, 1,036). The explanation for this is likely to vary from town to town, but one factor which was of general importance was that in all these areas trade unions had a long history of political activity, and it is therefore likely that activists were keen to establish a non-union base for the Labour party. Furthermore, in many of them, such as Preston, the trade unions had had a strong neighbourhood presence, for instance by collecting subscriptions not at work but through paid collectors who visited members at their homes. Most of these were also areas with high levels of women's economic activity, and the shift to neighbourhood politics can perhaps best be explained by the way in which women, initially mobilised through work experience, then helped shift the focus of politics to the neighbourhood.

The significance of women's organisation to the development of a neighbourhood-based Labour party has not been stressed hitherto, but in Preston it was crucial. There was indeed a dramatic national growth in women's organisations in the 1920s which needs to be emphasised: from the mere 5,500 members of the Women's Labour League in 1918 to 70,000 women members by 1921, 120,000 by 1923, and 200,000 by 1925. It was reported that 'in many cases the bulk of the Party in small towns and villages is women', and there are suggestions that Labour's electoral success of the later 1920s was based on the women's vote. 'There is increasing evidence that the awakened political consciousness of the women is more pronounced on the side of Labour than of any other political force in the Country.'[18] The tendency to assume that Women's Sections even at this date were of little political import is to extrapolate the situation obtaining in the 1930s back too far. Certainly the Labour party's Annual Reports show that women campaigned over a number of issues: women in paid employment, unemployment among women, social services, education for 'working women', Trade Boards, the need

Notes to Table 8.1 Local Labour parties covering two constituencies are included only where the total membership is over 2,000.
'Lib-Labs' (Liberals who declared themselves as also representing 'Labour' interests) are not counted as Labour candidates.
[a]The Woolwich 1929 vote is an average of the two seats.
[b]1903 by-election.
[c]1911 by-election.
[d]December 1910.
[e]1906.
[f]January 1910.
Source: Labour Party Annual Report 1930; Craig, *British Parliamentary Election Results.*

for equality in employment, minimum wages, the end of marriage bars and family allowances paid for out of a wealth tax.

Thirdly, there were those areas where the transition to neighbourhood politics relied mainly on the framework established by religious or ethnic organisations. Here no mass membership developed, and the greater democracy and accountability evident in the ward-based parties was not found: rather 'boss control' remained much more important. Liverpool and Glasgow provide the best examples of this (though in Glasgow the unions were also strong) and in London's docklands too the 'Catholic Mafia' reached great prominence (though Table 8.1 shows that in many London constituencies individual membership of the Labour party was also high).[19]

Finally there were those constituencies where the Labour party remained under trade union influence. In some single-industry areas, notably in mining, this reflected the dual role of the unions in life at work and out of work. In other areas the capacities for work-based politics remained strong, but there was little popular activism and trade union oligarchs held sway. Howard suggests that Coventry, Leicester, Llanelli, Doncaster, Cambridge, Wolverhampton and the Rhondda fall into this category.[20] It is notable that none of these had high levels of ward membership by the late 1920s. The process which was seen to be at work in Preston, whereby the former trade union leaders, notably Wooley and Francis, but also Wallwork (expelled 1929), were undermined by popular forces, was not observed in these constituencies.

Control of the local council was always of considerable importance in establishing Labour's credibility, whichever basis of support was relied upon. It was especially important in the 1930s in relation to unemployment. In Preston, where Labour never controlled the Council or other state bodies, the party seemed hostile to the unemployed, and it was only where the party could be seen to mitigate the effects of unemployment through the actions of its representatives on public bodies that it could hold the support of the unemployed.

Labour fared worst in those places where there was rapid population flux, usually related to high growth in employment. These were par excellence the new and expanding areas in the south and Midlands. Here new working practices frequently undermined craft capacities and workers' labour market control, while company housing eroded neighbourhood solidarity. The coalfields of the Dukeries were classic examples of this but similar processes could be found in such areas as Slough or Oxford where the Labour party remained exceptionally weak until World War II.[21]

In the 1930s a further important development took place in Preston: the growing capacity of unskilled workers to become collectively organised. Statist politics, which had previously been based upon neighbourhood and women's capacities, now got a further injection of support. The casualised and unskilled workers, who hitherto had few capacities for collective action, seized upon the potential of state employment which developed from the previous struggles of consumers to reduce their own insecurity. In doing so they changed the emphases of Labour politics, as their concern was for central state initiative and for the position of the worker in the provision of public services. It is unlikely that Preston was alone in seeing this transformation, but arguably this change in the labour market was more uneven, geographically. Many of the workers in the new municipal enterprises and amenities had been the most casualised in the labour market. Their de-casualisation under the aegis of the state could have had critical 'knock-on' effects on the condition of labour in the rest of the labour market. Where statist Labour parties controlled local authorities they had considerable potential to aid the de-casualisation of these workers, especially since at this time wages were not centrally negotiated. Thus the Labour-controlled 'Northern District' paid higher wages than any other district and, in London, Poplar paid wage levels well above rates set by the Joint Industrial Council. Several local authorities attempted to force their workers to join trade unions. In areas where statist Labour parties were weak, however, there may have been little move towards de-casualisation. White argues that, especially for men, there was little de-casualisation of labour in Islington in the inter-war years. An important development which took place in many parts of the country, however, was that security in the labour market was not determined simply by whether workers were able to develop their own barriers around particular occupations, but also by whether they might rely on the state for protection. This explains much of the agitation over 'sheltered occupations' which developed in the 1930s, with many private employers concerned that such workers were not affected by the demand and supply of the labour market.[22]

The expansion of public sector employment provided further opportunities for the trade unions to increase their membership. After the decline in membership in the 1920s, it was to the public sector that many unions looked for new support thereafter. The NUGMW for instance had 110,000 members in the public services in 1926 but 200,000 by 1938, a proportion of its total membership which increased from just under one-third to almost a half. By the 1930s most branches of public sector work were over 50 % unionised, despite the precipitate decline in other industrial sectors, and the strength of unions in the service sector was well established.[23]

In some areas casual employment was the subject of central state initiative, notably in dock-related work. As Phillips and Whiteside emphasise casualisation persisted in some respects, but its form was considerably changed.[24] As a result of unemployment insurance dockers were able to work regularly for a few days a week and sign on, collecting unemployment benefit, for the others. Underemployment was thereby institutionalised. Nonetheless these workers were stabilised by such changes which reduced internal competition between workers and so increased their capacities for collective action, and in these years they became much more highly unionised and more active Labour supporters, especially in London. The organisation of these casualised workers frequently related to the salience of neighbourhood capacities, since solidarity developed in the neighbourhood could then help lead to collective action at work.

Despite mass unemployment, then, it might be argued that state intervention had the effect of increasing the capacities for collective action of large numbers of unskilled or casualised workers, as they became somewhat isolated from operation of the harsh laws of supply and demand on the labour market. These capacities, furthermore, were increasingly likely to lead to statist struggles, as workers struggled to involve the state to help reduce the insecurity of the capitalist labour market.

The Labour party between the wars was a complex alliance of local parties, each based on various local capacities. The shift to neighbourhood capacities, which in turn overlapped with the growing powers of the unskilled, frequently helped produce statist labour politics, though in some areas, such as South Wales, local neighbourhood capacities were more amenable to mutualism. One thing does however stand out in this history of the early Labour movement: the party was strongest in electoral and other ways when it was less involved in conflicts over the price of labour and more concerned with struggles affecting the very conditions under which people sold their labour power. The Labour party of the inter-war years can best be seen as a party based on working-class interests when one considers its pioneering efforts to provide certain services and income in a non-commodified way, rather than its attempts to increase wages.

Employment change in Preston, 1891–1951

The following tables give Census data on employment change in Preston and should be consulted for much of the discussion in Chapter 4. It is however a difficult matter to put together a set of tables analysing change over time, since the headings under which the data are classified change considerably over the period 1891–1951. In particular, up to 1911 the main classification is industrial, with workers being classified by the industry in which they work, though the more numerous sectors are often broken down by occupation as well. Tables A.1 and A.2 give the details for change in Preston between 1891 and 1911, but many changes in classification have taken place which involve some reworking of the tables, as specified therein. From 1921 however occupational tables become available, and these are easier to use than the industrial tables, but in order to analyse change from 1911 to 1921 – a key period because of the impact of World War I on employment patterns – the 1911 tables have to be extensively reworked – by no means a perfect solution. The reworked data are presented in Table A.3. Finally, Table A.4 uses occupational Census data, again adjusted for comparability, to examine change from 1921 to 1951, but because no Census was taken in 1941 the table is an imperfect guide to the situation obtaining in the late 1930s.

A number of specific points should be noted. The suburbs of Fulwood and Penwortham are excluded from these tables and hence any over-literal reading of them would exaggerate the proletarian character of Preston's employment in the inter-war years. Unemployment is not specifically detailed until 1931, and even then it is underestimated since many workers laid off temporarily would have probably stated their previous occupation. The Census is a notoriously unreliable indicator of female work, particularly part-time work, but this is probably less the case in Preston than elsewhere since female textile employment was factory based and so less likely to be counted as part of domestic or 'housewifely' work.

Table A.1. *Occupations of males in Preston, 1891–1911 (percentage of males over 10)*

	1891	1901	1911
1. General or local government	1.10	1.30	1.76
2. Defence	0.17	0.32	0.35
3. Professional	2.69	2.28	2.28
4. Domestic officer or servant	0.44	0.76	1.17
5. Commercial occupations	3.25	3.80	4.02
6. Conveyance	7.17	9.68	10.18
7. Agriculture	1.45	1.25	1.25
8. Fishing	—	—	—
9. Miners and mine produce	0.61	0.52	0.46
10. Metals, engineering	7.83	10.65	10.97
11. Precious metals	0.53	1.37	1.97
12. Building	7.29	8.84	7.13
13. Wood, furniture	3.12	3.02	2.74
14. Brick, cement, pottery, glass	0.52	0.46	0.30
15. Chemicals	0.49	0.46	0.87
16. Skin, leather, hair, feather	0.48	0.40	0.38
17. Paper, prints, books, stationery	1.12	1.13	1.23
18. Textiles	27.89	20.54	23.02
19. Dress	3.53	3.80	3.55
20. Food, tobacco, drink, lodging	8.06	8.00	7.54
21. Gas, water, electricity, sanitary	0.73	0.78	0.77
22. Other, general, undefined	9.97	7.04	5.31
23. Unoccupied	11.52	13.58	12.67

Notes: 1901 categories are used. This has involved extensive reworking of 1891 categories, viz:

Order 9   Made up of 1891 Order 21, 1–2, excluding gas works service.

Order 10   Made up of 1891 Order 10, 1–2, Order 21, 8–12 and Order 13, 1 (shipwrights, iron).

Order 11   Made up of 1891 Order 10, 3–8 and Order 21, 7.

Order 12   Made up of 1891 Order 11, 1 and Order 21, 3 (pavoirs, road labourers, road contractors, railway contractors, navvies, other).

Order 13   Made up of 1891 Order 11, 2–3, Order 12, 1, Order 13, 1 (shipwrights, wood) and Order 20, 2–3.

Order 14   Made up of 1891 Order 21, 3 (stone quarries, dealers in stone), Order 21, 4–5.

Order 15   Made up of 1891 Order 14, Order 19, 1 and Order 20, 1.

Order 16   Made up of 1891 Order 12, 2 and Order 19, 2–3.

Order 17   Made up of 1891 Order 9 and Order 20, 4.

Order 21   Made up of 1891 Order 21, 2 (gas works service), Order 21, 6, and Order 23.

Order 20   Made up of 1891 Order 16 and Order 15.

Table A.2. *Occupations of females in Preston, 1891–1911 (percentage of females over 10)*

	1891	1901	1911
1. General or local government	0.03	0.04	0.10
2. Defence	—	—	—
3. Professional	1.73	1.64	1.67
4. Domestic officer or servant	7.68	6.14	5.07
5. Commercial occupations	0.08	0.12	0.27
6. Conveyance	0.02	0.07	0.04
7. Agriculture	0.04	0.03	0.03
8. Fishing	—		
9. Mines and mine produce	0.02	0.03	0.07
10. Metals, engineering	0.04	0.06	0.24
11. Precious metals	0.25	0.21	0.37
12. Building	—	—	—
13. Wood, furniture	0.19	0.14	0.16
14. Brick, cement, pottery, glass	0.02	0.01	0.01
15. Chemicals	0.05	0.08	0.12
16. Skin, leather, hair, feather	0.02	0.01	0.01
17. Paper, prints, books, stationery	0.18	0.22	0.59
18. Textiles	41.81	36.33	37.76
19. Dress	3.75	3.76	3.31
20. Food, tobacco, drink, lodging	2.50	2.76	4.07
21. Gas, water, electricity, sanitary	0.01	—	—
22. Other, general, undefined	0.66	0.39	0.42
23. Unoccupied	40.94	47.96	45.68

See notes to Table A.1.
Source: Censuses.

Notes to Table A.1. cont.

There is no reason to suppose that these adjustments lead to inaccuracy, since the basis of allotting job to industrial (sub)-orders remains the same between 1891 and 1911.

The only difference between 1901 and 1911 categories is that in the 1911 Census electrical apparatus workers were placed in order 10. For the purposes of this table they have been reclassified under Order 11.

Source: Censuses.

Table A.3. Occupational change in Preston, 1911–21

	Male			Female			Total		
	1911	1921	Change (%)[a]	1911	1921	Change (%)[a]	1911	1921	Change (%)[a]
1. Fishing	10	28		—	1		10	29	
2. Agriculture	530	542	+2.26	17	24		547	566	+3.47
3. Mining	82	80		32	1		114	81	
4. Coke, Lime, cement	100	10		—	45		100	55	
5. Bricks, pottery		69			27			96	
6. Chemicals	220	66		32	30		252	96	
7. Metals[b,c]	4,709	5,339	+19.98[d]	72	81		4,522	5,420	+19.85[d]
8. Precious metals	142	29		118	79		260	108	
9. Watches		52			3			55	
10. Electrical apparatus	639	580	−9.23	62	289		701	869	+23.97
11. Skins	130	119		5	8		135	127	
12. Textiles	9,426	6,523	−30.80	19,027	17,084	−10.21	28,453	23,607	−17.03
13. Dress	1,296	1,065	−17.82	1,536	1,296	−15.63	2,832	2,361	−16.63
14. Foods	823	613	−25.52	304	482	+58.55	1,127	1,095	−2.84
15. Wood[e]	1,024	1,773	+73.14	49	36		1,073	1,809	+68.59
16. Paper	372	348		205	286		577	634	
17. Builders[c]	2,745	1,409		2	7		3,006	1,416	
18. Painters[e]		765	−27.63		8			773	−27.18
19. Workers in other materials[b]	ſ	382		ſ	64		ſ	446	
20. Workers in undefined materials[b]	ſ	239		ſ	27		ſ	266	
21. Gas etc.	182	132		—	—		182	132	
22. Transport[g]	4,285	4,621	+7.84	22	151		4,307	4,772	+10.80
23. Commercial[h]	4,315	3,398	−18.49	1,997	1,595	−20.13	6,312	5,112	−19.01

24. Public administration	889	1,250	+40.61	51	231		940	1,481	+57.55
25. Professions	644	667	+3.57	750	805	+7.33	1,394	1,472	−5.60
26. Entertainment	315	230		103	124		418	354	
27. Personal service	1,099	1,054	−4.09	3,199	2,801	−12.44	4,298	3,855	−10.31
28. Clerks	894[i]	1,424	+59.28	110[i]	600	+445.45	1,004[i]	2,024	+101.89
29. Warehousemen etc.[g]		874			849			1,223	
30. Engine drivers	348	436		—	—		348	436	
31. Other workers (i.e. not in manufacturing) (+ unemployed)	1,532	3,808	+148.56	23	134	+6.16	1,555	3,942	+153.50
32. Unoccupied	5,731	3,915	−26.56	23,310	24,746		28,661	28,661	−0.70
Total population	53,915	53,993		63,173	63,413				

[a]Calculated only for categories in which 1% or more of workforce were employed in 1911.

[b]The figure for Order 7, Metals, in 1911 includes some workers (shipbuilders and vehicle workers) classified in Orders 19 and 20. Workers in other and undefined materials, in 1921.

[c]In 1911 plumbers were included in Order 17, Builders, in 1921 in Order 7, Metals. The plumbers of 1911 have been reclassified to Metals.

[d]In fact the percentage increase is greater because some of the metal workers of 1911 have been reclassified to Orders 19 and 20.

[e]In 1911 French-polishers were included in Order 15, Wood, in 1921 in Order 18, Painters.

[f]Figures for 1911 are included in Orders 4–18, depending on the nature of the occupation.

[g]The figure for Order 22, Transport, in 1911 includes some workers classified in Order 29, Warehousemen etc., in 1921.

[h]Dealers have been removed from other categories in the 1911 classification and put in Order 23.

[i]Figures for 1911 are included in Order 22, Transport, and Order 23, Commercial.

Source: Censuses.

Table A.4. Occupational change in Preston, 1921–51 (1951 Categories)

	Male			Female			Total		
	1921	1931	1951	1921	1931	1951	1921	1931	1951
1. Fishing	28	12	7	1	—	—	29	12	7
2. Agriculture	542	549	378	24	9	16	566	604	394
3. Mining	80	37	24	1	—	—	81	37	24
4. Ceramics, glass[a]	} 145	160	921	102	68	107	247	228	1,028
5. Chemicals[a]									
6. Metals	6,000	5,060	7,561	462	296	808	6,452	5,356	8,369
7. Textiles	6,523	3,846	1,712	17,084	14,537	6,624	23,607	18,383	8,336
8. Leather, fur	119	57	91	8	5	54	127	62	96
9. Dress[b]	1,065	1,089	695	1,296	1,319	1,275	2,361	2,408	1,970
10. Food	613	528	377	482	659	574	1,095	1,187	951
11. Wood	1,773	1,537	1,295	36	26	113	1,809	1,563	1,408
12. Paper, printers	348	392	381	286	322	344	634	714	725
13. Miscellaneous	621	534	317	91	109	44	712	643	361
14. Builders	1,409	1,990	2,344	7	3	5	1,416	1,993	2,349
15. Painters	765	928	1,096	8	55	59	773	983	1,155
16. Administration, managers[c]	} 4,648	4,887	4,592	1,826	2,128	2,682	6,474	7,015	7,274
18. Commercial, finance[c]									
20. Defence[c]									
21. Entertainment	230	272	170	124	44	41	354	316	211
22. Personal service	1,054	1,316	1,208	2,801	3,617	4,121	3,855	4,933	5,329
23. Clerks	1,424	2,139	2,266	600	946	2,917	2,024	3,085	5,183
24. Warehousemen etc.	874	922	1,226	349	573	701	1,223	1,495	1,927
25. Stationary engine drivers	436	438	715	—	—	9	436	438	724
26. Unskilled[d]	} 3,940	6,639	4,897	135	1,059	1,441	4,075	7,698	6,338
27. Other									

[a] These two orders made up three orders in 1921 and can be compared only as a joint category.

[b] In 1951 shoe- and bootmakers were placed in Leather rather than Dress as in 1921 and 1931. For the sake of comparability I have restored them to Dress.

[c] Order 16 was created in 1951 from Orders 18 and 20 which were thereby reduced. For comparability the three categories must be read together.

The 1881 Census Enumerators' returns for Preston

I chose to examine three distinct areas in toto, rather than to carry out a sample survey of every tenth house, because I felt that the latter procedure would average out neighbourhood differences within Preston into a meaningless set of figures. The three areas were chosen because they seemed the most distinctive, or extreme, examples of Preston neighbourhoods. The three areas are Marsh Lane, near the main engineering centres and the railway station, and so having a fair abundance of male labour; the area near the Lancaster Canal where there were a number of major cotton mills; and Fishwick, to the east of Preston, where there was an important craft sector. Altogether 4,812 people were recorded, about 5 % of Preston's population.

Map B.1 shows the areas selected and Table B.1 their basic social structure.

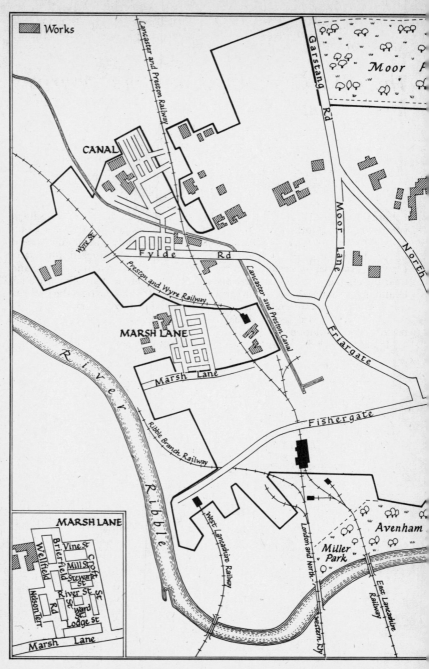

Map B.1 Preston neighbourhoods selected for analysis of 1881 Census returns (Source: Hewitson, *A History of Preston*)

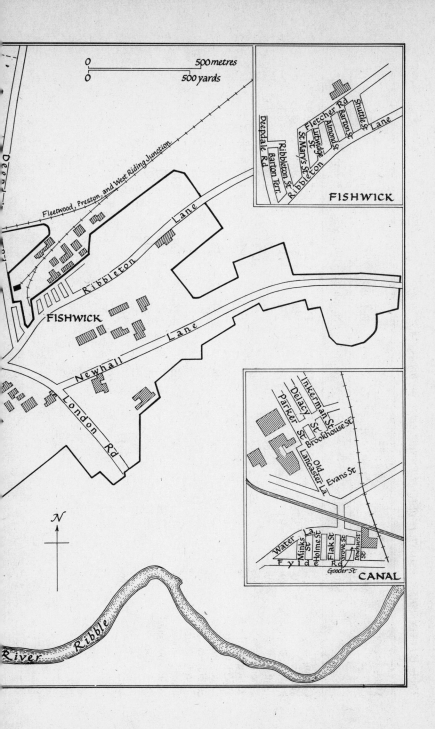

0 —— 500 metres
0 —— 500 yards

FISHWICK

Deepdale Rd
Ribbleton St
Barton Terr.
St. Mary's St.
Ribbleton
Fletcher Rd
Urydge St.
Almond St.
Barton St.
Shuttle St.
Lane

Fleetwood, Preston, and West Riding Junction

Ribbleton Lane

FISHWICK

Newhall Lane

London Rd

Inkerman St.
Delacy St.
Parker St.
Brookhouse St.
Old Lancaster La.
Evans St.

Water La.
Minks St.
Holmes St.
Flak St.
Stove St.
Dublin St.
Fylde Rd
Gooder St.

CANAL

N

River Ribble

Table B.1. *Occupational structure of three Preston neighbourhoods, 1881*

Males over 12	Marsh Lane		Canal		Fishwick		Total	
	Number	Percentage	Number	Percentage	Number	Percentage	Number	Percentage
Cotton	145	28.54	321	42.57	117	37.14	583	36.97
Metals	70	13.78	51	6.76	18	5.71	139	8.81
Railways	49	9.65	28	3.71	4	1.27	81	5.14
Crafts[a]	59	11.61	81	10.74	56	17.77	196	12.43
Labourers[b]	51	10.4	71	9.42	35	11.11	157	9.96
Agricultural	5	0.98	21	2.79	2	0.64	28	1.77
Miscellaneous working class	35	6.89	30	3.98	13	4.12	78	4.95
Employers/ professional/ white-collar[c]	8	1.51	20	2.65	15	4.76	43	2.73
Petits bourgeois[d]	18	3.54	53	7.03	19	6.03	90	5.71
Unoccupied	68	13.39	78	10.34	36	11.43	182	11.54
Total	508		754		315		1577	

Females over 12

Cotton	298	49.43	450	52.16	228	55.45	976	51.96
Tailoresses	21	3.39	27	3.15	25	6.05	73	3.86
Servants	6	0.97	22	2.57	9	2.18	37	1.96
Shop assistants	4	0.65	7	0.82	2	0.49	13	0.69
Other	19	3.07	34	3.97	23	5.57	76	4.02
Unoccupied	263	42.49	320	37.24	125	30.27	708	37.46
Total	611		857		413		1889

[a]Primarily in building; also tailors and shoemakers.
[b]Strictly general labourers. The small number of other labourers have been classified under the appropriate occupation.
[c]Mostly white-collar workers.
[d]In the case of builders, etc. it can be difficult to distinguish self-employed builder or small employer from worker. All 'master' builders, etc. are classified as petits bourgeois, together with small employers.
Source: 1881 Census Enumerators' returns for Preston.

Parliamentary election results in Preston, 1880–1945

It is extremely difficult to compare election results in Preston with the 'national' pattern, since Preston was (until 1950) a two-seat borough where voters had two votes. When there was only one candidate in opposition to the Tories examination of the share of the vote gives a misleading impression since Tory supporters were likely to have used both their votes but the opposition electors only one. Similarly, during the key period of its growth, until 1931, Labour stood only one candidate and it is impossible to use Labour's share of the vote as an indication of its popular support. Here I give the bare figures, and only in the text is there some attempt to evaluate their significance.

Election	Electors	Turnout (%)	Candidate	Party	Votes	Percentage of vote
1880			E. Hermon	Con	6,239	36.2
			Sir J. Holker	Con	5,641	32.7
			G.W. Bahr	Lib	5,355	31.1
1881			W.F. Ecroyd	Con	6,004	58.0
			H.Y. Thompson	Lib	4,340	42.0
1882 (April)†			H.C. Raikes	Con	6,045	58.9
			W.S. Simpson	Lib-Lab	4,212	41.1
1882 (November)†			W.E.M. Tomlinson	Ind Con	6,351	60.4
			R.W. Hanbury	Con	4,167	39.6
1885	14,876	91.1	W.E.M. Tomlinson	Con	8,459	38.5
			R.W. Hanbury	Con	7,971	36.4
			T.W. Russell	Lib	5,491	25.1
1886	14,876	83.9	W.E.M. Tomlinson	Con	7,497	30.6
			R.W. Hanbury	Con	7,296	29.7
			J.O. Pilkington	Lib	4,982	20.3
			G. Potter	Lib-Lab	4,771	19.4
1892	15,959	87.7	R.W. Hanbury	Con	8,070	36.6
			W.E.M. Tomlinson	Con	7,764	35.3
			C.J. Weld-Blundell	Lib	6,182	28.1
1895	16,395	76.3	Rt. Hon. R.W. Hanbury	Con	8,928	41.9
			W.E.M. Tomlinson	Con	7,622	35.7
			J. Tattersall	ILP	4,781	22.4
1900	16,867	76.4	Rt. Hon. R.W. Hanbury	Con	8,944	41.0
			W.E.M. Tomlinson	Con	8,067	36.9
			J.K. Hardie	Lab	4,834	22.1

Election	Electors	Turnout (%)	Candidate	Party	Votes	Percentage of vote
1900			Rt. Hon. R.W. Hanbury	Con	Unopposed	
1903†	17,973	84.2	J. Kerr	Con	8,639	57.1
			J. Hodge	Lab	6,490	42.9
1906	18,626	96.2	J.T. Macpherson	Lab	10,181	30.9
			H. Cox	Lib	8,538	26.0
			J. Kerr	Con	7,303	22.2
			Sir W.E.M. Tomlinson, Bt.	Con	6,856	20.9
1910 (January)	19,521	94.4	Hon. G.F. Stanley	Con	9,526	27.1
			A.A. Tobin	Con	9,160	26.0
			J.T. Macpherson	Lab	7,539	21.4
			Rt. Hon. Sir J.E. Gorst	Lib	6,281	17.8
			H. Cox[a]	FT	2,704	7.7
1910 (December)	19,521	88.9	Hon. G.F. Stanley	Con	9,184	26.8
			A.A. Tobin	Con	8,993	26.3
			E.H. Young	Lib	8,193	23.9
			W.H. Carr	Lab	7,855	23.0
1915			U.H. Broughton	Con	Unopposed	
1918	57,795	69.6	T. Shaw	Lab	19,213	25.8
			Hon. G.F. Stanley	Co C	18,970	25.4
			J.J. O'Neill	Lib	18,485	24.8
			W. Brookes	Co C	17,928	24.0
1922	57,953	87.8	T. Shaw	Lab	26,259	27.9
			J.P. Hodge	Lib	24,798	26.4
			Hon. G.F. Stanley	Con	20,410	21.7

Year	Electorate	Turnout %	Candidate	Party	Votes	%
1923	59,406	87.2	T. Shaw	Lab	25,816	34.4
			J.P. Hodge	Lib	25,155	33.6
			W.M. Kirkpatrick	Con	23,962	32.0
1924	60,840	88.8	Rt. Hon. T. Shaw	Lab	27,009	26.3
			A.R. Kennedy	Con	25,887	25.2
			J.P. Hodge	Lib	25,327	24.6
			G. Barnes	Con	24,557	23.9
1929	81,866	87.9	Rt. Hon. T. Shaw	Lab	37,705	29.5
			W.A. Jowitt	Lib	31,277	24.4
			Dr. A.B. Howitt	Con	29,116	22.8
			C.E.G.C. Emmott	Con	27,754	21.7
			S.M. Holden[b]	Ind Lab	2,111*	1.6
1929†	81,866	79.6	Sir W.A. Jowitt	Lab (N Lab)	35,608	54.6
			Dr. A.B. Howitt	Con	29,168	44.8
			S.M. Holden[b]	Ind Lab	410*	0.6
1931	84,243	85.7	W.M. Kirkpatrick	Con	46,276	32.5
			A.C. Moreing	Con	45,843	32.2
			Rt. Hon. T. Shaw	Lab	25,710	18.0
			E. Porter	Lab	24,660	17.3
1935	84,291	82.6	A.C. Moreing	Con	37,219	26.9
			W.M. Kirkpatrick	Con	36,797	26.7
			Dr. R.A. Lyster	Lab	32,225	23.3
			R.L. Reiss	Lab	31,827	23.1
1936†	84,535	79.0	E.C. Cobb	Con	32,575	48.8
			F.G. Bowles	Lab	30,970	46.4
			Miss F. White[c]	Ind	3,221*	4.8
1940			R.F.E.S. Churchill	Con	Unopposed	

Election	Electors	Turnout (%)	Candidate	Party	Votes	Percentage of vote
1945	88,535	80.2	Dr. S. Segal	Lab	33,053	24.2
			J.W. Sunderland	Lab	32,889	24.1
			R.F.E.S. Churchill	Con	29,129	21.4
			J. Amery	Con	27,885	20.4
			J.M. Toulmin	Lib	8,251*	6.1
			P.J. Devine	Com	5,168*	3.8

Notes:

Co C   = Coalition Conservative
Com   = Communist
Con   = Conservative
FT   = Free Trade
ILP   = Independent Labour Party
Ind   = Independent
Lab   = Labour
Lib   = Liberal
Lib-Lab = Liberal who declared himself as also representing 'Labour' interests
N Lab   = National Labour
*   = Loss of deposit
†   = by-election

[a]Cox had been refused re-adoption by the local Liberal Association on account of his frequent criticism of the Liberal governments' social policy.

[b]Holden stated at the General Election that he was the nominee of an organisation called the British Reform and Women's Party (with headquarters in Manchester), which supported local option. At the by-election he was the nominee of the Preston Progressive Labour Party which was formed shortly after the General Election.

[c]Miss White was the founder and nominee of the Spinsters' Pensions' Association.

Source: Craig (ed.), *British Parliamentary Election Results, 1832–85; 1885–1918; 1918–49.*

Local election results in Preston, 1900–38

These results are presented in two ways. Before 1914 there were few contested candidatures, so individual results of contested wards are presented in full. It is often difficult to ascertain the political affiliation of uncontested victors (though most would have been Tory) and this is not given. On some occasions the political affiliation of candidates even in contested elections is not clear and a question mark follows the party affiliation if this is deduced from other sources (the candidates' known politics on other issues, etc.). After 1918 there are more contests and results are presented thematically with Table D.2 listing the affiliation of the victor (not always known) and Table D.3 listing the percentage vote achieved by Labour in those seats it contested.

Table D.1. Municipal election results in Preston, 1900–14

Year	Ward[a]	Candidate	Party[b]	Votes	Labour's percentage of vote
1900	Deepdale	W. Worden	Prog?	678	
		W. Whiteside	Ind	356	
		T.P. Parkinson	Prog	321	
	Maudland	R.S. Simpson		622	
		H. Cartmell	Prog	419	
	St John's	J.R. Hodgson		895	
		E. Barker		328	
		A. Lees	Ind	296	
	Fishwick	A.M. Birley		554	
		J. Eccles		542	
	Ribbleton	J. Ainsworth		645	
		W. Johnson	Prog	617	
	Moorbrook	D.W. Brown		1,117	
		J. Allsup		219	
1901	Avenham	E.J. Andrew	Prog	647	
		J. Holland		38	
	Christ Church	T. Houghton		706	
		B. Jackson		141	
	Moorbrook	T. Parkinson	Prog	762	
		J. Foster		640	
	Park	W. Johnson	Prog	1,126	
		J. Whittingham		769	
		F. Ogle	ILP	120	11.2
	Fishwick	H. Cartmell	Ind	618	
		J. Hesketh		508	

Year	Ward	Candidate	Party	Votes	%
	Trinity	W. Hale		940	
		R.E. Treasure		409	
1902	No contests				
1903	Park	J.R. Smith	Lib	1,440	
		J. Swarbrick	Lab	771	34.9
		D. McDade	Con	682	
	Fishwick	W.H. Francis	Lab	494	42.0
1904	Moorbrook	T. Parkinson	Prog	940	
		E.G. Hothersall	Ind	596	
1905	Deepdale	C. Middlebrook		722	
		W. Eastham	Lab	701	49.3
	Ribbleton	J. Hodgson	Ind Lab	662	53.5
		J.W. Pateson	Con	576	
	Moorbrook	R.W. Smith		799	
		W.H. Francis	Lab	587	42.4
1906	St John's	J.R. Hodgson	Con	1,206	
		W.S. Coates	Lab	506	29.6
	Deepdale	W. Worden	Con	1,089	
		W.H. Francis	Lab	493	31.2
	Ribbleton	H. Mallott	Ind	779	
		J. Sumner	Lab	526	40.3
1907	Trinity	C. Winter	Con	1,072	
		J. Wooley	Lab	565	34.5
	Christ Church	W. Houghton	Con	930	
		J. Billington	Lab	338	26.7
	Park	Holderness	Con	1,345	
		Metcalfe	Lab	750	35.8
	St John's	G. Hale	Con	1,112	
		W. Eastham	Lab	592	34.7

Table D.1. *Cont.*

Year	Ward[a]	Candidate	Party[b]	Votes	Labour's percentage of vote
	Ribbleton	J. Hubbertsey	Ind	675	
		W.H. Francis	Lab	494	42.2
1908	Deepdale	C. Middlebrook	Con	1,118	
		Mason	ILP	470	29.6
	Fishwick	Breakell	Con	877	
		Mason	ILP	394	31.0
1909	Trinity	J. Sherlow	Ind Protestant	1,030	
		T. Archer	Ind Catholic	737	
	Moorbrook	D.W. Brown	(Mayor-elect)	913	
		T. Drury	Ratepayers'	697	
	Deepdale	W. Worden		969	
		W. Hargreaves	Lab	643	39.9
	Maudland	J. Billington	Lab	752	56.3
		R.S. Simpson		583	
	St Peter's	W.H. Ainsworth	1,055		
		D. Metcalfe	Lab	662	38.6
	St John's	J. Hodgson	1,049		
		R. Swarbrick	Lab	774	42.5
	Fishwick	J. Rigby	Ratepayers'	846	
		R.E. Towler	ILP	363	30.0
1910	No contests				
1911	No contests				
1912	St John's	J. Hodgson		902	
		R. Swarbrick	Lab	808	47.2

Christ Church	C.J. Sumber		748	
	G. Howarth	Lab	539	41.9
Deepdale	H. Leigh		934	
	J. Herbert	Lab	636	40.5
Ribbleton	G. Billington		650	
	J. Wooley	Lab	643	49.7
1913 Christ Church	A. Burnie	Ratepayers'	1,007	
	W. Houghton	Con	526	

Notes:

Con = Conservative
ILP = Independent Labour Party
Ind = Independent
Lab = Labour (LRC)
Lib = Liberal
Prog = Progressive

[a]Wards were redivided in 1900: the six wards of the 1890s which elected two councillors a year were split into twelve wards electing one councillor a year.

[b]It is not always possible to determine the politics of candidates but candidates whose political affiliation is not specified are usually Conservatives.

Source: Preston Guardian.

Table D.2. *Ward results in municipal elections in Preston, 1919–38 (excluding by-elections)*

	Ashton	Avenham	Christ Church	Deepdale	Fishwick	Maudland	Moorbrook	Park	Ribbleton	St John's	St Peter's	Trinity
1919	Con	?[a]	Lab	Lab	Prog	Lab	Prog	?	Lab	Prog	Lab	Lab
1920	?	Ind	Prog	Prog	Municipal Reform	Prog	Lab	Lab	Lab	Lab	Lab	Lab
1921	?	?	?	Ind	Lab	Ind	Con	Ind	Lab	?	Ind	Con
1922	?	?	?	?	?	Con	?	?	Lab	?	Lab	Lab
1923	?	Ind	?	?	Con	Lab	Lab	Con	Lab	Lab	Con	Lab
1924	Con	Con	Con	Con	Con	Ind	Con	Con	Lab	Con	Ind	Con
1925	Con	Con	Lab?	Con	Lib	Con	Lab	Con	Lab	Ind	Lab	Con
1926	Ind	Ind	Lab	Con	Con	Lab	Lab	Con	Lab	Lab	Lab	Lab
1927	Ind	Ind	Lab	Ind	Con	Lab	Ind	Ind	Lab	Con	Ind	Lab
1928	Con	Ind	Lab	Lab	Con	Lab	Lab	Lab	Lab	Ind	Lab	Lab
1929	?	?	Lab	Con	Women's Rep.	Lab	Lab	Lab	Ind	Lab	Lab	Lab
1930	Ind	Con	Lab	Ind	Con	Con	Ind	Ind	Lab	Lab	Ind	Lab
1931	Con	Con	Con	Con	Ind	Con	Ind	Con	Con	?	Lab	Con
1932	Con	Ind	Lab	Con	Lab	Lab	Ind	Con	Con	Lab	Lab	Lab
1933	Lib	Con	Lab	Ind	Lab	Con	Lab	?	Lab	Lab	Ind	Lab
1934	Con	Con	Lab	Con, Lab[b]	?	Con	Lab	Con	Lab	Con	Lab	Lab
1935	Con	Ind	Lab	Con	Lab	Con	Ind	Lab	Ind	Con	Ind, Ind[b]	Lab
1936	Ind	Con	Lab	Con	Lab	Con	Ind	Con	Lab	Lab	Ind	Lab
1937	Con	Con	Con	Con	Lab	Lab	Lab	Con	Lab	Lab	Ind	Con
1938	Con	Con	Con	Con	Lab	Lab	Ind	Lab	Ind	Con	Ind	Lab
Number of Labour victories	0	0	11	3	7	7	9	5	15	9	10	15

Notes:

Con = Conservative
Ind = Independent
Lab = Labour
Lib = Liberal

Prog = Progressive
[a] Independent or Conservative.
[b] Two seats.
Source: *Preston Guardian*

Table D.3. Labour vote in contested wards in municipal elections in Preston, 1919–38 (percentages)

	Ashton	Avenham	Christ Church	Deepdale	Fishwick	Maudland	Moorbrook	Park	Ribbleton	St John's	St Peter's	Trinity
1919	46.73		57.24	51.25		55.23	41.43		60.45	46.53	56.93	53.27
1920			43.57		44.43	46.63						
1921			42.09[a]								42.91	40.55
1922				44.54		46.01			60.53			
1923				40.14	37.93	51.23	42.62	44.40	50.93	59.37	49.14	56.48
1924			44.14		39.26		52.73		68.76	44.16		45.23
1925			59.72	48.47	28.44				61.11	48.99	59.06	48.58
1926	42.04		56.67	47.96	46.88	59.49	42.98		63.93	53.93	54.35	
1927				43.55	48.66	56.03	57.07	51.11		46.74		51.95
1928	34.89		61.08	53.61	45.34	48.69		61.02	56.21		58.65	51.08
1929				45.34	42.08[b]	60.64[b]	57.07	61.02	44.34	57.22	58.20	
1930			52.40		45.61[b]	49.51				53.65	39.76	50.87
1931		21.87	49.71	45.37[b]		39.96[c]	47.46	43.38	47.20		93.46[d]	40.94
1932				47.66	52.50	52.94	52.96		44.93		52.33	57.97[b]
1933					55.50	47.51						55.60
1934		27.16	52.30	39.55[e,f]		48.00	50.11	50.30	65.87	48.57		49.62[b]
1935				43.38	58.29	47.99		42.97	41.92		40.85[e]	50.53
1936		26.28	58.52	44.41	60.46	43.21[b]	48.82	45.49	52.59	53.52	38.31	51.75
1937			48.65	46.36			50.09		52.79	51.37		43.07
1938		29.98	43.75	48.44		54.96	48.62	53.99	40.24	42.95	44.89	50.28

[a] Independent Labour.

[b] Three candidates: Labour, Conservative and left-wing opposition to Labour.

[c] Four candidates: Labour, Liberal, Conservative and left-wing opposition to Labour.

[d] Labour was opposed by left wing.

[e] Two seats.

[f] Four candidates: Labour, Independent Labour, Conservative and Married Women.

Source: Preston Guardian.

Notes

ABBREVIATIONS

AEU	Amalgamated Engineering Union
ARTLC	Preston Trades Council and Labour Party, Annual Reports of Trades and Labour Council
BSP	British Sessional Papers
CFT	*Cotton Factory Times*
CWCM	Preston Labour party, Central Women's Council Meetings minutes
ECO	Cotton Employers' Association, Correspondence with loom overlookers
EJM	Cotton Employers' Association, Joint meetings with representatives of operatives' associations, minutes
EM	Cotton Employers' Association, Annual members . . . meetings
ERT	Oral history transcripts by Elizabeth Roberts
ILP	Independent Labour Party
LCRO	Lancashire County Record Office
LDP	*Lancashire Daily Post*
LPM	Preston Trades Council and Labour Party, Minute books
LRC	Labour Representation Committee
NUGMW	National Union of General and Municipal Workers
NWLHSS	North West Labour History Society
PCM	Preston County Borough Council, minutes of meetings
PG	*Preston Guardian*
PH	*Preston Herald*
PRO	Public Record Office
SM	Preston Spinners' Union, Committee meeting minute books
SO	*Slough Observer*
TCM	Preston Trades Council and Labour Party, Minute book of Trades Council
TGWU	Transport and General Workers' Union
TIBG	*Transactions of the Institute of British Geographers*
TM	Preston Typographical Association, Minute book
TTF	Preston Textile Trades Federation, Minutes, accounts and register of attendance
UTFWA	United Textile Factory Workers' Association

WC   Preston Weavers' Union, Book of cases and complaints
WCA   Women's Citizen Association
WRM   Preston Weavers' Union, Minute book of meetings of mill
            representatives
WSPU   Women's Suffrage and Political Union

PREFACE

1 The best-known account of the decline of class is A. Gorz, *Farewell to the Working Class*, London: Pluto, 1982; see also P. Saunders, 'Beyond housing classes: the sociological significance of private property rights in the means of consumption', *International Journal of Urban and Regional Research*, 8, 2, 1984; J. Urry, 'Localities, regions, and social class', *International Journal of Urban and Regional Research*, 5, 4, 1981, and A. Touraine, *The Post-industrial Society: Tomorrow's Social History*, London: Wildwood, 1971.

2 See especially the comments of G.S. Jones and R. Samuel, 'The Labour party and social democracy', in G.S. Jones and R. Samuel (eds.), *Culture, Ideology and Politics*, London: Routledge & Kegan Paul, 1983.

3 For Britain the best account is J. Cronin, *Labour and Society in Britain 1918–1979*, London: Batsford, 1984; though see also J. Hinton, *Labour and Socialism: A History of the British Labour Movement 1867–1974*, Brighton: Wheatsheaf, 1983, and K. Burgess, *The Challenge of Labour: Shaping British Society 1850–1930*, London: Croom Helm, 1980. For international perspectives see A. Przeworski, *Capitalism and Social Democracy*, Cambridge University Press, 1985.

I POLITICAL PRACTICES AND THE SOCIAL STRUCTURE

1 *Lancashire Daily Post* (LDP), Oct. 1922.

2 R. McKibbin, *The Evolution of the Labour Party 1910–1924*, Oxford University Press, 1974, p. xiv. His argument is elaborated in his 'Why was there no Marxism in Great Britain?', *English Historical Review*, 9, 1984.

3 D. Lockwood, 'Sources of variation in working class images of society', *Sociological Review*, 14, 1966, and the discussion in M. Bulmer (ed.), *Working-Class Images of Society*, London: Routledge & Kegan Paul, 1975.

4 J. Goldthorpe and D. Lockwood, *The Affluent Worker in the Class Structure*, Cambridge University Press, 1968, 1969. See esp. volume 2.

5 P. Joyce, *Work, Society and Politics*, Brighton: Harvester, 1980.

6 R. Williams, *Culture and Society*, Harmondsworth: Penguin, 1963, p. 311; also *The Long Revolution*, Harmondsworth: Penguin, 1963, pp. 41ff.

7 E.P. Thompson, *The Making of the English Working Class*, London: Gollancz, 1963. This issue is particularly important in the use of autobiographies. See the comments of D. Vincent, *Bread, Knowledge and Freedom: A Study of Nineteenth Century Working Class Autobiography*, London: Europa, 1981; G.S. Jones, 'Working class culture and working class politics in London 1870–1900', *Journal of Social History*, 7, 1974; Joyce, *Work, Society and Politics*, passim.

8 A useful discussion of this is H. Newby, *The Deferential Worker*, Harmondsworth: Penguin, 1977.

9 There have been some imaginative efforts to deal with these problems. See many of the papers in P. Thompson (ed.), *Our Common History*, London: Pluto, 1982, especially that by L. Passerini. See also the discussion by the Popular Memory Group, 'Popular memory: Theory, politics, methods', in Centre for Contemporary Cultural Studies, *Making Histories*, London: Hutchinson, 1982.

10 R. Williams, *Culture and Society*, p. 313.

11 J. Winter, 'Trade unions and the Labour party in Britain', in H.J. Momsen and H.G. Huring (eds.), *The Development of Trade Unionism in Great Britain and Germany 1880–1914*, London: George Allen & Unwin, 1985, p. 363. Jones, 'Working class culture'.

12 Winter, 'Trade unions', pp. 368, 361; Jones, *Language of Class*, Cambridge University Press, 1983.

13 A. Gramsci, *Selections from Prison Notebooks*, London: Lawrence and Wishart, 1971, p. 423.

14 For instance in the work of the Centre for Contemporary Cultural Studies. See the articles by Johnson in J. Clarke, C. Critcher and R. Johnson (eds.), *Working Class Culture*, London: Hutchinson, 1979, esp. p. 234.

15 A. Giddens, *The Constitution of Society*, Cambridge: Polity, 1984, pp. 41ff. and glossary.

16 H. Newby, *The Deferential Worker*, pp. 371, 383, 406.

17 M. Burawoy, *Manufacturing Consent*, Chicago University Press, 1979.

18 R. Price, 'Rethinking Labour history', in J. Cronin and J. Schneer (eds.), *Social Conflict and the Political Order in Modern Britain*, London: Croom Helm, 1982.

19 Burgess, *The Challenge of Labour*; J. Hinton, *The First Shop Stewards' Movement*, London; George Allen & Unwin, 1973; R. Price, *Masters, Unions, and Men: Work Control in Building and the Rise of Labour, 1830–1914*, Cambridge University Press, 1980.

20 S.M. Lipset, *Political Man*, London: Heinemann, 1981, p. 231; R. Alford, 'Class voting in the Anglo-American political system', in S.M. Lipset and S. Rokkan (eds.), *Party Systems and Voter Alignments*, New York: Free Press, 1965, pp. 68–9.

21 See for instance S.M. Lipset, *Political Man*, pp. 126ff., and the critique by M. Rogin, *The Intellectuals and MacCarthy: The Radical Specter*, Massachusetts Institute of Technology Press, 1967.

22 See for example S. Halebsky, *Mass Society and Political Conflict*, Cambridge University Press, 1976.

23 Halebsky, *Mass Society*, p. 188.

24 S. Berger, 'Introduction', *Organising Interests in Western Europe*, Cambridge University Press, 1981, p. 11.

25 M. Schafter, 'Party and patronage: Germany, England and Italy', *Politics and Society*, 1977, p. 417. Compare Lipset and Rokkan: 'the decisive contrasts among the [party] systems had emerged before the entry of working class parties into the political arena, and the character of the mass parties was heavily influenced by the constellation of ideologies, movements, and organisations they had to confront in that arena', in 'Cleavage structure, party systems and voter alignments: An introduction', in S.M. Lipset and S. Rokkan (eds.), *Party Systems and Voter Alignments*, p. 413.

26 J. Cronin, *Labour and Society*, p. 11.

27 I. Katznelson, 'Working class formation and the state: nineteenth century England in American perspective', in P.B. Evans, D. Rueschemeyer and T. Skocpol (eds.), *Bringing the State Back In*, Cambridge University Press, 1985, p. 274. See also S. Tolliday and J. Zeitlin (eds.), *Shop Floor Bargaining and the State*, Cambridge University Press, 1985, especially the articles by Reid and Zeitlin.

28 J. Urry, *The Anatomy of Capitalist Societies*, London: Macmillan, 1981.

29 E.P. Thompson, *The Making of the English Working Class*; G. Phillips and N. Whiteside, *Casual Labour: The Unemployment Question in the Port Transport Industry 1880–1970*, Oxford: Clarendon, 1985.

30 See Katznelson, 'Working class formation', and his *City Trenches*, Chicago University Press, 1982.

31 M. Olson, *The Logic of Collective Action*, Cambridge, Mass.: Harvard University Press, 1965.

32 C. Offe and H. Wisenthal, 'Two logics of collective action: theoretical notes on social class and organisational form', in M. Zeitlin (ed.), *Political Power and Social Theory*, Greenwich, Conn.: Connecticut University Press, 1980.

33 Offe and Wisenthal give two further reasons why employers find it easier to act on their interests: because in capitalist society their interests are regarded as legitimate, and because their interests are supported by the state, 'Two logics', p. 198.

34 Offe and Wisenthal, 'Two logics', p. 193.

35 For examples see P. Saunders, *Urban Politics: A Sociological Interpretation*, London: Hutchinson, 1979, esp. p. 129.

36 N. Abercrombie and J. Urry, *Capital, Labour and the Middle Class*, London: George Allen & Unwin, 1983. On realism see A. Sayer, *Method in Social Science: A Realist Approach*, London: Heinemann, 1984, and R. Keat and J. Urry, *Social Theory as Science*, London: Routledge & Kegan Paul, 2nd edition, 1982.

37 McEachern for instance distinguishes between the working classes' defensive and revolutionary interest: *A Class against Itself?*, Cambridge University Press, 1980, pp. 42–3. It should be added that I am not objecting to realist epistemology, but rather to the failure in this case to consider adequate the nature of causal mechanisms in generating political practice.

38 T. Benton, '"Objective" interests and the sociology of power', *Sociology*, 1981.

39 E.O. Wright, *Classes*, London: Verso, 1985.

40 See J. Roemer, *A General Theory of Exploitation and Class*, Cambridge, Mass.: Harvard University Press, 1982.

41 Wright, *Classes*, p. 249.

42 There is of course a long debate about the nature of pre-capitalist modes of production, and some writers have argued that workers are separated from their means of production in all modes. J. Martin, *Feudalism to Capitalism*, London: Hutchinson, 1983, argues that in feudal England workers were also separated from the means of production (in this case primarily from the land) yet it is clear that he is referring to legal rather than de facto separation. MacFarlane's work on the existence of a land market among peasants from the twelfth century is instructive in this regard, however: A. MacFarlane, *The Origins of English Individualism*, Oxford: Blackwell, 1978. Giddens's distinc-

tion between class-divided society (in which class differences are not a central feature) and class society (in which they are) is similar to the one presented here: A. Giddens, *A Contemporary Critique of Historical Materialism*, Vol. 1, London: Macmillan, 1981.

43 I am not arguing that wage bargaining and practical politics are unrelated. One way of increasing wages may be to reduce the commodity status of labour. Wage bargaining need not imply the de-commodification of labour, however.

44 This development has been emphasised by J. Gershuny and I. Miles, *The New Service Economy: The Transformation of Employment in Industrial Societies*, London: Pinter, 1983. See also R. Pahl, *Divisions of Labour*, Oxford: Blackwell, 1984.

2 THE DIVERSITY OF WORKING-CLASS POLITICS

1 There is a certain amount of ambiguity surrounding the term 'patriarchy': whether it refers to the rule of the father over the rest of the family, or the rule of all men over all women. See M. Barrett, *Women's Oppression Today*, London: Verso, 1980, and S. Walby, *Patriarchy at Work*, Cambridge: Polity, 1986. In this book I follow Walby's usage of the term to refer to men's power over women; the issue is further discussed in Section 3.2.

2 B. Moss, *The Origins of the French Labour Movement*, Berkeley: California University Press, 1976; W. Sewell, *Work and Revolution in France: The Language and Labour of the Old Regime*, Cambridge University Press, 1980.

3 A.M. Hadfield, *The Chartist Land Company*, Newton Abbot: David & Charles, 1970; J. McAskill, 'The Chartist land plan', in A. Briggs (ed.), *Chartist Studies*, London: Macmillan, 1959; D. Thompson, *The Chartists*, London: Temple Smith, 1984, esp. pp. 299–306; D. Farnie, *The English Cotton Industry and the World Market 1815–1896*, Oxford University Press, 1979, chapter 7.

4 Centre for Contemporary Cultural Studies, *Unpopular Education*, London: Hutchinson, 1981, p. 36; T.W. Laqueur, *Religion and Respectability: Sunday Schools and Working Class Culture 1780–1850*, Yale University Press, 1976.

5 There are no good recent analyses of these associations but see P.J.H. Gosden, *The Friendly Societies in England 1815–1875*, Manchester University Press, 1961.

6 C. Sowerwine, *Sisters or Citizens? Women and Socialism in France since 1876*, Cambridge University Press, 1982.

7 Notably Pahl, *Divisions of Labour*.

8 S. Yeo, 'Working class association, private capital, welfare and the state', in N. Parry *et al.* (eds.), *Social Work, Welfare and the State*, London: Edward Arnold, 1979; S. Yeo, 'State and anti-state: reflections on social forms and struggles from 1850', in P. Corrigan (ed.), *Capitalism, State Formation and Marxist Theory*, London: Quartet, 1980.

9 See Sowerwine, *Sisters or Citizens?*.

10 For a discussion of these issues see D. Lyddon, 'Workplace organisation in the British car industry: A critique of Jonathan Zeitlin', *History Workshop*, 15, 1983. See also Burawoy, *Manufacturing Consent*.

11 See C. Cockburn, Brothers: *Male Dominance and Technological Change*, London: Pluto, 1983 and, more generally, Walby, *Patriarchy at Work*.

12 H. Hartmann, 'The unhappy marriage of Marxism and feminism: towards a more progressive union', *Capital and Class*, 8, 1979; M. Barrett, *Women's Oppression Today*; J. Brenner and M. Ramas, 'Rethinking women's oppression', *New Left Review*, 144, 1984.

13 J. Urry, *The Anatomy of Capitalist Societies*, discusses this.

14 On nationalisation see R.E. Barry, *Nationalisation in British Politics*, London: Cape, 1965. It should be emphasised that I am not arguing that working-class pressure was necessarily the main social force behind nationalisation.

15 J. Bush, *Behind the Lines: East London Labour 1914–19*, London: Merlin, 1984.

16 On Poplarism See N. Branson, *Poplarism*, London: Lawrence & Wishart, 1979. Again I am not arguing that the working class was the only force behind the creation of the 'welfare' state. Here I focus only on demands for state intervention, rather than on what actually happened. An adequate historical account would need to examine the role of the 'service class' and the pressures exerted by capital. See I. Gough, *The Political Economy of the Welfare State*, London: Macmillan, 1979, for a good interim account.

17 On these see N.H. Buck, 'The analysis of state intervention in nineteenth century cities: the case of municipal labour policy in east London 1886–1914', in M. Dear and N. Scott (eds.), *Urbanisation and Urban Planning in Capitalist Society*, London: Methuen, 1981.

18 J. Gershuny, *After Industrial Society: The Emerging Self-service Economy*, London: Macmillan, 1978, and J. Gershuny and I. Miles, *The New Service Economy*.

19 D.G. Green, *Working Class Patients and the Medical Establishment*, Aldershot: Gower, 1985.

20 Report as to the Practice of Medicine and Surgery by Unqualified Persons in the UK, British Sessional Papers (BSP) Cd 5422, 1910, Vol. XLIII. For general interpretations see V. Navarro, *Class Struggle, the State and Medicine: An Historical and Contemporary Analysis of the Medical Sector in Great Britain*, London: Martin Robertson, 1978, and especially R. Earwicker, 'The Labour movement and the creation of the National Health Service', unpublished Ph.D. thesis, University of Birmingham, 1982–3.

21 See generally Green, *Working Class Patients*.

22 R. Earwicker, 'Miners' medical services before the First World War: the South Wales Coalfield', *Llafur*, 1983.

23 PRO file MH 49/30.

24 Ibid.

25 Welsh Board of Health, *The Hospital Survey: The Hospital Services of South Wales*, London: His Majesty's Stationery Office, 1945, and PRO file MH 49. See especially the records of the Neath Society (PRO MH 49/30).

26 PRO file MH 49 and MH 42/28 (for the Gawr Society); Welsh Board of Health, *The Hospital Survey*. Green, *Working Class Patients*, argues that mutualist societies were not geared to wage earners, but perhaps overstates the case.

27 Green, *Working Class Patients*.

28 Earwicker, 'The Labour movement', p. 151.

29 All details from PRO file MH 66/872. I owe the reference to Jane Mark-Lawson.

30 On Nelson see J. Mark-Lawson, 'Women and welfare', forthcoming Ph.D. thesis, University of Lancaster. On Poplar see PRO file MH 52/191, and MH

66, which observes that the Public Health Department was 'live and active', and the Town Council 'exuberant'.

31 *The Insurance Gem*, Feb. 1930.

32 See the various election addresses of local Labour candidates, in which the problem of health care is usually seen as one which would be resolved by higher wages: *Slough Observer*, *(SO)*, especially 1 Apr. 1927. The story is reported from a different angle in *SO*, 14 Mar. 1930.

33 *SO*, 18 Nov. 1932; 23 Feb. 1934.

34 M. Daunton, 'Miners' houses: South Wales and the Great Northern Coalfield 1880–1914', *International Review of Society History*, 1980. See also the continuing research of Mark Bhatti on housing in Merthyr. More generally see M. Daunton, *House and Home in the Victorian City: Working Class Housing 1850–1914*, London: Edward Arnold, 1983.

35 *Building Society Gazette*, Jan. 1930.

36 *Building Society Gazette*, Feb. 1930, Mar. 1930. The Amalgamated Engineering Union spent £100,000 on mortgage finance in 1929.

37 Much analysis of the social forces behind public housing fails to appreciate this. See J. Melling (ed.), *Housing, Social Policy and the State*, London: Croom Helm, 1980. P. Dickens, S. Duncan, M. Goodwin and F. Gray, *Housing, States and Localities*, London: Methuen, 1985, chapter 5, and M. Daunton (ed.), *Councillors and Tenants: Local Authority Housing in English Cities 1919–1939*, Leicester University Press, 1984, are more circumspect.

38 *SO*, 12 Aug. 1932; 29 July 1932; 11 Sept. 1931.

39 PRO files HLG 49/884 and HLG 101/20.

40 Dickens *et al.*, *Housing, States and Localities*; PRO file HLG 49/884.

41 PRO file HLG 101/20.

42 A. Alexander, *Borough Government and Politics: Reading 1835–1985*, London: George Allen & Unwin, 1985, esp. p. 198.

43 *SO*, 14 Aug. 1931; 2 May 1930; 18 Dec. 1931.

44 *SO*, 14 Aug. 1931; 2 May 1931.

45 *SO*, 5 Feb. 1932.

46 On Glasgow see J. Melling, *Rent Strike; People's Struggles for Housing in Industrial Scotland 1890–1916*, Edinburgh: Polygon, 1983.

47 Some examples of this usage would include P. Cooke, 'Radical regions', in G. Rees *et al.* (eds.), *Political Action and Social Identity*, London: Macmillan, 1985; S. McIntyre, *Little Moscows*, London: Croom Helm, 1980, (though this is a careful study which also emphasises that radicalism measured in terms of voting may not be related to radicalism in other issues); P. Joyce, *Work, Society and Politics* (on deference and paternalism).

3 THE LOCAL BASES OF PRACTICAL POLITICS

1 S. Lash, *The Militant Worker: Class and Radicalism in France and America*, London: Heinemann, 1984; S. Lash and J. Urry, 'The New Marxism of collective action: a critical analysis', *Sociology*, 18, 1984; C. Tilly and L. Tilly, *Class Conflict and Collective Action*, New York: Sage, 1981.

2 Some writers have emphasised the significance of 'local cultures' but their analytical importance remains to be proven. See P. Cooke, 'Class practices as regional markers', in D. Gregory and J. Urry, *Social Relations and Spatial*

Structures, London: Macmillan, 1985, for one example. This question is more fully discussed in my 'Understanding political alignments in contemporary Britain: do localities matter?', *Political Geography Quarterly*, 1987.

3 E.O. Wright, *Class, Crisis and the State*, London: Verso, 1978.

4 Though this is not spelled out by Wright, and in more recent work he seems to have played down the importance of these capacities: Wright, *Classes*.

5 This is a generalisation which should not obscure important exceptions, such as the increased mobility of labour in certain conditions, for instance the migration of many Welsh workers from Wales in the inter-war years, or the practice of the tramping worker, which will be discussed below. Even in this case mobility often takes place once and for all: members of other social classes may however see people outside their locality frequently (at conferences, during business trips and the like).

6 The concept of locality is a problematic one, as S. Duncan points out in *What is Locality?*, University of Sussex Working Paper in Urban and Regional Studies 54, 1986. I refer primarily to processes which are local by virtue of their affecting working-class capacities through their effects on face-to-face relations. This leaves the actual physical spatial scale undefined (in large urban sites it will be bigger than in small mining villages, for instance). I make frequent reference to local studies in order to uncover these processes at work in specific places.

7 J. Foster, *Class Struggle in the Industrial Revolution*, London: Methuen, 1973.

8 E.J. Hobsbawm, 'The labour aristocracy in nineteenth century Britain', in E.J. Hobsbawm, *Labouring Men*, London: Weidenfeld, 1964.

9 The various criticisms are to be found in H.F. Moorhouse, 'The Marxist theory of the labour aristocracy', *Social History*, 3, 1, 1978; A. Reid, 'Politics and economics in the formation of the British working class: a response to H.F. Moorhouse', *Social History*, 3, 3, 1978; H.F. Moorhouse, 'History, sociology and the quiescence of the British working class: a reply to Reid', *Social History*, 4, 3, 1979; A. Reid, 'Response to Moorhouse', *Social History*, 4, 3, 1979; G. McLennan, 'The "labour aristocracy" and "incorporation": notes on some terms in the social history of the working class', *Social History*, 6, 1, 1981; H.F. Moorhouse, 'The significance of the labour aristocracy', *Social History*, 6, 2, 1981; J. Field, 'British historians and the concept of the labour aristocracy', *Radical History Review*, 1978; R. Gray, *The Aristocracy of Labour in Nineteenth Century Britain*, London: Macmillan, 1981.

10 Hobsbawm, 'The labour aristocracy'; R. Gray, *The Labour Aristocracy in Mid-Victorian Edinburgh*, Oxford University Press, 1976; G. Crossick, *An Artisan Elite in Victorian Society*, London: Croom Helm, 1978.

11 M. Hanagan, 'Artisans and industrial workers: Work structure, technological change and worker militancy in three French towns 1830–1914', unpublished Ph.D. thesis, University of Michigan, 1976, p. 34.

12 C. More, *Skill and the English Working Class*, London: Croom Helm, 1980; J. Melling, 'The foreman: a forgotten figure in nineteenth century industry', unpublished paper, University of Strathclyde, 1978.

13 H.A. Turner, *Trade Union Growth, Policy and Structure*, Toronto University Press, 1963, p. 114.

14 C. More, *Skill and the English Working Class*.

15 B. and S. Webb, *Industrial Democracy*, London: Longman, 1902, p. 474. The

Webbs' work was based on an extensive survey of all British unions in the 1890s. It is important to recognise, however, that their political purpose lay in arguing that a rational economic order could be built up around trade unions and they therefore tended to play down elements of union practice which could be construed as restrictive.

16 A. Stinchcombe, 'Bureaucratic and craft administration of production: a comparative study', *Administrative Science Quarterly*, 4, 1959.

17 On railways see F. McKenna, *The Railway Worker*, London: Faber, 1980; on iron and steel see C. Littler, *The Development of the Labour Process in Capitalist Societies*, London: Heinemann, 1982.

18 H. Davis, *Beyond Class Images*, London: Croom Helm, 1979. Davis's sample was drawn from a large corporation where chances of promotion would have been greater than in small workshops.

19 D. Wedderburn and R. Crompton, *Workers' Attitudes and Technology*, Cambridge University Press, 1972, pp. 36, 57; C. Sabel, *Work and Politics*, Cambridge University Press, 1982, chapter 3, p. 89.

20 Crossick, *An Artisan Elite*; J. Foster, *Class Struggle*, and 'British imperialism and the labour aristocracy', in J. Skelley (ed.), *The General Strike*, London: Lawrence & Wishart, 1976. Gray, *Mid-Victorian Edinburgh*.

21 R. Gray, *Mid-Victorian Edinburgh*, p. 108.

22 Gray, *Mid-Victorian Edinburgh*, pp. 106–10. By skilled Gray means, in my definition, craft-skilled.

23 Gray, *Mid-Victorian Edinburgh*, pp. 122–3.

24 Gray, *Mid-Victorian Edinburgh*, pp. 102–3, 92–3, 143, 141. The tendency for artisans to have distinctive religious sentiments, usually non-conformist, in opposition to the more hierarchical Anglican church, is discussed by H. McLeod in *Class and Religion in the Late Victorian City*, London: Croom Helm, 1974.

25 G. McKenzie, *The Aristocracy of Labour: The Skilled Worker in the US Class Structure*, Cambridge University Press, 1973. See his remarks p. 31: 'In nearly all cases the craftsman will be able to set up his business doing what he did when he worked for someone else. The non skilled or clerical employee however cannot simply utilise his talents as a business enterprise but will in most cases have to go into something completely different.'

26 A. Williams, *Life in a Railway Factory*, London: Tavistock, 1969, pp. 92, 102.

27 I. Prothero, *Artisans and Politics: The Life and Times of John Gast*, Folkestone: Dawson, 1979.

28 See M. Daunton, 'Down the pit: work in the Great Northern and South Wales coalfields, 1870–1914', *Economic History Review*, 34, 1981. P. Cooke, 'Class relations and uneven development in Wales', in G. Day and D. Robbins (eds.), *Diversity and Decomposition in the Labour Market*, Aldershot: Gower, 1982, argues that differences between the two coalfields are to be explained by the greater homogeneity of the South Wales miners. This is however by no means self-evident and it is not clear that homogeneity necessarily leads to concerted collective action. See my 'Ethnic divisions in the labour market and working class politics', paper given at the Economic and Social Research Council Symposium on Segregation in Employment, University of Lancaster, 1985.

29 R.J. Holton, *British Syndicalism 1900–14*, London: Pluto, 1976, chapter 5.

30 J. Zeitlin, 'The emergence of shop steward organisation, and job control in the British car industry', *History Workshop*, 10, 1980; H. Clegg, *General Union: A Study of the National Union of General and Municipal Workers*, Oxford: Blackwell, 1954.

31 B. Williams, 'The beginnings of Jewish Trade Unionism in Manchester 1881–1891', in K. Lunn (ed.), *Hosts, Immigrants and Minorities*, Folkestone: Dawson, 1980.

32 M. Hanagan, 'Artisans and industrial workers'. See also J. Zeitlin, 'Craft control and the division of labour: engineers and compositors in Britain 1880–1930', *Cambridge Journal of Economics*, 1979.

33 F. McKenna, *The Railway Worker*; C. More, *Skill and the English Working Class*.

34 In Middlesbrough in 1907 Lady Bell noted that, in one iron works, of 230 workers she questioned seventy-six had worked there all their lives, or for over thirty years. M. Bell, *At the Works*, Newton Abbot: David & Charles, 1969, p. 17.

35 More, *Skill and the English Working Class*; S. Yeo, *Religion and Voluntary Organisations in Crisis*, London: Croom Helm, 1976, pp. 130, 40.

36 More, *Skill and the English Working Class*, p. 114; N. Todd, 'A history of Labour in Lancaster and Barrow-in-Furness *c*.1890–1920', unpublished in Ph.D. thesis, University of Lancaster, 1976. See also P. Gooderson, 'A Social History of Lancaster 1780–1914', unpublished Ph.D. thesis, University of Lancaster, 1975, and J. Mark-Lawson, M. Savage and A. Warde, 'Gender and local politics: struggles over welfare 1918–1939', in L. Murgatroyd *et al.* (eds.), *Localities, Class and Gender*, London: Pion, 1985.

37 The traditional accounts are R. Bendix, *Work and Authority in Industry*, New York: Free Press, 1963; G.K. Ingham, 'Organisational size, orientation to work and industrial behaviour', *Sociology*, 1967, and *Size of Industrial Organisation and Worker Behaviour*, Cambridge University Press, 1970. More recent approaches are P. Joyce, *Work, Society and Politics*; G. Norris, 'Industrial paternalist capitalism and local labour markets', *Sociology*, 1978.

38 D. Smith, *Conflict and Compromise: Class Formation in English Society 1830–1914*, London: Routledge & Kegan Paul, 1982.

39 More, *Skill and the English Working Class*, p. 112.

40 See Clegg, *General Union*; A. Clinton, *Post Office Workers: A Trade Union and Social History*, London: George Allen & Unwin, 1984.

41 'Ingot', *The Socialisation of Iron and Steel*, London: Gollancz, 1936, p. 102.

42 G.S. Jones, *Outcast London*, Harmondsworth: Penguin, 1971.

43 A. Shallice, 'Liverpool Labourism and Irish Nationalism in the 1920s and 1930s', *North West Labour History Society (NWLHS) Bulletin*, 8, 1982; A. Shallice, 'Orange and Green and militancy: Sectarianism and working class politics in Liverpool 1900–1914', *NWLHS Bulletin*, 6, 1979–80; R.S.W. Davies, 'The Liverpool Labour party and the Liverpool working class 1900–1939', *NWLHS Bulletin*, 6, 1979–80; P. Waller, *Democracy and Sectarianism*, Liverpool University Press, 1981, and my 'Ethnic divisions in the labour market and working class politics'.

44 H. Hartmann, 'The unhappy marriage of Marxism and feminism', p. 11.

45 See C. Hakim, *Occupational Segregation: A Comparative Study of the Degree and Patterns of the Differentiation between Men and Women's Work in Britain and the United States*, Department of Employment Research Paper 9, 1979; L.

Murgatroyd, 'Occupational stratification and segregation by sex', in L. Murgatroyd *et al.* (eds.), *Localities, Class and Gender*.

46 A. John, *By the Sweat of our Brow: Women Workers at Victorian Mines*, London: Croom Helm, 1980; N. Dennis, F. Henriques and C. Slaughter, *Coal is our Life*, London: Tavistock, 1956, p. 144.

47 B. Campbell, *Wigan Pier Revisited*, London: Virago, 1984, pp. 97–116.

48 H. Francis and D. Smith, *The Fed: A History of the South Wales Miners in the Twentieth Century*, London: Lawrence & Wishart, 1980, pp. 134, 65.

49 S. Damer, 'State, class, housing: Glasgow 1915', and J. Melling, 'Clydeside housing and the evolution of state rent control', both in J. Melling (ed.), *Housing, Social Policy and the State*. Todd, 'A history of labour in Lancaster and Barrow-in-Furness', and R. McKibbin, *The Evolution of the Labour Party 1910–1924*, show that Barrow had one of the largest Women's Sections of the Labour Party in the early 1920s.

50 In Burnley in 1901 there were 4,557 male weavers over twenty-five and 4,875 female weavers over twenty-five – almost identical proportions: Royal Commission on Labour, Group C, BSP 1892, Vol. XXXV.

51 D. Gittins, *Fair Sex*, London: Hutchinson, 1982. She observes that 'among those weaving couples, however, household duties were shared quite evenly and equally between husband and wife': p. 130.

52 J. Mark-Lawson, 'Women and welfare'; G. Trodd, 'Political change and the working class in Blackburn and Burnley 1890–1914', unpublished Ph.D. thesis, University of Lancaster, 1978.

53 J. Liddington and J. Norris, *One Hand Tied Behind Us*, London: Virago, 1978. The authors do not specify which areas were most active, but from their evidence it is clear that Burnley, Nelson and Colne were the most important.

54 W. Walker, *Juteopolis*, Dundee University Press, 1979, p. 40.

55 Walker, *Juteopolis*, p. 41.

56 This point remains tentative since Walker does not discuss these issues in detail. The Scottish Prohibition Party which was strong in the area and derived considerable support from women appears to have been generally suspicious of the state.

57 J. Lewis, 'The working class wife and mother and state intervention, 1870–1918', in J. Lewis (ed.), *Labour and Love: Women's Experience of Home and Family 1850–1940*, Oxford: Blackwell, 1986.

58 P. Willmott and M. Young, *Family and Kinship in East London*, Harmondsworth: Penguin, 1962, and R. Frankenburg, *Communities in Britain*, Harmondsworth: Penguin, 1966, chapters 7 and 8. The connections between 'communities' and support for the Labour party are drawn in J.J. Seabrook, *What Went Wrong: Working People and the Ideals of the Labour Movement*, London; Gollancz, 1978; E. Hobsbawm, 'The forward march of labour halted?', in M. Jacques and F. Mulhearn (eds.), *The Forward March of Labour Halted?*, London: Verso, 1981, and implicitly by writers discussing the 'neighbourhood effect' in electoral studies, such as W. Miller, *Electoral Dynamics*, London: Macmillan, 1977. The reservations about the 'decline of community' are expressed by P. Willmott, *The Evolution of Community: A Study of Dagenham after 40 Years*, London: Routledge & Kegan Paul, 1963, pp. 109ff., and Cronin, *Labour and Society*, chapter 9.

59 Willmott and Young, *Family and Kinship*, p. 94.

60 Dennis *et al.*, *Coal is Our Life*, p. 136.

61 C. Calhoun, *The Question of Class Struggle*, Oxford: Blackwell, 1982, p. 227.

62 See for instance his rather strange statement, *The Question of Class Struggle*, p. 202, that 'the most politically active were not low skilled workers, however, but urban artisans, members of the building trades and in specifically trade union activity the privileged spinners. This points to the importance of community . . .'

63 The classic demonstration of this is G. Tupling, *The Economic History of Rossendale*, Manchester University Press, 1927.

64 This line of argument could be derived from M. Castells, *The Urban Question: A Marxist Approach*, London: Edward Arnold, 1977. It could easily lead to a form of spatial determinism criticised by P. Saunders, *Social Theory and Urban Question*, London: Hutchinson, 1981.

65 C. Pooley, 'Residential mobility in the Victorian city', *Transactions of the Institute of British Geographers (TIBG)*, 1979; Joyce, *Work, Society and Politics*, p. 202.

66 Pooley, 'Residential mobility', p. 268.

67 M. Daunton, *Coal Metropolis Cardiff*, Leicester University Press, 1977, p. 111.

68 G. Trodd, 'Political change and the working class'.

69 Pooley, 'Residential mobility': 'in the short term many working class areas remained communities simply because of the short distances over which people moved', p. 272.

70 Calhoun, *The Question of Class Struggle*; Thompson, *The Making of the English Working Class*, chapter 15; Joyce, *Work, Society and Politics*.

71 G. Crossick and H. Haupt, 'Shopkeepers, master artisans and the historian: the petite bourgeoisie in comparative focus', in G. Crossick and H. Haupt (eds.), *Shopkeepers and Master Artisans in the Nineteenth Century*, London: Methuen, 1984, p. 19. More generally on the ties binding the petite bourgeoisie and the working class see M. Tebbutt, *Making Ends Meet: Pawnbroking and Working Class Credit*, Leicester University Press, 1983.

72 E.J. Hobsbawm and J. Scott, 'Political shoemakers', *Past and Present*, 1982.

73 For example Colne Valley in Yorkshire: D. Clark, *Colne Valley: Radicalism to Socialism*, London: Longman, 1981; and Glasgow: K. Middlemass, *The Clydesiders*, London: Macmillan, 1965.

74 Crossick and Haupt, 'Shopkeepers, master artisans and the historian'; A. Offer, *Property and Politics 1870–1914: Landownership, Law, Ideology, and Urban Development in England*, Cambridge University Press, 1981.

75 See the comments of R. Dennis, *English Industrial Cities of the Nineteenth Century*, Cambridge University Press, 1984, and D. Cannadine, 'Residential segregation in nineteenth century towns: from shapes on the ground to shapes in society', in J.H. Johnson and C. Pooley (eds.), *The Structure of Nineteenth Century Cities*, London: Croom Helm, 1982.

76 G. Trodd, 'Political change and the working class'.

77 G.S. Jones, *Language of Class*.

4 LABOUR MARKET STRUCTURE IN PRESTON, 1880–1940

1 The three other towns were Lancaster, Liverpool and Wigan. See A. Hewitson, *A History of Preston*, Preston: Chronicle Offices, 1883, and H.W.

Clemesha, *A History of Preston in Amounderness*, Manchester University Press, 1912. The Preston Guild is now held every twenty years and is of only ceremonial importance.

2 Dickens's novel *Hard Times* is based around the events of the Preston strike and lock-out of 1853–4. Lewis Mumford chose an unnamed picture of Preston as an example of the 'industrial coketown' in *The City in History*, New York: Secker, 1961 (plate 39, top). M. Anderson, *Family Structure in Nineteenth Century Lancashire*, Cambridge University Press, 1971, p. 19.

3 D. Farnie, *The English Cotton Industry*.

4 Figures from Hewitson, *A History of Preston*.

5 See Mark-Lawson *et al.*, 'Gender and local politics', for some discussion of Lancaster.

6 Farnie, *The English Cotton Industry*.

7 Interdepartmental Committee on Physical Deterioration, BSP 1904, Vol. XXXII, p. 131.

8 T. Banks, *A Sketch of the Cotton Trade of Preston*, Preston: Toulmin, 1888.

9 Hewitson, *A History of Preston*, p. 188.

10 Banks, *A Sketch of the Cotton Trade of Preston*, pp. 14, 16.

11 The following passages summarise the argument developed fully in M. Savage, 'Capitalist and patriarchal relations in Preston cotton weaving 1890–1940', in L. Murgatroyd *et al.* (eds.), *Localities, Class and Gender*, and 'Control at work: north Lancashire cotton weaving 1890–1940', Lancaster Regionalism Group Working Paper 7, 1982.

12 E. Roberts, *A Woman's Place*, Oxford: Blackwell, 1984, noted: 'The investigator receives the impression that attitudes [about sexual morality] were perhaps stricter in Preston than in Barrow and Lancaster, certainly over the question of pre-marital pregnancy' (p. 76). Apparently a well-known Preston story concerned a father who killed his unmarried pregnant daughter.

13 D. Thompson, 'Courtship and marriage in Preston between the wars', *Oral History*, 3, 2, 1975.

14 Savage, 'Control at work', and 'Capitalist and patriarchal relations'.

15 Walker, *Juteopolis*; Gittins, quoted in Roberts, *A Woman's Place*, p. 118.

16 Report of Interdepartmental Committee on Physical Deterioration, appendix V, pp. 125–6. Painters earned £89 p.a., and bricklayers £94 p.a., well above the male average in 1906. See G. Routh, *Occupation and Pay in Great Britain 1906–79*, London: Macmillan, 1980. Roberts, *A Woman's Place*, p. 147.

17 B. Bristow, 'Residential differentiation in mid nineteenth century Preston', unpublished Ph.D. thesis, University of Lancaster, 1982, reaches similar conclusions from the 1851 Census of Preston.

18 Roberts, *A Woman's Place*, pp. 118–21.

19 These points can be established because of some excellent primary sources on working practices in Preston, notably very full records of individual grievances which weavers made to their union, which give details of expected practices and departures from them. They are used in Savage, 'Capitalist and patriarchal relations'. J. Lambertz, 'Sexual harassment in the cotton industry', *History Workshop Journal*, 19, 1985, comes to similar conclusions.

20 Joyce, *Work, Society and Politics*, p. 177.

21 Preston Overlookers' Union, Rules and Minute book, *passim*.

22 Preston Overlookers' Union, Minute book, 11 July 1905; 25 July 1905.

23 Preston Weavers' Union, Book of cases and complaints (WC), 8 May 1912.

24 *Cotton Factory Times* (CFT), 16 June 1911.

25 Most of the records of the Amalgamated Association of Beamers, Twisters and Drawers (Hand and Machine), Preston Branch, have been lost. See the bibliography for a list of those that have survived. See also H.A. Turner, *Trade Union Growth*, pp. 155, 274 and, for the beamers and drawers, J.B. Brooks, *Lancashire Bred*, Cowley: Church Army Free Press, 1950, pp. 120–3. See Cotton Employers' Association, Annual, members . . . meetings (EM), 27 Nov. 1912; 27 Jan. 1913; 1 Sept. 1915.

26 Preston Weavers' Union, Minute book of meetings of mill representatives (WRM), 29 Sept. 1897; 5 May 1898.

27 WRM, 5 May 1898.

28 Turner, *Trade Union Growth*; R. Penn, *Skilled Manual Workers in the Class Structure*, Cambridge University Press, 1984.

29 See my 'The social bases of working class politics: The Labour movement in Preston 1890–1940', unpublished Ph.D. thesis, University of Lancaster, 1984, pp. 197–9. The Cardroom Workers' Union became even less powerful after 1914, when the secretary was caught fiddling union funds.

30 See Chapter 5 for further details.

31 *Preston Co-operative Society Souvenir*, 1902, and C. Laker, 'Co-operative stores and private traders in Preston, 1870–1906', unpublished M.A. dissertation, University of Lancaster, 1981. More generally on the mutualism of overlookers, see D. Healey, 'Overlookers', unpublished paper, University of Manchester, 1978.

32 Notably by Turner, *Trade Union Growth*, and Penn, *Skilled Manual Workers*.

33 The best descriptions to be found in H. Catling, *The Spinning Mule*, London: Tavistock, 1969, and W. Lazonick, 'Industrial relations and technical change: the case of the self-acting mule', *Cambridge Journal of Economics*, 1979.

34 G.H. Wood, *The History of Wages in the Cotton Trade During the Past Hundred Years*, London: Sheratt & Hughes, 1910.

35 Turner, *Trade Union Growth*. These features are also stressed by writers who do not argue that spinning should be seen as a craft: for instance Lazonick, 'The self-acting mule', and C. Littler, 'The bureaucratisation of the shop floor: The development of modern work systems', unpublished Ph.D. thesis, University of London, 1980.

36 Preston Spinners' Union, Committee meeting minute books (SM), 15 Nov. 1898. See also SM, 7 Mar. 1909; 4 Jan. 1910; 21 July 1914; 4 Dec. 1913.

37 M. Holbrook-Jones, *Supremacy and Subordination of Labour: The Hierarchy of Work in the Early Labour Movement*, London: Heinemann, 1982, presents some evidence to the effect that in Bolton spinners were able to nominate piecers for promotion – if common this was much more akin to a craft system.

38 SM, 5 May 1914; 22 June 1907; 2 Jan. 1906.

39 Turner, *Trade Union Growth*.

40 Royal Commission on Labour, Vol. XXXV, p. 746.

41 B. and S. Webb, *Industrial Democracy*, p. 494.

42 SM, 28 Oct. 1890.

43 Lazonick, 'The self-acting mule'.

44 M. Freifield, 'Technical change and the "self-acting" mule: a study of skill and the social division of labour', *Social History*, 11, 3, 1986.

45 Joyce, *Work, Society and Politics*; Jones, *Language of Class*, chapter 2.

46 K. Burgess, *The Origins of English Industrial Relations*, London: Croom Helm, 1975, p. 269. Bolton was something of an exception however: see E. Thorpe, 'Industrial relations and the social structure: a case study of Bolton cotton mule spinners', unpublished Ph.D. thesis, University of Salford, 1969.

47 R.F. Dyson, 'The development of collective bargaining in the cotton spinning industry 1893–1914', unpublished Ph.D. thesis, University of Leeds, 1971; J.L. White, *The Limits of Trade Union Militancy*, New York: Greenwood, 1978.

48 SM, 29 Jan. 1912; EM, 12 Feb. 1912.

49 *Preston Guardian* (PG), 29 Nov. 1929.

50 The records of both these companies are held at the Lancashire County Record Office, Preston.

51 It has been argued (see W. Lazonick, 'The decline of the British cotton industry', in B. Elbaum and W. Lazonick (eds.), *The Decline of the British Economy*, Oxford University Press, 1985), that it was the strength of trade union restrictive practices which prevented employers from improving productivity. Such accounts overemphasise the strength of unions and fail to recognise that it was the structure of capital ownership which was of major importance in weakening the employers. See B. Bowker, *Lancashire Under the Hammer*, London: Hogarth, 1928; Political and Economic Planning, *Report on the British Cotton Industry*, London, 1934, and Report of the Economic Advisory Committee on the Cotton Industry, BSP 1929–30, Vol. XII.

52 EM, 11 Mar. 1915; 13 Apr. 1916.

53 One of Elizabeth Roberts's respondents (in her oral history transcripts (ERT)) was forced to go to the village of Longridge, several kilometres from Preston, to take a job. See also *CFT*, 24 Oct. 1930.

54 This is fully discussed in Savage, 'Capitalist and patriarchal relations', esp. pp. 186–90, and in his 'The social bases of working class politics', esp. pp. 161–8.

55 J. Jewkes and S. Jewkes, *The Juvenile Labour Market*, London: Gollancz, 1938, p. 34.

56 H. Clay, *The Post-war Unemployment Problem*, London: Macmillan, 1929; A. Glynn and S. Oxborrow, *Inter-war Britain: A Social and Economic History*, London: George Allen & Unwin, 1976.

57 Preston Textile Trades Federation, Minutes, accounts and register of attendance (TTF), 13 Dec. 1915; 6 Jan. 1916.

58 EM, 24 Mar. 1917.

59 Cotton Employers' Association, Joint meetings with representatives of operatives' associations, minutes (EJM), 4 Aug. 1920.

60 Cotton Employers' Association, Correspondence with loom overlookers (ECO), 16 Oct. 1920.

61 See Savage, 'Capitalist and patriarchal relations', pp. 190–2; and his 'The social bases of working class politics', pp. 184–9, for more details.

62 ERT, Mrs A1P.

63 ERT, Mrs L1P, Mrs P2P, Mrs T4P; *CFT*, 15 Nov. 1929; 7 Feb. 1930; 29 Nov.

1929; see Savage, 'The social bases of working class politics', p. 183, for details.

64   *CFT*, 2 June 1916; 9 June 1916.
65   *CFT*, 29 Jan. 1915.
66   EM, 12 Jan. 1916; the Preston Spinners' Union, Piecers' and spinners' contribution books give details of joiners for 1893; for 1935 see J. Jewkes and R. Gray, *Wages and Conditions in the Cotton Spinning Industry*, Manchester University Press, 1935, p. 189.
67   SM, 21 Jan. 1930; 28 Jan. 1930; 4 Feb. 1930.
68   SM, 17 Dec. 1921 (ten attended); 14 Feb. 1924 (six attended); 16 May 1923.
69   SM, 15 May 1934; 24 July 1934, and the general complaints in SM, 30 Oct. 1937.
70   SM, 10 Dec. 1935; 26 Jan. 1937.
71   P. Waller, *Town, City and Nation*, Oxford University Press, 1983, pp. 95–6.
72   The Enquiry by the Board of Trade into the Cost of Living, 1906, shows that only Worcester had lower rates; E. Hunt, *Regional Wage Differentials in Britain 1850–1914*, Oxford: Clarendon, 1973.
73   R. Hyman, *The Workers' Union*, Oxford: Clarendon, 1971.
74   Preston Trades Council and Labour Party, Minute books (LPM), 25 Sept. 1919; 6 Nov. 1919; 27 Nov. 1919.
75   *PG*, 22 Apr. 1922; Labour Party Annual Report 1922.
76   See more generally J. Zeitlin, 'Craft control and the division of labour', and 'Engineers and compositors: a comparison', in R. Harrison and J. Zeitlin (eds.), *Divisions of Labour*, Brighton: Harvester, 1985.
77   A.E. Musson, *The Typographical Association: Its Origins and History up to 1949*, Oxford University Press, 1954, chapter 11; Preston Typographical Association, Minute books (TM), 31 Jan. 1894; 24 Feb. 1894; 27 Mar. 1895; 22 May 1895; 29 Aug. 1895; 28 Mar. 1896; 24 Oct. 1906; 27 Oct. 1906; 29 Oct. 1906; 28 Sept. 1895; and more generally Cockburn, *Brothers*.
78   TM, 27 May 1907; 30 July 1912; 25 Jan. 1922; 23 Jan. 1907; 25 Apr. 1917; Musson, *Typographical Association*, chapter 11. Machinemen had originally been excluded from Preston: TM, 20 Jan. 1925.
79   On the AEU see *PG*, 16 Oct. 1937. Sabel, *Work and Politics*; C. Sabel and J. Zeitlin, 'Historical alternatives to mass production: politics, markets and technology in nineteenth-century industrialisation', *Past and Present*, 108, 1985.
80   See L. Tilly and J. Scott, *Women, Work, and the Family*, London: Holt, 1978.

5   URBAN STRUCTURE AND ASSOCIATIONAL PRACTICES

1   C. Booth, *Life and Labour of the People of London*, London: Macmillan, 17 vols., 1902–3; R. Lawton and C. Pooley, *The Social Geography of Merseyside in the Nineteenth Century*, final report to Social Science Research Council, 1976; H. Carter, *An Introduction to Urban Historical Geography*, London: Edward Arnold, 1983, chapter 10; T.J. Jackson, 'Housing areas in mid-Victorian Wigan and St Helens', 1981; K. Cowland, 'The identification of social (class) areas and their place in nineteenth century urban development', *TIBG*, 1979. For the debate more generally see R. Dennis, *English Industrial Cities*.
2   D. Ward, 'Victorian cities: How modern?', *Journal of Historical Geography*,

1975, and 'Environs and neighbours in the "Two Nations": residential differentiation in mid-nineteenth century Leeds', *Journal of Historical Geography*, 1980.

3 Joyce, *Work, Society and Politics*, chapter 3, esp. p. 111.

4 B. Bristow, 'Residential differentiation', esp. pp. 195, 281. See also F.P. Atkinson, 'Common elements in the urban morphology of three Lancashire mill towns', unpublished M.Phil. thesis, University of Nottingham, 1972.

5 A contemporary report also noted the mixing of skilled and unskilled workers: Enquiry by the Board of Trade into the Cost of Living, 1906.

6 Bristow notes the clustering of railway workers in 1851: 45 % lived within 400 metres of the station, and 91 % within 1 kilometre: 'Residential differentiation', pp. 247ff.

7 ERT, Mr C1P.

8 H. Dutton and J. King, *Ten Per Cent and No Surrender*, Cambridge University Press, 1981.

9 All details from *Barratt's Directory of Preston*, Preston: Barratt's, 1892.

10 G. Sjoberg, *The Pre-industrial City: Past and Present*, New York: Free Press, 1960. On the 'monkey rack' see ERT, passim. On the suburban middle class see L. Davidoff, *The Best Circles: Society, Etiquette and the Season*, London: Croom Helm, 1973.

11 See Daunton, *House and Home*, on Preston's landownership. On estate development more generally see D. Cannadine, *Lords and Landlords: The Aristocracy and the Towns 1774–1967*, Leicester University Press, 1980.

12 McLeod, *Class and Religion*.

13 Hewitson, *A History of Preston*, pp. 452–75. More generally on the influence of the bourgeoisie on urban structure see R.J. Morris, 'The middle class and British towns and cities of the Industrial Revolution, 1780–1870', in D. Fraser and A. Sutcliffe (eds.), *The Pursuit of Urban History*, London: Edward Arnold, 1983.

14 H. Cartmell, *Preston Churches and Sunday Schools*, Preston: Snape, 1892, p. 90.

15 St Saviour's Scrap book containing press cuttings, pamphlets etc. relating to the parish.

16 See generally Morris, 'The middle class'.

17 K. Inglis, *Churches and the Working Class*, London: Routledge & Kegan Paul, 1963, pp. 48–57, argues that this system was almost extinct by 1900.

18 Christ Church, *Outline of the History of Christ Church* (n.d.).

19 Cartmell, *Preston Churches and Sunday Schools*, p. 199.

20 Inglis, *Churches and the Working Class*; H. Pelling, *Popular Politics and Society in late Victorian Britain*, London: Macmillan, 1968, chapter 2; H. Mann, *Religious Worship in England and Wales*, London: Her Majesty's Stationery Office, 1854; H. Perkin, *The Origins of Modern English Society*, London: Routledge & Kegan Paul, 1968, pp. 199–201.

21 A.D. Gilbert, *Religion and Society in Industrial England*, London: Longman, 1976; E.R. Wickham, *Church and People in an Industrial City*, London: Butterworth, 1957; Joyce, *Work, Society and Politics*; P.F. Clarke, *Lancashire and the New Liberalism*, Cambridge University Press, 1971.

22 Christ Church, Parish magazine, 1872. This point is somewhat tenuous, as it relies on negative evidence, but records from this period give this impression. See also D.G. Smith, 'The social and political significance of the Church of

England in mid-nineteenth century textile Lancashire with particular reference to Preston', unpublished M.A. dissertation, University of Lancaster, 1984.

23 The eligible population comprises those aged over 15. This is calculated by taking the percentage of those over 15 for the Preston registration district as a whole and applying the same ratio to each parish. The five parishes were St Saviour's, St Paul's, Christ Church, St Mark's and St James's. For Christ Church figures from 1890 are used. For the national picture, see Gilbert, *Religion and Society*, p. 28.

24 See St Saviour's Service register for 1881, 1883, 1884, 1885 and 1894. The number of attendants is usually only slightly higher than the number of communicants, however: St James's Service register, 7 Oct. 1883; 21 Sept. 1885 (?). A similar inference can be drawn from St Paul's Service register.

25 J. Bossy, *The English Catholic Community 1570–1850*, London: Darton, Longman & Todd, 1975; I. Porter, *A History of the Fylde of Lancashire*, Fleetwood (no publ.), 1876, chapter 3.

26 B.F. Page, *The First Catholic Charitable Society of Preston*, Preston: Snape, 1923, pp. 39, 50.

27 Other Catholic records, 'Historical Notes on St Walburge's' (n.d.), p. 15; Bossy, *The English Catholic Community*, p. 246; Anderson, *Family Structure*.

28 St Ignatius Roman Catholic Church, Marriage registers; I also consulted E. MacLysarght, *The Surnames of Ireland*, Dublin: Irish Academic Press, 1980. Most of the 24 % whose names might have been Irish were indeed Irish for they originated from Protestant settlers in Ireland. There were 125 couples in all.

29 St Ignatius's, opened in 1833, was placed at the north-eastern corner of Preston, an area not built up until the late Victorian period. The Church of English Martyrs, built in the north of Preston, always lay close to terraced housing on the west, but had open ground to the east until the building up of Deepdale, and St Joseph's church, when built, lay at the eastern edge of Preston. See Map 2.

30 Hewitson, *A History of Preston*, p. 318.

31 Other Catholic records, *Catholic Truth Society Official Guide 1907*.

32 W. Pilkington, *Flashes of Preston Methodism*, Preston: privately printed, 1890; Methodist records, Wesley Circuit: Local preachers' minutes; Lune Street Circuit: Leader's meetings, minutes.

33 Data from *Barratt's Directories*, various editions.

34 On Newcastle under Lyme see F. Bealey, J. Blondel and W. McCann, *Constituency Politics: A Study of Newcastle under Lyme*, London: Faber, 1965.

35 See A. Gallagher, 'The social control of working class leisure in Preston, c.1850–1975', unpublished M.A. dissertation, University of Lancaster, 1975.

36 In 1818 all thirty-five members of the Lodge of Peace and Unity were working class except for three innkeepers; they included six cotton spinners, four weavers, three joiners and three mechanics. See A.J. Berry, *The Lodge of Peace and Unity: Its History and Significance Thereof*, Preston: Snape, 1923, pp. 41, 119.

37 ERT, Mr B7P, Mr C6P.

38 *PG*, 28 Oct. 1922; 14 Apr. 1923. A call for business ethics was made in 1925: *PG*, 28 Mar. 1925.

39 Two Rotary Club projects included a 'big brother' scheme whereby

businessmen would encourage a young man to get on, and a scheme for finding odd jobs round the house for the unemployed. *PG*, 13 Dec. 1934; 11 Feb. 1928; 26 Oct. 1929; 18 Feb. 1933; 25 Feb. 1931; 25 Mar. 1933; 1 Apr. 1933.

40 In St John's the population fell from 6,226 in 1871 to 4,705 in 1901 and 3,594 in 1931. In St George's it fell from 2,908 to 1,414 and 923 over the same period. (Data from Censuses.)

41 St David's Road, St Michael's Road, St Martin's Road and St Cuthbert's Road. All calculations based on data from *Barratt's Directories*, 1901, 1907, 1926, 1932. There were 104 residents in 1907. The few cases where a relative (assumed because of same surname) lived at the same address are included as instances of continuity.

42 Wickham, *Church and People*, p. 169; R. Currie, A. Gilbert and L. Horsley, *Churches and Churchgoers: Patterns of Church Growth in the British Isles since 1700*, Oxford: Clarendon, 1977.

43 St Jude's Anglican church, Service register.

44 *PG*, 10 Dec. 1927.

45 *PG*, 17 Dec. 1927.

46 St Peter's Anglican church, Pew book.

47 St Paul's Anglican church, Pew rents. This church might have been expected to retain elite influence the longest since it was the official Infirmary church, where paternalist links remained into the inter-war years.

48 *PG*, 16 Feb. 1929; 31 Jan. 1925; 28 May 1927; 26 July 1930.

49 *PG*, 14 Mar. 1906.

50 *PG*, 14 Mar. 1938.

51 *PG*, 10 Nov. 1906.

52 Cartmell, *Preston Churches and Sunday Schools*, p. 114.

53 An example of another initiative of a similar type is provided by the formation of the 'Ashton British Workman's Social Club' in 1880: see Other Anglican records, *St Michael's New Church Bazaar Souvenir*, 1908.

54 Christ Church, 4th Report of Mutual Improvement Society, minutes, 29 Sept. 1891; *Preston Herald (PH)*, 8 Nov. 1893.

55 *PH*, 31 Jan. 1893; 1 Oct. 1894. The vicar was opposed to the billiards but was overruled.

56 Christ Church, Parish magazine, Dec. 1908.

57 Christ Church, Council minutes, 21 Feb. 1906; 19 Sept. 1906.

58 See Other Anglican records, *Preston National Schools Improvement Fund Bazaar*, 1908. One of the parents elected was a pork butcher, the other is unidentified.

59 Christ Church, Papers re freeing of sittings, including accounts of income from pew rents.

60 St Paul's, Church Institute committee (Social Club) minutes, 14 Nov. 1926.

61 St Paul's, Church Institute committee (Social Club) minutes, 14 July 1932; St Paul's Church Institute committee minutes, 6 Mar. 1917.

62 B. Seebohm Rowntree and B.R. Lavers, *English Life and Leisure*, London: Longman, 1951, chapter 13.

63 See Savage, 'The social bases of working class politics', p. 252, for further details.

64 Hewitson, *A History of Preston: Whitehead's Preston Yearbook*, Preston: Whitehead, 1910; *PG*, 22 Jan. 1907; 1 Feb. 1908.

65 P. Wild, 'Recreation in Rochdale 1900–1940', in J. Clarke, C. Critcher and R. Johnson (eds.), *Working Class Culture*, London: Hutchinson, 1979; the Marsh Lane Methodist Chapel's Marriage register shows that only fourteen of the thirty-eight grooms married there between 1929 and 1938 were manual workers. See also Fylde Road and Moor Lane Circuit, List of Trustees, which shows the dominance of petit-bourgeois groups.

66 Preston Overlookers' Union, Minute book, 20 Sept. 1904; 7 Sept. 1905; 21 Sept. 1905; 19 Sept. 1910; 1 Nov. 1910; 24 Oct. 1911; 8 Jan. 1915.

67 Preston Weavers' Union, Minute book of committee, quarterly and special meetings, 20 Nov. 1906.

68 The Bolton case is discussed in Dyson, 'The development of collective bargaining'; SM, 7 Feb. 1901; 1 Aug. 1901.

69 TM, 13 Dec. 1902; PG, 23 Apr. 1904; 23 July 1904; 30 July 1904; *Whitehead's Preston Yearbook*, 1910.

70 CFT, 7 May 1915; PG, 7 Mar. 1920.

71 B. Harrison, *Drink and the Victorians*, London: Faber, 1971. Preston was a major centre of the temperance movement in the 1830s and 1840s. See J. Livesey, *The Life and Times of J. Livesey*, London: National Temperance Publications, 1885.

72 This 'spatial' element of respectability has not been much discussed by historians. For general discussions see T. Tholfsen, *Working Class Radicalism in Mid-Victorian Britain*, London: Croom Helm, 1976; P. Bailey, *Leisure and Class in Victorian England*, London: Routledge & Kegan Paul, 1978; Crossick, *An Artisan Elite*; Gray, *The Aristocracy of Labour*.

73 See also C. Laker, 'Co-operative stores and private traders in Preston, 1870–1906', unpublished M.A. dissertation, University of Lancaster, 1981; more generally M. Winstanley, *The Shopkeeper's World, 1830–1914*, Manchester University Press, 1983.

74 Laker, 'Co-Operative stores', p. 37; more generally Crossick and Haupt, 'Shopkeepers, master artisans and the historian'.

75 The Co-op paid for members to take evening classes at the Harris Technical School and in 1902 2,000 members took advantage of this.

76 Tebbutt, *Making Ends Meet*; E. Ross, 'Survival networks: Women's neighbourhood sharing before World War I', *History Workshop*, 15, 1983.

77 *Preston Co-operative Society Souvenir*, 1902.

78 ERT, Mrs C7P.

79 R. Price, *An Imperial War and the British Working Class*, London: Routledge & Kegan Paul, 1972, p. 59; S. Shipley, *Club Life and Socialism*, London: History Workshop, 1980.

80 PG, 21 Sept. 1907.

81 Statistics as to the Operation of Laws Relating to the Sale of Intoxicating Liquor, Parliamentary Papers, passim.

82 In 1927 the local newspaper recorded that Deepdale Labour Club had 370 male and 150 female members, yet only 101 members were recorded in the official returns: PG, 30 July 1927.

83 PG, 30 July 1927.

84 PG, 30 July 1927; 11 Aug. 1928; 1 Mar. 1930; 17 May 1930; 1 Jan. 1923; 3 Jan. 1931; 2 Jan. 1932; 4 July 1931.

244 *Notes to pages 134–9*

6 THE EMERGENCE OF INDEPENDENT LABOUR POLITICS, 1880–1914

1 On urban Liberalism see J.R. Vincent, *The Formation of the Liberal Party, 1857–1868*, London: Constable, 1966; D. Fraser, *Urban Politics in Victorian England*, Leicester University Press, 1976; T.J. Nossiter, *Influence, Opinion, and Political Idiom in Reformed England: Case Studies from the North East 1832–1874*, Brighton: Harvester, 1975. My paper 'Understanding political alignments' summarises the literature on contemporary urban–rural alignments. On the creation of the suburban base of Conservatism in the later nineteenth century see J. Cornford, 'The transformation of Conservatism in the late nineteenth century', *Victorian Studies*, 1963; on Lancashire's exceptionalism, Clarke, *Lancashire and the New Liberalism*.

2 Furthermore, not all middle-class people would have had the vote as adult sons living at home were generally disenfranchised. See the arguments of P.F. Clarke, 'Liberals, Labour and the franchise', *English Historical Review*, 92, 1977.

3 *PH*, 30 June 1886. See also Joyce, *Work, Society and Politics*, for further observations.

4 Before 1832 Preston had an unusually wide male franchise, so encouraging radical candidatures. See Hewitson, *A History of Preston*; H.N.B. Morgan, 'Social and political leadership in Preston 1820–1860', unpublished M.Litt. thesis, University of Lancaster, 1980. Preston's radical history was also revealed by its centrality in the early Victorian temperance movement; see Harrison, *Drink and the Victorians*.

5 Clarke, *Lancashire and the New Liberalism*; see also H. Pelling, *Social Geography of British Elections, 1885–1910*, London: Macmillan, 1967; on the importance of religious cleavage more generally see N. Kirk, *The Growth of Working Class Reformism in Mid-Victorian England*, London: Croom Helm, 1984; P.T. Phillips, *The Sectarian Spirit: Sectarianism, Society and Politics in Victorian Cotton Towns*, Toronto University Press, 1983, p. 60.

6 Joyce, *Work, Society and Politics*. See also R.L. Greenall, 'Popular Conservatism in Salford, 1868–1886', *Northern History*, 1974.

7 J. Barron, *A History of the Ribble Navigation from Preston to the Sea*, Preston Corporation, 1938 and, for early disputes, Morgan, 'Social and political leadership in Preston'.

8 Calculated from Preston County Borough Council, minutes of meetings (PCM), budget figures.

9 D. Englander, *Landlord and Tenant in Urban England 1838–1918*, Oxford: Clarendon, 1983. The Preston situation is very different from that discussed by Hennock in which the large employers are the big municipal spenders: see E.P. Hennock, *Fit and Proper Persons: Ideal and Reality in Nineteenth-century Urban Government*, London: Edward Arnold, 1973.

10 Banks, *A Sketch of the Cotton Trade of Preston*, p. 16.

11 *PH*, 31 Oct. 1888.

12 *PH*, 23 Oct. 1888.

13 *LDP*, 28 Oct. 1888; 31 Oct. 1888; *PH*, 27 Oct. 1888. On the politics of influence more generally see Joyce, *Work, Society and Politics*.

14 *PH*, 3 Nov. 1888.

15 Joyce, *Work, Society and Politics*. For a more balanced account see J. Garrard,

Leadership and Power in Victorian Industrial Towns, 1830–1880, Manchester University Press, 1983.

16 From *PCM*. Sanitation-related expenditure is defined as that spent on roads, paving, flagging, gas and electricity, nightsoil, scavenging, hospitals, sewers and watering the streets. For the death rates, Preston County Borough, Medical Officer of Health, Annual Report 1901.

17 *LDP*, 21 Oct. 1891.

18 *LDP*, 19 Oct. 1891; 22 Oct. 1891, though in the end Simpson did not stand.

19 *LDP*, 22 Oct. 1891; 31 Oct. 1891.

20 *PH*, 8 Nov. 1882; Hewitson, *A History of Preston*, p. 251.

21 *PG*, 21 Jan. 1882.

22 *PH*, 22 Nov. 1882; 18 Nov. 1882.

23 *PH*, 11 Nov. 1882.

24 *PH*, 22 Nov. 1882, election address.

25 Ibid.

26 On Liverpool see Waller, *Democracy and Sectarianism*; J. Smith, 'Commonsense thought and working class consciousness: Some aspects of the Glasgow and Liverpool labour movements in the early years of the twentieth century', unpublished Ph.D. thesis, University of Edinburgh, 1980; Clarke, *Lancashire and the New Liberalism*.

27 *PH*, 5 Oct. 1895.

28 This is an example of how 'local social movements', which Urry sees as being characteristic of the modern period, have their older analogues: Urry, 'Localities, regions and social class'.

29 *PH*, 13 July 1895; 3 Aug. 1895.

30 Hewitson, *A History of Preston*, p. 252; *PH*, 26 June 1895.

31 *LDP*, 27 Oct. 1891; 28 Oct. 1891; *PG*, 5 Mar. 1900.

32 *LDP*, 20 Oct. 1893; 27 Oct. 1893; *PG*, 5 Mar. 1900.

33 *LDP*, 30 Oct. 1895; 25 Oct. 1895; 26 Oct. 1897; *PH*, 10 Aug. 1896. For further details on the Preston contests see D. Howell, *British Workers and the Independent Labour Party 1888–1906*, Manchester University Press, 1983, pp. 213–17. Joyce emphasises the significance of the socialist movement in the later nineteenth century in undermining the old Toryism: Joyce, *Work, Society and Politics*. A.J. Ainsworth, 'Religion in the working class community and the evolution of socialism in the late nineteenth century: a case of working class consciousness', *Histoire Sociale – Social History*, 1977. For another influential account over-emphasising the significance of the socialists, see S. Yeo, 'A new life: the religion of socialism in Britain 1883–1896', *History Workshop Journal*, 4, 1977.

34 For evidence of Labour's advance elsewhere see M. Shepherd and J. Halstead, 'Labour's municipal election performance in provincial England and Wales 1900–1913', *Bulletin of the Society for the Study of Labour History*, 39, 1979.

35 *PG*, 7 Apr. 1900; 10 Mar. 1900.

36 Labour Party Archive, LRC files 6/175, 6/194.

37 *PH*, 13 May 1903; 7 May 1903.

38 On the national context see F. Bealey and H. Pelling, *Labour and Politics 1900–1906: A History of the Labour Representation Committee*, London: Macmillan, 1958; *PH*, 16 May 1903.

39 *PG*, 6 Jan. 1906; 20 Jan. 1906.

40 EM, 23 Jan. 1895; 17 Feb. 1897; 6 Jan. 1898; 10 Aug. 1898; 10 Apr. 1897.
41 EM, 13 Oct. 1904; 27 Oct. 1904.
42 *PH,* 27 Oct. 1903; 31 Oct. 1903.
43 Speeches by Johnson: *PG,* 20 Oct. 1900; White: *LDP,* 25 Oct. 1899; Brown:
    LDP, 27 Oct. 1899; Cartmell: *LDP,* 31 Oct. 1901, 27 Oct. 1900.
44 *PH,* 29 Oct. 1904.
45 Derived from budget returns of PCM. On the massive rise in rates elsewhere
    see Offer, *Property and Politics*; A. Sutcliffe, 'In search of the urban variable',
    in Fraser and Sutcliffe (eds.), *The Pursuit of Urban History.*
46 *LDP,* 27 Oct. 1899. The importance of 'tradespeople' (those most strongly
    affected by rates) voting for the Progressives was noted by *LDP,* 1 Nov. 1898.
    PG, 20 Oct. 1900.
47 *LDP,* 30 Oct. 1907.
48 *LDP,* 25 Oct. 1906, and Wooley's speech, *LDP,* 22 June 1907.
49 *PG,* 8 Aug. 1900; speeches by Francis: *PH,* 3 Oct. 1903; Coates: *LDP,* 25 Oct.
    1906; Francis: *LDP,* 26 Oct. 1906.
50 *PG,* 27 July 1907; *LDP,* 1 Nov. 1893.
51 *LDP,* 30 Oct. 1906.
52 *PG,* 6 Oct. 1906. He later condemned the practice of employing women: *PG,*
    10 Oct. 1908.
53 Details from *PG,* 17 Feb. 1906; 8 Dec. 1906; 26 Jan. 1907; 2 Mar. 1907.
54 *PG,* 30 Mar. 1907.
55 *PG,* 8 June 1907; 9 Nov. 1908; *PH,* 12 June 1913.
56 *PG,* 13 Oct. 1906; 15 Dec. 1906; 8 Dec. 1906.
57 Preston Trades Council Labour Party, Minute book of Trades Council (TCM),
    5 Dec. 1913; 14 Jan. 1914; 3 Jan. 1914; *PG,* 16 Dec. 1909.
58 *LDP,* 1 Nov. 1893; Labour Party Archive, LRC files 6/194.
59 TM, 2 Oct. 1899; 30 Oct. 1899; 3 July 1900; Labour Party Archive, LRC file
    1/82; TM, 16 Aug. 1900. A meeting of the Typographical Association voted
    thirty-nine to one in favour of Labour representation.
60 Preston Overlookers' Union, Minute book, 17 Feb. 1904; 7 Mar. 1905; 3 July
    1905; *PG,* 15 Feb. 1908.
61 N.K. Scott, 'The architectural development of cotton mills in Preston and
    district', unpublished M.A. dissertation, University of Liverpool, 1952;
    Labour Party Archive, LRC file 1/95.
62 *PH,* 10 July 1912; *LDP,* 15 Oct. 1912.
63 Figures on councillors from PCM and *Barratt's Directories.* On Labour's
    weakness see Labour Party Archive, LRC files 9/208, 13/411. On the
    Primrose League see *PH,* 10 Feb. 1912; 17 Feb. 1912, and M. Pugh, *The Tories
    and the People, 1880–1935,* Oxford: Blackwell, 1985.
64 Offer, *Property and Politics*; *LDP,* 29 Oct. 1901; also Mallott in *LDP,* 31 Oct.
    1906.
65 *PG,* 2 June 1900.
66 See B.K. Murray, *The People's Budget 1909/10: Lloyd George and Liberal
    Politics,* Oxford University Press, 1980.
67 *LDP,* 2 Nov. 1907; *PG,* 8 Jan. 1910; 10 Feb. 1910.
68 *PG,* 22 Aug. 1900; Labour Party Archive, LRC file 9/189.
69 A motion in favour of secular, rate-funded education was defeated by the
    Trades Council, twenty-one votes to ten: *PG,* 8 Sept. 1906; 3 Nov. 1906; 5 Jan.

1907; Preston Trades Council and Labour Party, Annual Reports of Trades and Labour Council (ARTLC), 1906.
70 *PG*, 2 Nov. 1907; 11 Jan. 1908; ARTLC, 1907.
71 *PG*, 1 May 1909; 11 Apr. 1908; 8 Aug. 1908; 29 Aug. 1908.
72 *PG*, 30 Oct. 1909.
73 *LDP*, 2 Nov. 1912.
74 Clarke, *Lancashire and the New Liberalism*; for the weakness of Liberals at the municipal level, see G.L. Bernstein, 'Liberals, and the Progressive Alliance in the constituencies 1900–1914', *Historical Journal*, 26, 1983; M. Shepherd, 'The effect of the franchise on the social and sexual composition of the municipal electorate 1882–1914', *Bulletin of the Society for the Study of Labour History*, 45, 1982.
75 See for example *PG*, 12 May 1906.

7 THE TRANSFORMATION OF THE LABOUR PARTY, 1914–40

1 C. Cook and J. Stevenson, *The Slump: Politics and Society in the Great Depression*, London: Quartet, 1979.
2 Burgess, *The Challenge of Labour*, and Hinton, *The First Shop Stewards' Movement*, concentrate on wartime changes in the industrial position of skilled workers. A. Reid, 'Politics and the division of labour 1880–1920', in H.J. Momsen and H.G. Huring (eds.), *The Development of Trade Unionism in Great Britain and Germany 1880–1914*, London: George Allen & Unwin, 1985, offers a critique of Burgess and Hinton and focuses upon the state. See also his 'Dilution, trade unionism and the state in Britain during the First World War', in Tolliday and Zeitlin (eds.), *Shop Floor Bargaining*.
3 TTF, 18 Nov. 1907; 9 Mar. 1908; 4 Mar. 1910; 10 June 1910; 7 Nov. 1910; 6 Mar. 1911; 29 Jan. 1912; 5 Feb. 1912; 21 Aug. 1913; 29 Sept. 1913. The unions were successful some time after 1913 when the Cotton Employers' Association supported their request.
4 Preston Board of Guardians, minute book, passim. W.H. Francis, the insurance agent and Non-conformist preacher, was the most active Labour representative.
5 TCM, 7 Oct. 1914; 5 Apr. 1916; 29 July 1918; TTF, 23 Aug. 1915.
6 TTF, 28 Mar. 1915; EM, 10 Nov. 1915.
7 Wooley in *LDP*, 3 Nov. 1919; *LDP*, 27 Oct. 1920; 1 Nov. 1921.
8 Reid, 'Dilution, trade unionism and the state'. The state is also emphasised in many of the essays in M. Lanagan and B. Schwarz (eds.), *Crises in the British State 1880–1930*, London: Hutchinson, 1985.
9 EM, 10 Nov. 1915. The employers on the committee pledged themselves to respect the unions' demands over female employment: EM, 22 Nov. 1915.
10 See H.D. Henderson, *The Cotton Control Board*, Oxford: Clarendon, 1922.
11 *CFT*, 25 June 1915.
12 *CFT*, 23 June 1916.
13 TCM, 24 Feb. 1915.
14 TCM, 2 June 1916; 19 May 1917; 22 May 1917; 6 June 1917; ARTLC, 1919.
15 *LDP*, 22 Oct. 1925; 27 Oct. 1922.
16 N. Whiteside, 'Welfare legislation and the unions during the First World War', *Historical Journal*, 23, 4, 1980.

17 TCM, 24 Feb. 1915; LPM, 7 Aug. 1918; *PG,* 19 Feb. 1919.
18 Labour Party Annual Report 1922.
19 *PG,* 29 May 1921; more generally on the Labour party and health, Earwicker, 'The Labour movement', and A. Clinton, *The Trade Union Rank and File: Trades Councils in Britain 1900–1940,* Manchester University Press, 1977, esp. pp. 36–8.
20 *PG,* 2 Feb. 1922.
21 *PG,* 10 Apr. 1926.
22 *PG,* 11 Jan. 1925.
23 TCM, 24 Feb. 1915; *PG,* 23 Nov. 1929; 27 Oct. 1923.
24 *PG,* 27 Oct. 1923; *LDP,* 25 Oct. 1923.
25 See for example the speeches of Howarth and Edwards: *LDP,* 28 Oct. 1919; LPM, 24 April 1919.
26 LPM, 6 Nov. 1919; 29 Jan. 1920; D. Hayden, *The Grand Domestic Revolution: A History of Feminist Designs for American Homes, Neighborhoods and Cities,* Massachusetts Institute of Technology Press, 1983.
27 *LDP,* 29 Oct. 1925.
28 J. Williamson, the Workers' Union organiser, was a Labour activist before 1914: see *PH,* 24 Aug. 1912.
29 See *PG,* 31 May 1919; 27 Oct. 1923; 30 Oct. 1926; 6 Dec. 1924.
30 LPM, 29 Apr. 1920; *PG,* 20 Oct. 1920.
31 *PG,* 29 Oct. 1921.
32 *PG,* 18 Feb. 1919; 15 Apr. 1922; 12 Nov. 1921.
33 *PG,* 27 Oct. 1923.
34 See the speeches of Handley, Mason and Atherton in *PG,* 27 Oct. 1923.
35 *PG,* 27 Oct. 1923.
36 *PG,* 6 Nov. 1920; LPM, 18 Jan. 1923; 26 June 1923; 21 Aug. 1923; 10 July 1923.
37 ARTLC, 1924; 1925; LPM, 13 Feb. 1924; 20 Aug. 1925; 22 May 1920; 18 Jan. 1931; 1 Apr. 1931; 3 Nov. 1927; 17 Nov. 1927; 5 May 1931.
38 LPM, 19 Mar. 1923; ARTLC, 1925; 1929; LPM, 21 Feb. 1929.
39 Preston Labour party, Central Women's Council Meetings minutes (CWCM), 3 Feb. 1930; 28 Mar. 1929; 22 Oct. 1927; ARTLC, 1928.
40 ARTLC, 1924; 1928; 1929.
41 A.J.P. Taylor, *A Personal History,* London: Hamish Hamilton, 1983. Taylor was in the Preston ILP in the 1920s. For details on membership see ARTLC.
42 LPM, May 1921.
43 LPM, 28 Apr. 1938; ARTLC, 1919; LPM, 29 Mar. 1923.
44 LPM, 3 Dec. 1924; 29 Sept. 1926; 4 Dec. 1930.
45 LPM, passim, is full of this controversy.
46 ARTLC, 1938.
47 LPM, 30 Aug. 1928.
48 No representatives were sent to a Manchester conference on nursery schools: LPM, 2 Nov. 1927. The first references to nursery schools were by women candidates: *LDP,* 18 Oct. 1927; 30 Oct. 1929; CWCM, 19 Sept. 1929 (on open-air schools); 20 July 1930 (on slipper baths). For baths as a campaign issue see speeches by Partington: *LDP,* 31 Oct. 1928; Coates and Gordon: *LDP,* 30 Oct. 1929; Higginson: *LDP,* 30 Oct. 1930; 27 May 1933. On

medical services see CWCM, 27 Mar. 1931. On washhouses see CWCM, 11 May 1931; *LDP*, 31 Oct. 1927.
49 See speeches by Mason: *LDP*, 1 Nov. 1924; Dunlevy: *LDP*, 30 Oct. 1925; Cook: *LDP*, 27 Oct. 1926; Rhodes: *LDP*, 29 Oct. 1926; Leggett: *LDP*, 29 Oct. 1926.
50 *LDP*, 31 Oct. 1929; 1 Nov. 1929.
51 LPM, 25 June 1931. For examples of concern before 1914, see TCM, 7 Sept. 1910; 26 Oct. 1910; 2 Aug. 1911; 1 Nov. 1911; 1 Oct. 1913.
52 See for example the speech by Taylor: *LDP*, 23 Oct. 1925; LPM, 20 Sept. 1923; 23 July 1930.
53 *LDP*, 27 Oct. 1927.
54 LPM, 30 Jan. 1930; *LDP*, 31 Oct. 1933.
55 *LDP*, 3 Nov. 1925; *The Times*, 25 July 1929.
56 ARTLC, 1938.
57 This proved to be the only occasion known to me where religion divided the Labour movement: Butler, a Protestant, was replaced by a Catholic candidate. See my 'Ethnic divisions in the labour market and working class politics'.
58 *LDP*, 1 Aug. 1929.
59 On the Anomalies Act see B. Gilbert, *British Social Policy 1914–1939*, London: Batsford, 1970; *PG*, 6 Dec. 1930.
60 *PG*, 30 July 1932.
61 See for example CWCM, 30 Apr. 1934; 13 Sept. 1934.
62 *PG*, 27 Apr. 1929.
63 CWCM, 15 June 1928; 18 May 1928; 13 Oct. 1930.
64 *PG*, 9 Jan. 1926; LPM, 5 May 1931.
65 LPM, 31 May 1933; 7 Jan. 1937.
66 *PG*, 5 May 1934.
67 *PG*, 12 Nov. 1932.
68 *PG*, 12 Nov. 1932; 23 Nov. 1935.
69 *PG*, 6 Jan. 1934; 1 Oct. 1932; 30 Jan. 1934; 23 Dec. 1932; 14 Jan. 1933; 11 Feb. 1934. These centres were particularly strong in Lancashire: see R.H. Hayburn, 'The voluntary occupational centre movements 1932–9', *Journal of Contemporary History*, 1971.
70 See for example *PG*, 1 Feb. 1936.
71 Cook and Stevenson, *The Slump*.
72 See for example the speech by Ellison: *LDP*, 29 Oct. 1925; SM, 4 June 1929.
73 LPM, 23 Feb. 1919. More generally see P.H. Taylor, 'Preston Trades and Labour Council: Its role in Preston politics and society', unpublished M.A. dissertation, University of Lancaster, 1978.
74 *PG*, 29 Nov. 1919.
75 SM, 17 Oct. 1930.
76 LPM, 24 Aug. 1932.
77 *PG*, 12 Mar. 1938; 18 June 1938; 16 July 1938; 6 Aug. 1938.
78 LPM, 26 July 1934; 27 Sept. 1934; Mar. 1935.
79 LPM, 21 Dec. 1933; 14 Feb. 1934; 22 Apr. 1931.
80 *LDP*, 30 Oct. 1936; 28 Oct. 1936.
81 This point is discussed further in my paper 'Understanding political alignments'.

8 CONCLUSIONS

1 On Salvidge, see Waller *Democracy and Sectarianism*. The Chamberlain family was of similar importance in Birmingham: see Smith, *Conflict and Compromise*.

2 P. Thane, 'The Labour party and state "welfare"', in K.D. Brown (ed.), *The First Labour Party 1906–1910*, London: Croom Helm, 1985, p. 185. M. Lanagan, 'Reorganising the labour market: Unemployment, the state and the labour market 1880–1913', in M. Lanagan and B. Schwarz (eds.), *Crises in the British State*, p. 104. More generally see McKibbin, 'Why was there no Marxism?'

3 For instance see Hennock, *Fit and Proper Persons*.

4 Pugh, *The Tories and the People*, p. 154; H.V. Emy, *Liberals, Radicals and Social Politics, 1892–1914*, Cambridge University Press, 1973.

5 See A. Sykes, *Tariff Reform in British Politics 1903–1913*, Oxford: Clarendon, 1979.

6 On the Liberals' problems with coming to terms with trade unions see G.R. Searle, 'The Edwardian Liberal party and business', *English Historical Review*, 1983. Royal Commission on Labour, Group C, BSP 1892, Vols. XXXIV, XXXVI; BSP 1893–4, Vols. XXXII, XXXIX; BSP 1895, Vol. XXXV.

7 Howell, in *British Workers*, cites these two areas as ILP strongholds. On Leicester, see B. Lancaster, 'Local elections and the consolidation of class politics in Leicester', paper presented at the Conference of the Society for the Study of Labour History, May 1986.

8 Shepherd and Halstead, 'Labour's municipal election performance'; J. Cronin, *Industrial Conflict in Modern Britain*, London: Croom Helm, 1979.

9 White, *Trade Union Militancy*.

10 Cronin, *Industrial Conflict*, p. 130; C. Cook, 'Liberals, Labour and local elections', in C. Cook and G. Peele (eds.), *The Politics of Reappraisal*, London: Macmillan, 1975.

11 See H. Matthew, R. McKibbin and J. Kay, 'The franchise factor in the rise of the Labour party', *English Historical Review*, October 1976, but see M. Pugh, *Electoral Reform in War and Peace*, London: Routledge & Kegan Paul, 1978.

12 Reid, 'Politics and the division of labour' and 'Dilution, trade unionism and the state'.

13 Clarke, *Lancashire and the New Liberalism*.

14 I. McLean, *The Legend of Red Clydeside*, Edinburgh: Donald, 1983; R. Whiting, *The View from Cowley: The Impact of Industrialisation on Oxford 1918–1939*, Oxford: Clarendon, 1983.

15 C. Howard, 'Expectations borne unto death: Local Labour party expansion in the 1920s', in J. Winter (ed.), *The Working Class in Modern British Politics*, Cambridge University Press, 1983.

16 R.M. Pritchard, *Housing and the Spatial Structure of the City: Residential Mobility and the Housing Market in an English City since the Industrial Revolution*, Cambridge University Press, 1976, p. 115.

17 Tebbutt, *Making Ends Meet*.

18 Labour Party Annual Report 1926.

19 On Liverpool and Glasgow see P. Seyd and L. Minkin, 'The Labour party and its members', *New Society*, 27 Sept. 1979. See also Savage, 'Ethnic divisions in the labour market and working class politics'.

20 Howard, 'Expectations borne unto death'.
21 Whiting, *The View from Cowley*; R.J. Waller, *The Dukeries Transformed: The Social and Political Development of a Twentieth-century Coalfield*, Oxford: Clarendon, 1983.
22 Clegg, *General Union*, Part 2, Ch. 3; J. White, *The Worst Street in North London: Campbell Bunk, Islington, between the Wars*, London: Routledge & Kegan Paul, 1986.
23 H. Clegg, *A History of British Trade Unions since 1889*, Vol. 2, Oxford: Clarendon, 1985, esp. pp. 545f.
24 Phillips and Whiteside, *Casual Labour*.

Bibliography

I MANUSCRIPT SOURCES

(a) Trade unions

Preston and District Power Loom Weavers', Winders' and Warpers' Association (Preston Weavers' Union)
    Minute book of committee, quarterly and special meetings 1903–38
    Minute book of meetings of mill representatives 1892–1909
    Minute book of representatives of the cotton trade to consider the general holidays 1892–5
    Register of members
    Book of cases and complaints 1904–40
    Strike pay and stoppage book 1890–1938
    Wages calculation book for different mills 1906–45
    Correspondence, agreements and working calculations 1918–45
Scrap book of newspaper cuttings re cotton trade and union activities
    Rules of Preston and District Power Loom Weavers' Association (LCRO, file DDX 1089)
Amalgamated Association of Operative Cotton Spinners and Twiners, Preston Branch (Preston Spinners' Union)
    Committee meeting minute books 1889–1940
    Membership books
    Centenary New Preston Mills material 1970
    Piecers' and spinners' contribution books 1890–1914
    Rules
    Annual Reports of the Amalgamation 1915–40
    (Harris Library, Preston)
Preston and District Association of Power Loom Overlookers (Preston Overlookers' Union)
    Minute book 1892–1940
    Secretary's journal 1925–35
    Almanacs
    Rules 1923
    Letter book 1921–40
    Members' register 1921–40
    Members' register c.1900

Delegation book with list of cotton mills closed down 1920–41

Correspondence with: Whittle and Turner Ltd, J. and A. Leigh Ltd, Hartley Bros., J. Bibby and Sons Ltd, Joshua Hoyle and Sons (Preston) Ltd, Turnbull and Yates, Brook Mill (Leyland), G and R. Dewhurst

General Union of the Association of Loom Overlookers: objects, rules, regulations etc., 1905, 1909, 1920

(LCRO, file DDX 1151)

Amalgamated Textile Warehousemen, Preston and District Branch

Minutes 1906–40

Contribution books, passim

Agreements and memorials 1920–40

Printed agenda for meetings 1920–40

(LCRO, file DDX 1142)

Amalgamated Association of Beamers, Twisters and Drawers (Hand and Machine), Preston Branch

Minutes 1929–34

Cash book, previously used by 'St Ignatius'

Secretary's copy letter book 1913–26

Contribution book 1929–34

(LCRO, file DDX 1269, and Harris Library, Preston)

North Lancashire Card, Blowing Room and Ring Spinners' Association (Cardroom Workers' Union)

Minutes of quarterly and committee meetings 1913–15

Minutes of committee and representatives' meetings, 1914–18

Minutes of committee, council and special meetings, 1913–22, 1930–3

Minutes of Council and executive meetings 1933–6

Reports of disputes

Register of members

Contribution records

Stoppage book 1914–40

Amalgamated Association of Card, Blowing and Ring Room Operatives, Golden Jubilee Souvenir 1886–1936

(LCRO, file DDX 1102)

Preston and District Textile Trades Federation (Preston Textile Trades Federation)

Minutes, accounts and register of attendance 1907–38

(LCRO, file DDX 1089)

Typographical Association, Preston Branch (Preston Typographical Association)

Souvenir of Preston Guild 1902

Minute books 1890–1930

(Harris Library, Preston)

(b) Employers' records

Horrocks, Crewdson and Co. Ltd

Centenary Mill wages book 1936–9

Weavers' sick fund book 1886–1946

Private wages 1900–26

Preston Royal Infirmary Fund book 1919–29
Salaries and pension book 1881–1911
Newscuttings book
Monthly wages and salaries book
Preston mills private ledger
(LCRO, file DDHs)
John Hawkins and Sons Ltd
Memoranda and articles of association 1899
Directors' meetings minutes 1899–1900
General and directors' meetings minutes 1899–1940
Register of members and share ledger, register of transfers, register of directors
and survey of capital and shares 1899–1905
Survey of share capital and shares 1918–27
(LCRO, file DDX 868)
Ribblesdale Mill
Salaries book 1935–8
General wage book 1935–45
Drawers wage book 1935–47
(LCRO, file DDX 1081)
North Lancashire Master Cotton Spinners' and Manufacturers' Association
(Cotton Employers' Association)
Annual, members', executive and sub-committee meetings minutes
1894–1906
Annual, members', executive, finance, sub-committee meetings, and joint
meetings with representatives of Operatives' Associations 1906–20
Annual, members', and executive meetings minutes 1920–40
Joint meetings with representatives of Operatives' Associations, minutes
1920–40
Letter book, passim
Correspondence with: Textile Trades Federation 1919–40, Operative Spinners
1919–40, Tapesizers 1919–40, Warehousemen 1919–40, Weavers, Warpers
and Winders 1919–40, Mill Engineers, Joiners and Others 1920–40, Card,
Blowing Room and Ring Spinners 1921–40, Beamers, Twisters and Drawers
1937–40, Loom Overlookers 1937–40
Preston Guild file 1902, 1922
Book of particulars: rules, lists of members and number of looms etc. 1929
List of officer and directory of members 1927, 1931
Memoranda book containing notes concerning disputes 1919–21, 1926–32
Letter book of Joint Local Committee for Cotton Control 1917–18
(LCRO, file DDX 1116)

(c) Friendly Societies

Independent Order of Rechabites, Preston
Welcome Tent: Minutes 1886–1904; Book of rules of Welcome Tent; Annual
returns: number of members and state of finances; Contribution book
1904–23
War of Freedom Tent: Minutes 1886–1903; Contribution book 1886–96; Book
of Juvenile Tent Ritual *c*.1900

Crystal Spring Tent: Minutes 1887–90
Jubilee Tent: Candidates' declaration book 1885–98, 1915–19
(LCRO)
Preston Oddfellows
Pleasant Retreat Lodge: Register of members 1846–51, 1875, 1876–7,
    1882–91; Declaration book 1871–82; Minutes 1913–23
Preston Joint Lodges of Oddfellows: Widows' and Orphans' Committee
    minutes 1891–1919
Preston: the Whit Disturbances 1888
(LCRO)

(d) Church records (including published brochures etc. of specific churches)

St Saviour's Anglican church
Service register 1890–1940
Scrap book containing press cuttings, pamphlets etc. relating to the parish
    1869–1945
St Saviour's Church Centenary 1868–1968 commemorative brochure
(LCRO, file PR 2900)
St James's Anglican church
Service register 1890–1940
Statistical summary of parochial work, lists of assistant clergy and churchwar-
    dens and records of principal events 1872–1902
(LCRO, file PR 2901)
St Peter's Anglican church
Vestry book 1898–1922
Service book 1922–40
Temperate society minute book 1912–23
Pew book 1924–42
St Peter's Church, Preston (1975), by W. Makin
(LCRO)
Christ Church Anglican church
Service register 1888–1903
Parish magazine 1872, 1895, 1896 and passim
Mutual Improvement Society minutes 1889–96
Book of newspaper cuttings re Mutual Improvement Society 1890–6
Book of newspaper cuttings re National Schools Bazaar, 1896
Pew rent book 1902–24
Papers re freeing of sittings, including accounts of income from pew rents
'Outline of the history of Christ Church' (n.d.)
Council minutes, passim
(LCRO, file PR 2952)
St Jude's Anglican church
Service register 1902–40
Parochial statistics
(LCRO, file PR 2972)
St Paul's Anglican church
Service register 1890–1940
Pew rents 1920–35

Bible class attendance books 1895–1909
Church Institute committee minutes 1921–40
Parish magazine, passim
(LCRO)
St Mark's Anglican church
Meetings of seat holders
Statistics on Sunday school attendance 1913–40
(LCRO)
Sunday Schools' Association
Minute book, passim
Annual reports 1882–4, 1890–1914
Subscription list for Whit treat
(LCRO)
Other Anglican records
St Michael's New Church Bazaar Souvenir, 1908 (LCRO)
Preston National Schools Improvement Fund Bazaar Souvenir, 1908 (LCRO, file PR
2952 5/5)
St Ignatius Roman Catholic church
Marriage register 1868–1930
List of inhabitants of St Ignatius Place and Square 1841–81
A History of St Ignatius 1833–1933, by A. Holden
St Ignatius: A Preston Congregation 1833–1983 (1983), by L. Warren
(LCRO, file RCPg)
The First Catholic Charitable Society
Minutes 1883–1940
Minutes of the Catholic Guardian Committee and the Compact Committee
1900–10
Register of Members 1888–1940
(LCRO)
Other Catholic records
Preston United Catholic Burial Collecting Society: Annual reports 1903–34;
Collectors' registers
'Historical Notes on St. Walburge's' (n.d.)
Catholic Truth Society Official Guide 1907
(LCRO)
Methodist records
Wesley Circuit: Local preachers' minutes 1897–1914
Fylde Road and Moor Lane Circuit: List of Trustees and details of trust deeds for
various churches in the circuit 1923–53
Lune Street Circuit: Leaders' meetings minutes 1917–40
Marsh Lane Methodist Chapel: Marriage register
(LCRO, file MPr)
Records of other religious associations
Congregational Union: Preston and Fylde District: Preston district minute
book 1890–1908
(LCRO)

(e) Political records

Preston Trades Council and Labour Party

Minute book of Trades Council 1910–18
Minute book of Executive Committee of Trades Council 1912–17
Annual Reports of Trades Council 1902–4, 1906–7, 1910
Minute book of Trades and Labour Council 1918–20
Minute book of Executive Committee of Trades and Labour Council 1920–3
Minute book of all committee meetings of Trades and Labour Council 1923–40
Central Women's Council meetings minutes 1925–35
Annual Reports of Trades and Labour Council 1906, 1907, 1919, 1921–3, 1924/5–38
(Harris Library, Preston)
Labour Party Archive
Annual Reports 1900–40
LRC files
Organisation files
WNC files
FAS files
PA files
(Transport House)
Other political records
Folder on Liberal campaign in January 1910 general election
Scrapbook of newscuttings on Liberal campaign in January 1910 general election
Folder on various municipal contests in the 1930s
Preston Junior Conservative Club Bazaar Gazette 1890
(Harris Library, Preston)

(f) Local authority records

Preston County Borough Council minutes and departmental reports 1880–1940
Minutes of the Distress Committee 1905–9
Minutes of the Committee for the Relief of Distress by War, including the Belgian Refugee Reception Committee, 1914–19
Minutes of the General Strike Emergency Committee 1926
Papers relating to the passing of the Ribble Navigation Acts, 1883, 1888, 1889, 1890
(LCRO, file CBP)
Medical Officer of Health of Preston County Borough: Annual Reports 1896–1940
(Harris Library, Preston)
Preston Board of Guardians, minute book 1890–1930, passim
(LCRO, file PJG)

(g) Miscellaneous records

Typescript commentary on the activities of the Preston Branch of the WSPU (1966) (Harris Library, Preston)
Letter from Miss Grace Alderman, Chelmsford, to Mr R. Towler, concerning the lives and activities of Preston suffragettes, 20–1 Sept. 1964 (LCRO)
Preston Infant Welfare Voluntary Workers' Association
Annual Report 1926/7–35/6

Brochure: 'Preston Infant Welfare Voluntary Workers' Association 1916–37'
(Harris Library, Preston)
'Early Recollections': essay contest entries of old Lancashire residents (LCRO)
Preston Co-operative Society Souvenir, 1902 (Harris Library, Preston)

2 NEWSPAPERS

Building Society Gazette
Co-operative Record
Cotton Factory Times 1890–1937
The Insurance Gem
Lancashire Daily Post
Northern Voice 1929
Preston Chronicle
Preston Guardian 1890–1940
Preston Herald
Preston Labour News 1937–40
Slough Observer
Textile Mercury
The Times

3 PUBLIC PAPERS

(a) **Parliamentary Papers**

Census, 1881, 1891, 1901, 1911, 1921, 1931, 1951.
Returns Relating to Wages, BSP 5172, 1883.
Royal Commission on Labour, Group C, BSP 1892, Vols. XXXIV, XXXV, XXXVI;
BSP 1893–4, Vols. XXXII, XXXIV, XXXIX; BSP 1895, Vol. XXXV.
Report of Interdepartmental Committee on Physical Deterioration, BSP 1904,
Vol. XXXII.
Statistics as to the Operation of Laws Relating to the Sale of Intoxicating Liquor,
1905–38.
Report of an Enquiry by the Board of Trade into the Cost of Living, BSP 1906, Vol.
CVII.
Report as to the Practice of Medicine and Surgery by Unqualified Persons in the
UK, BSP Cd 5422, 1910, Vol. XLIII.
Interim Report of the Central Committee on Women's Employment, BSP
1914–16, Vol. XXXVII.
Report of the Board of Trade on the Increased Employment of Women in the UK
during the War, with Statistics to April 1918, BSP 1918, Vol. XIV.
Report of the Economic Advisory Committee on the Cotton Industry, BSP
1929–30, Vol. XII.

(b) **Public Record Office**

Files HLG 49, HLG 101, MH 42, MH 49, MH 52, MH 66.

4 ORAL HISTORY TRANSCRIPTS

Elizabeth Roberts, Transcripts of Interviews with Preston Respondents (University of Lancaster Library).

5 SECONDARY WORKS

Abercrombie, N. and J. Urry, *Capital, Labour and the Middle Class*, London: George Allen & Unwin, 1983.

Ainsworth, A.J. 'Religion in the working class community and the evolution of socialism in the late nineteenth century: A case of working class consciousness', *Histoire Sociale – Social History*, 1977.

Alexander, A. *Borough Government and Politics: Reading 1835–1985*, London: George Allen & Unwin, 1985.

Alford, R. 'Class voting in the Anglo-American political system', in S.M. Lipset and S. Rokkan (eds.), *Party Systems and Voter Alignments*, New York: Free Press, 1965.

Amalgamated Cotton Mills Trust. *Concerning Cotton*, London: A.J. Wilson & Co., 1920.

Anderson, M. *Family Structure in Nineteenth Century Lancashire*, Cambridge University Press, 1971.

Atkinson, F.P. 'Common elements in the urban morphology of three Lancashire Mill towns', unpublished M.Phil. thesis, University of Nottingham, 1972.

Bailey, P. *Leisure and Class in Victorian England*, London: Routledge & Kegan Paul, 1978.

Banks, T. *A Sketch of the Cotton Trade of Preston*, Preston: Toulmin, 1888.

Barratt's Directory of Preston, Preston: Barratt, various editions.

Barrett, M. *Women's Oppression Today*, London: Verso, 1980.

Barron, J. *A History of the Ribble Navigation from Preston to the Sea*, Preston Corporation, 1938.

Barry, R.E. *Nationalisation in British Politics*, London: Cape, 1965.

Bealey, F., J. Blondel and W. McCann, *Constituency Politics: A Study of Newcastle under Lyme*, London: Faber, 1965.

Bealey, F. and H. Pelling, *Labour and Politics 1900–1906: A History of the Labour Representation Committee*, London: Macmillan, 1958.

Bell, M. *At the Works*, Newton Abbot: David & Charles, 1969.

Bendix, R. *Work and Authority in Industry*, New York: Free Press, 1963.

Benton, T. '"Objective" interests and the sociology of power', *Sociology*, 1981.

Berger, S. (ed.), *Organising Interests in Western Europe*, Cambridge University Press, 1981.

Bernstein, G.L. 'Liberals and the Progressive Alliance in the constituencies 1900–1914', *Historical Journal*, 26, 1983.

Berry, A.J. *The Lodge of Peace and Unity: Its History and Significance Thereof*, Preston: Snape, 1923.

Bohstedt, J. *Riots and Community Politics in England and Wales 1790–1810*, Cambridge, Mass.: Harvard University Press, 1983.

Booth, C. *Life and Labour of the People of London*, London: Macmillan, 17 vols., 1902–3.

Bossy, J. *The English Catholic Community 1570–1850*, London: Darton, Longman & Todd, 1975.

Bott, E. *Family and Social Network*, London: Tavistock, 1959.

Bowker, B. *Lancashire under the Hammer*, London: Hogarth, 1928.

Branson, N. *Poplarism*, London: Lawrence & Wishart, 1979.

Braverman, H. *Labour and Monopoly Capitalism*, New York: Monthly Review of Books, 1974.

Braybon, G. *Women Workers in the First World War*, London: Croom Helm, 1980.

Brenner, J. and M. Ramas, 'Rethinking women's oppression', *New Left Review*, 144, 1984.

Briggs, A. (ed.), *Chartist Studies*, London: Macmillan, 1959.

Bristow, B. 'Residential differentiation in mid-nineteenth century Preston', unpublished Ph.D. thesis, University of Lancaster, 1982.

Brooks, J.B. *Lancashire Bred*, Cowley: Church Army Free Press, 1950.

Buck, N.H. 'The analysis of state intervention in nineteenth century cities: The case of municipal labour policy in east London 1886–1914', in M. Dear and N. Scott (eds.), *Urbanisation and Urban Planning in Capitalist Society*, London: Methuen, 1981.

Bulmer, M. (ed.), *Working Class Images of Society*, London: Routledge & Kegan Paul, 1975.

Burawoy, M. *Manufacturing Consent*, Chicago University Press, 1979.

Burgess, K. *The Origins of English Industrial Relations*, London: Croom Helm, 1975.
   The Challenge of Labour: Shaping British Society 1850–1930, London: Croom Helm, 1980.

Bush, J. *Behind the Lines: East London Labour 1914–19*, London: Merlin, 1984.

Calhoun, C. *The Question of Class Struggle*, Oxford: Blackwell, 1982.
   'Industrialisation and social radicalism: British and French workers' movements and the mid-nineteenth century crisis', *Theory and Society*, 12, 3, 1984.

Campbell, B. *Wigan Pier Revisited*, London: Virago, 1984.

Cannadine, D. *Lords and Landlords: The Aristocracy and the Towns 1774–1967*, Leicester University Press, 1980.
   'Residential segregation in nineteenth century towns: From shapes on the ground to shapes in society', in J.H. Johnson and C. Pooley (eds.), *The Structure of Nineteenth Century Cities*, London: Croom Helm, 1982.

Carr, F.W. 'Engineering workers and the rise of Labour in Coventry', unpublished Ph.D. thesis, University of Warwick, 1978.

Carter, H. *An Introduction to Urban Historical Geography*, London: Edward Arnold, 1983.

Cartmell, H. *Preston Churches and Sunday Schools*, Preston: Snape, 1892.
   For Remembrance: An Account of Some Fateful Years, Preston: Toulmin, 1919.

Castells, M. *The Urban Question: A Marxist Approach*, London: Edward Arnold, 1977.

Catling, H. *The Spinning Mule*, London: Tavistock, 1969.

Centre for Contemporary Cultural Studies, *Unpopular Education*, London: Hutchinson, 1981.

Clark, D. *Colne Valley: Radicalism to Socialism*, London: Longman, 1981.

Clarke, J., C. Critcher and R. Johnson (eds.), *Working Class Culture*, London: Hutchinson, 1979.

Clarke, P.F. *Lancashire and the New Liberalism*, Cambridge University Press, 1971.
  'Liberals, Labour and the franchise', *English Historical Review*, 92, 1977.
Clay, H. *The Post-war Unemployment Problem*, London: Macmillan, 1929.
Cleary, E.J. *The Building Society Movement*, London: Elek, 1983.
Clegg, H. *General Union: A Study of the National Union of General and Municipal Workers*, Oxford: Blackwell, 1954.
  A History of British Trade Unions since 1889, Vol. 2, Oxford: Clarendon, 1985.
Clemesha, H.W. *A History of Preston in Amounderness*, Manchester University Press, 1912.
Clinton, A. *The Trade Union Rank and File: Trades Councils in Britain 1900–1940*, Manchester University Press, 1977.
  Post Office Workers: A Trade Union and Social History, London: George Allen & Unwin, 1984.
Cockburn, C. *Brothers: Male Dominance and Technological Change*, London: Pluto, 1983.
Cook, C. *The Age of Alignment*, London: Macmillan, 1975.
  'Liberals, Labour and local elections', in C. Cook and G. Peele (eds.), *The Politics of Reappraisal*, London: Macmillan, 1975.
Cook, C. and J. Stevenson, *The Slump: Politics and Society in the Great Depression*, London: Quartet, 1979.
Cooke, P. 'Class relations and uneven development in Wales', in G. Day and D. Robbins (eds.), *Diversity and Decomposition in the Labour Market*, Aldershot: Gower, 1982.
  'Radical regions', in G. Rees *et al.* (eds.), *Political Action and Social Identity*, London: Macmillan, 1985.
  'Class practices as regional markers', in D. Gregory and J. Urry, *Social Relations and Spatial Structures*, London: Macmillan, 1985.
Cornford, J. 'The transformation of Conservatism in the late nineteenth century', *Victorian Studies*, 1963.
Cowland, K. 'The identification of social (class) areas and their place in nineteenth-century urban development', *TIBG*, 1979.
Craig, F.W.S. (ed.), *British Parliamentary Election Results, 1885–1918*, London: Macmillan, 1974.
  British Parliamentary Election Results, 1832–85, London: Macmillan, 1977.
  British Parliamentary Election Results, 1918–49, London: Macmillan, 1977.
Cronin, J. *Industrial Conflict in Modern Britain*, London: Croom Helm, 1979.
  Labour and Society in Britain 1918–1979, London: Batsford, 1984.
Crossick, G. *An Artisan Elite in Victorian Society*, London: Croom Helm, 1978.
Crossick, G. and H. Haupt, 'Shopkeepers, master artisans and the historian: The petite bourgeoisie in comparative focus', in G. Crossick and H. Haupt (eds.), *Shopkeepers and Master Artisans in the Nineteenth Century*, London: Methuen, 1984.
Currie, R., A. Gilbert and L. Horsley, *Churches and Churchgoers: Patterns of Church Growth in the British Isles since 1700*, Oxford: Clarendon, 1977.
Damer, S. 'State, class, housing: Glasgow 1915', in J. Melling (ed.), *Housing, Social Policy and the State*, London: Croom Helm, 1980.
Daunton, M. *Coal Metropolis Cardiff*, Leicester University Press, 1977.
  'Miners' houses: South Wales and the Great Northern Coalfield 1880–1914', *International Review of Social History*, 1980.

'Down the pit: Work in the Great Northern and South Wales coalfields, 1870–1914', *Economic History Review*, 34, 1981.

House and Home in the Victorian City: Working Class Housing 1850–1914, London: Edward Arnold, 1983.

Daunton, M. (ed.), *Councillors and Tenants: Local Authority Housing in English Cities 1919–1939*, Leicester University Press, 1984.

Davidoff, L. *The Best Circles: Society, Etiquette and the Season*, London: Croom Helm, 1973.

Davies, R.S.W. 'The Liverpool Labour party and the Liverpool working class 1900–1939', *NWLHS Bulletin*, 6, 1979–80.

Davis, H. *Beyond Class Images*, London: Croom Helm, 1979.

Dennis, N., F. Henriques and C. Slaughter, *Coal is our Life*, London: Tavistock, 1956.

Dennis, R. *English Industrial Cities of the Nineteenth Century*, Cambridge University Press, 1984.

Dickens, P., S. Duncan, M. Goodwin and F. Gray, *Housing, States and Localities*, London: Methuen, 1985.

Dublin, T. *Women and Work: The Transformation of Work and Community in Lowell, Massachusetts 1826–1860*, Columbia University Press, 1981.

Duncan, S. 'What is locality?', University of Sussex Working Paper in Urban and Regional Studies 54, 1986.

Dutton, H. and J. King, *Ten Per Cent and No Surrender*, Cambridge University Press, 1981.

'The limits of paternalism: The cotton tyrants of North Lancashire 1836–1854', *Social History*, 7, 1982.

Dyson, R.F. 'The development of collective bargaining in the cotton spinning industry 1893–1914', unpublished Ph.D. thesis, University of Leeds, 1971.

Earwicker, R. 'The Labour movement and the creation of the National Health Service', unpublished Ph.D. thesis, University of Birmingham, 1982–3.

'Miners' medical services before the first world war: The South Wales Coalfield', *Llafur*, 1983.

Emy, H.V. *Liberals, Radicals and Social Politics, 1892–1914*, Cambridge University Press, 1973.

Englander, D. *Landlord and Tenant in Urban England 1838–1918*, Oxford: Clarendon, 1983.

Evans, P.B., D. Rueschemeyer and T. Skocpol (eds.), *Bringing the State back in*, Cambridge University Press, 1985.

Farnie, D. *The English Cotton Industry and the World Market 1815–1896*, Oxford University Press, 1979.

Field, J. 'British historians and the concept of the labour aristocracy', *Radical History Review*, 1978.

Foster, J. *Class Struggle in the Industrial Revolution*, London: Methuen, 1973.

'British imperialism and the labour aristocracy', in J. Skelley (ed.), *The General Strike*, London: Lawrence & Wishart, 1976.

Francis, H. and D. Smith, *The Fed: A History of the South Wales Miners in the Twentieth Century*, London: Lawrence & Wishart, 1980.

Frankenburg, R. *Communities in Britain*, Harmondsworth: Penguin, 1966.

Fraser, D. *Urban Politics in Victorian England*, Leicester University Press, 1976.

Fraser, D. and A. Sutcliffe (eds.), *The Pursuit of Urban History*, London: Edward Arnold, 1983.

Freifield, M. 'Technical change and the "self-acting" mule: A study of skill and the social division of labour', *Social History*, 11, 3, 1986.

Gallagher, A. 'The social control of working class leisure in Preston, *c.* 1850–1975', unpublished M.A. dissertation, University of Lancaster, 1975.

Garrard, J. *Leadership and Power in Victorian Industrial Towns, 1830–1880*, Manchester University Press, 1983.

Gershuny, J. *After Industrial Society: The Emerging Self-service Economy*, London: Macmillan, 1978.

Gershuny, J. and I. Miles, *The New Service Economy: The Transformation of Employment in Industrial Societies*, London: Pinter, 1983.

Giddens, A. *A Contemporary Critique of Historical Materialism*, Vol. 1, London: Macmillan, 1981.

  The Constitution of Society, Cambridge: Polity, 1984.

Gilbert, A.D. *Religion and Society in Industrial England*, London: Longman, 1976.

Gilbert, B. *British Social Policy 1914–1939*, London: Batsford, 1970.

Gittins, D. *Fair Sex*, London: Hutchinson, 1982.

Glynn, A. and S. Oxborrow, *Inter-war Britain: A Social and Economic History*, London: George Allen & Unwin, 1976.

Goldthorpe, J. and D. Lockwood, *The Affluent Worker in the Class Structure*, Cambridge University Press, 1968, 1969.

Gooderson, P. 'A social history of Lancaster 1780–1914', unpublished Ph.D. thesis, University of Lancaster, 1975.

Gorz, A. *Farewell to the Working Class*, London: Pluto, 1982.

Gosden, P.J.H. *The Friendly Societies in England 1815–1875*, Manchester University Press, 1961.

Gough, I. *The Political Economy of the Welfare State*, London: Macmillan, 1979.

Gramsci, A. *Selections from Prison Notebooks*, London: Lawrence & Wishart, 1971.

Gray, R. *The Labour Aristocracy in Mid-Victorian Edinburgh*, Oxford University Press, 1976.

  The Aristocracy of Labour in Nineteenth Century Britain, London: Macmillan, 1981.

Green, D.G. *Working Class Patients and the Medical Establishment*, Aldershot: Gower, 1985.

Greenall, R.L. 'Popular Conservatism in Salford, 1868–1886', *Northern History*, 1974.

Hadfield, A.M. *The Chartist Land Company*, Newton Abbot: David & Charles, 1970.

Hakim, C. *Occupational Segregation: A Comparative Study of the Degree and Patterns of the Differentiation between Men and Women's Work in Britain and the United States*, Department of Employment Research Paper 9, 1979.

Halebsky, S. *Mass Society and Political Conflict*, Cambridge University Press, 1976.

Hall, A.A. 'Social control and the working class challenge in Ashton-under-Lyne 1886–1914', unpublished M.A. dissertation, University of Lancaster, 1975.

Hanagan, M. 'Artisans and industrial workers: Work structure, technological change and worker militancy in three French towns 1830–1914', unpublished Ph.D. thesis, University of Michigan, 1976.

  The Logic of Solidarity: Artisans and Industrial Workers in Three French Towns 1871–1914, Urbana, Ill.: Illinois University Press, 1980.

Harrison, B. *Drink and the Victorians*, London: Faber, 1971.

Hartmann, H. 'The unhappy marriage of Marxism and feminism: Towards a more progressive union', *Capital and Class*, 8, 1979.

Haw, G. *Today's Work: Municipal Government, the Hope of Democracy*, London: Clarion, 1901.

Hayburn, R.H. 'The voluntary occupational centre movements 1932–9', *Journal of Contemporary History*, 1971.

Hayden, D. *The Grand Domestic Revolution: A History of Feminist Designs for American Homes, Neighborhoods and Cities*, Massachusetts Institute of Technology Press, 1983.

Haynes, L. 'Unemployment in Preston', unpublished M.A. dissertation, University of Lancaster, 1978.

Healey, D. 'Overlookers', unpublished paper, University of Manchester, 1978.

Henderson, H.D. *The Cotton Control Board*, Oxford: Clarendon, 1922.

Hennock, E.P. *Fit and Proper Persons: Ideal and Reality in Nineteenth-century Urban Government*, London: Edward Arnold, 1973.

Hesketh, P. *My Aunt Edith*, London: Peter Davies, 1966.

Hewitson, A. *A History of Preston*, Preston: Chronicle Offices, 1883.

Hinton, J. *The First Shop Stewards' Movement*, London: George Allen & Unwin, 1973.

   Labour and Socialism: A History of the British Labour Movement 1867–1974, Brighton: Wheatsheaf, 1983.

Hobsbawm, E.J. 'The labour aristocracy in nineteenth century Britain', in E.J. Hobsbawm, *Labouring Men*, London: Weidenfeld, 1964.

   'The forward march of labour halted?', in M. Jacques and F. Mulhearn (eds.), *The Forward March of Labour Halted?*, London: Verso, 1981.

Hobsbawm, E.J. and J. Scott, 'Political Shoemakers', *Past and Present*, 1982.

Holbrook-Jones, M. *Supremacy and Subordination of Labour: The Hierarchy of Work in the Early Labour Movement*, London: Heinemann, 1982.

Holton, R.J. *British Syndicalism 1900–14*, London: Pluto, 1976.

Howard, C. 'Expectations borne unto death: Local Labour party expansion in the 1920s', in J. Winter (ed.), *The Working Class in Modern British Politics*, Cambridge University Press, 1983.

Howell, D. *British Workers and the Independent Labour Party 1888–1906*, Manchester University Press, 1983.

Hunt, E. *Regional Wage Differentials in Britain 1850–1914*, Oxford: Clarendon, 1973.

Hyman, R. *The Workers' Union*, Oxford: Clarendon, 1971.

Ingham, G.K. 'Organisational size, orientation to work and industrial behaviour', *Sociology*, 1967.

   Size of Industrial Organisation and Worker Behaviour, Cambridge University Press, 1970.

Inglis, K. *Churches and the Working Class*, London: Routledge & Kegan Paul, 1963.

'Ingot', *The Socialisation of Iron and Steel*, London: Gollancz, 1936.

Jackson, T.J. 'Housing areas in mid-Victorian Wigan and St Helens', *TIBG*, 1981.

Jewkes, J. and R. Gray, *Wages and Conditions in the Cotton Spinning Industry*, Manchester University Press, 1935.

Jewkes, J. and S. Jewkes, *The Juvenile Labour Market*, London: Gollancz, 1938.

John, A. *By the Sweat of our Brow: Women Workers at Victorian Mines*, London: Croom Helm, 1980.

Jones, G.S. *Outcast London*, Harmondsworth: Penguin, 1971.

   'Working class culture and working class politics in London 1870–1900', *Journal of Social History*, 7, 1974.

Language of Class, Cambridge University Press, 1983.

Jones, G.S. and R. Samuel, 'The Labour party and social democracy', in G.S. Jones and R. Samuel (eds.), *Culture, Ideology and Politics*, London: Routledge & Kegan Paul, 1983.

Joyce, P. *Work, Society and Politics*, Brighton: Harvester, 1980.

Katznelson, I. *City Trenches*, Chicago University Press, 1982.

'Working class formation and the state: Nineteenth century England in American perspective', in P.B. Evans, D. Rueschmeyer and T. Skocpol (eds.), *Bringing the State back in*, Cambridge University Press, 1985.

Keat, R. and J. Urry, *Social Theory as Science*, London: Routledge & Kegan Paul, 2nd edition, 1982.

Kirby, M.W. 'The Lancashire cotton industry in the inter-war years: A study of organisational change', *Business History*, 16, 1974.

Kirk, N. *The Growth of Working Class Reformism in mid-Victorian England*, London: Croom Helm, 1984.

Laker, C. 'Co-operative stores and private traders in Preston, 1870–1906', unpublished M.A. dissertation, University of Lancaster, 1981.

Lambertz, J. 'Sexual harassment in the cotton industry', *History Workshop Journal*, 19, 1985.

Lanagan, M. 'Reorganising the labour market: Unemployment, the state and the labour market 1880–1913', in M. Lanagan and B. Schwarz (eds.), *Crises in the British State 1880–1930*, London: Hutchinson, 1985.

Lanagan, M. and B. Schwarz (eds.), *Crises in the British State 1880–1930*, London: Hutchinson, 1985.

Lancaster, B. 'Local elections and the consolidation of class politics in Leicester', paper presented at the Conference of the Society for the Study of Labour History, May 1986.

Laqueur, T.W. *Religion and Respectability: Sunday Schools and Working Class Culture 1780–1850*, New Haven, Conn.: Yale University Press, 1976.

Lash, S. *The Militant Worker: Class and Radicalism in France and America*, London: Heinemann, 1984.

Lash, S. and J. Urry, 'The New Marxism of collective action: A critical analysis', *Sociology*, 18, 1984.

Lawton, R. and C. Pooley, *The Social Geography of Merseyside in the Nineteenth Century*, final report to Social Science Research Council, 1976.

Lazonick, W. 'Industrial relations and technical change: The case of the self-acting mule', *Cambridge Journal of Economics*, 1979.

'The decline of the British cotton industry', in B. Elbaum and W. Lazonick (eds.), *The Decline of the British Economy*, Oxford University Press, 1985.

Lewis, J. *The Politics of Motherhood*, London: Croom Helm, 1980.

'The working class wife and mother and state intervention, 1870–1918', in J. Lewis (ed.), *Labour and Love: Women's Experience of Home and Family 1850–1940*, Oxford: Blackwell, 1986.

Liddington, J. and J. Norris, *One Hand Tied Behind Us*, London: Virago, 1978.

Lipset, S.M. *Political Man*, London: Heinemann, 1981.

Lipset, S.M. and S. Rokkan, 'Cleavage structure, party systems and voter alignments: An introduction', in S.M. Lipset and S. Rokkan (eds.), *Party Systems and Voter Alignments*, New York: Free Press, 1965.

Littler, C. 'The bureaucratisation of the shop floor: The development of modern work systems', unpublished Ph.D. thesis, University of London, 1980.

The Development of the Labour Process in Capitalist Societies, London: Heinemann, 1982.

Livesey, J. *The Life and Times of J. Livesey*, London: National Temperance Publications, 1885.

Lockwood, D. 'Sources of variation in working class images of society', *Sociological Review*, 14, 1966.

Lyddon, D. 'Workplace organisation in the British car industry: A critique of Jonathan Zeitlin', *History Workshop*, 15, 1983.

McAskill, J. 'The Chartist land plan', in A. Briggs (ed.), *Chartist Studies*, London: Macmillan, 1959.

McEachern, D. *A Class against Itself?*, Cambridge University Press, 1980.

MacFarlane, A. *The Origins of English Individualism*, Oxford: Blackwell, 1978.

McIntyre, S. *Little Moscows*, London: Croom Helm, 1980.

McKenna, F. *The Railway Worker*, London: Faber, 1980.

McKenzie, G. *The Aristocracy of Labour: The Skilled Worker in the US Class Structure*, Cambridge University Press, 1973.

McKibbin, R. *The Evolution of the Labour Party 1910–1924*, Oxford University Press, 1974.

'Why was there no Marxism in Great Britain?', *English Historical Review*, 9, 1984.

McLean, I. *The Legend of Red Clydeside*, Edinburgh: Donald, 1983.

McLennan, G. 'The "labour aristocracy" and "incorporation": Notes on some terms in the social history of the working class', *Social History*, 6, 1, 1981.

McLeod, H. *Class and Religion in the Late Victorian City*, London: Croom Helm, 1974.

MacLysarght, E. *The Surnames of Ireland*, Dublin: Irish Academic Press, 1980.

Mann, H. *Religious Worship in England and Wales*, London: Her Majesty's Stationery Office, 1854.

Mark-Lawson, J. 'Women and welfare', forthcoming Ph.D. thesis, University of Lancaster.

Mark-Lawson, J., M. Savage and A. Warde, 'Gender and local politics: Struggles over welfare 1918–1939', in L. Murgatroyd *et al.* (eds.), *Localities, Class and Gender*, London: Pion, 1985.

Martin, J. *Feudalism to Capitalism*, London: Hutchinson, 1983.

Matthew, H., R. McKibbin and J. Kay, 'The franchise factor in the rise of the Labour party', *English Historical Review*, October 1976.

Melling, J. 'The foreman: A forgotten figure in nineteenth century industry', unpublished paper, University of Strathclyde, 1978.

'Clydeside housing and the evolution of state rent control', in J. Melling (ed.), *Housing, Social Policy and the State*, London: Croom Helm, 1980.

Rent Strike: People's Struggles for Housing in Industrial Scotland 1890–1916, Edinburgh: Polygon, 1983.

Melling, J. (ed.), *Housing, Social Policy and the State*, London: Croom Helm, 1980.

Middlemass, K. *The Clydesiders*, London: Macmillan, 1965.

Miliband, R. *Parliamentary Socialism: A Study in the Politics of Labour*, London: Merlin, 1961.

Miller, W. *Electoral Dynamics*, London: Macmillan, 1977.

Moorhouse, H.F. 'The Marxist theory of the labour aristocracy', *Social History* 3, 1, 1978.

'History, sociology and the quiescence of the British working class: A reply to Reid', *Social History*, 4, 3, 1979.

'The significance of the labour aristocracy', *Social History*, 6, 2, 1981.

More, C. *Skill and the English Working Class*, London: Croom Helm, 1980.

Morgan, H.N.B. 'Social and political leadership in Preston 1820–1860', unpublished M.Litt. thesis, University of Lancaster, 1980.

Morris, R.J. 'The middle class and British towns and cities of the Industrial Revolution, 1780–1870', in D. Fraser and A. Sutcliffe (eds.), *The Pursuit of Urban History*, London: Edward Arnold, 1983.

Moss, B. *The Origins of the French Labour Movement*, Berkeley: California University Press, 1976.

Mumford, L. *The City in History*, New York: Secker, 1961.

Murgatroyd, L. 'Occupational stratification and segregation by sex', in L. Murgatroyd *et al.* (eds.), *Localities, Class and Gender*, London: Pion, 1985.

Murgatroyd, L. *et al.* (eds.), *Localities, Class and Gender*, London: Pion, 1985.

Murray, B.K. *The People's Budget 1909–10: Lloyd George and Liberal Politics*, Oxford University Press, 1980.

Musson, A.E. *The Typographical Association: Its Origins and History up to 1949*, Oxford University Press, 1954.

Navarro, V. *Class Struggle, the State and Medicine: An Historical and Contemporary Analysis of the Medical Sector in Great Britain*, London: Martin Robertson, 1978.

Newby, H. *The Deferential Worker*, Harmondsworth: Penguin, 1977.

Norris, G. 'Industrial paternalist capitalism and local labour markets', *Sociology*, 1978.

Nossiter, T.J. *Influence, Opinion, and Political Idiom in Reformed England: Case Studies from the North East 1832–1874*, Brighton: Harvester, 1975.

Offe, C. and H. Wisenthal, 'Two logics of collective action: Theoretical notes on social class and organisational form', in M. Zeitlin (ed.), *Political Power and Social Theory*, Greenwich, Conn.: Connecticut University Press, 1980.

Offer, A. *Property and Politics 1870–1914: Landownership, Law, Ideology, and Urban Development in England*, Cambridge University Press, 1981.

Olson, M. *The Logic of Collective Action*, Cambridge, Mass.: Harvard University Press, 1965.

Page, B.F. *The First Catholic Charitable Society of Preston*, Preston: Snape, 1923.

Pahl, R. *Divisions of Labour*, Oxford: Blackwell, 1984.

Pelling, H. *Social Geography of British Elections, 1885–1910*, London: Macmillan, 1967.

Popular Politics and Society in Late Victorian Britain, London: Macmillan, 1968.

Penn, R. *Skilled Manual Workers in the Class Structure*, Cambridge University Press, 1984.

Perkin, H. *The Origins of Modern English Society*, London: Routledge & Kegan Paul, 1968.

Phillips, G. and N. Whiteside, *Casual Labour: The Unemployment Question in the Port Transport Industry 1880–1970*, Oxford: Clarendon, 1985.

Phillips, P.T. *The Sectarian Spirit: Sectarianism, Society and Politics in Victorian Cotton Towns*, Toronto University Press, 1983.

Pilkington, W. *Flashes of Preston Methodism*, Preston: privately printed, 1890.

Political and Economic Planning, *Report on the British Cotton Industry*, London, 1934.

Pooley, C. 'Residential mobility in the Victorian City', *TIBG*, 1979.

Popular Memory Group, 'Popular memory: Theory, politics, methods', in Centre for Contemporary Cultural Studies, *Making Histories*, London: Hutchinson, 1982.

Porter, I. *A History of the Fylde of Lancashire*, Fleetwood (no publ.), 1876.

Preston Corporation, *Towards a Prouder Preston*, Preston Corporation [c. 1948].

Price, R. *An Imperial War and the British Working Class*, London: Routledge & Kegan Paul, 1972.

 Masters, Unions, and Men: Work Control in Building and the Rise of Labour, 1830–1914, Cambridge University Press, 1980.

 'Rethinking Labour history', in J. Cronin and J. Schneer (eds.), *Social Conflict and the Political Order in Modern Britain*, London: Croom Helm, 1982.

Pritchard, R.M. *Housing and the Spatial Structure of the City: Residential Mobility and the Housing Market in an English City since the Industrial Revolution*, Cambridge University Press, 1976.

Prothero, I. *Artisans and Politics: The Life and Times of John Gast*, Folkestone: Dawson, 1979.

Przeworski, A. *Capitalism and Social Democracy*, Cambridge University Press, 1985.

Pugh, M. *Electoral Reform in War and Peace*, London: Routledge & Kegan Paul, 1978.

 The Tories and the People, 1880–1935, Oxford: Blackwell, 1985.

Reid, A. 'Politics and economics in the formation of the British working class: A response to H.F. Moorhouse', *Social History*, 3, 3, 1978.

 'Response to Moorhouse', *Social History*, 4, 3, 1979.

 'Dilution, trade unionism and the state in Britain during the First World War', in S. Tolliday and J. Zeitlin (eds.), *Shop Floor Bargaining and the State*, Cambridge University Press, 1985.

 'Politics and the division of labour 1880–1920', in H.J. Momsen and H.G. Huring (eds.), *The Development of Trade Unionism in Great Britain and Germany 1880–1914*, London: George Allen & Unwin, 1985.

Roberts, E. *A Woman's Place*, Oxford: Blackwell, 1984.

Roemer, J. *A General Theory of Exploitation and Class*, Cambridge, Mass.: Harvard University Press, 1982.

Rogin, M. *The Intellectuals and McCarthy: The Radical Specter*, Massachusetts Institute of Technology Press, 1967.

Rosen, A. *Rise Up Women: The Militant Campaign of the Women's Social and Political Union*, London: Routledge & Kegan Paul, 1974.

Ross, E. 'Survival networks: Women's neighbourhood sharing before World War 1', *History Workshop*, 15, 1983.

Routh, G. *Occupation and Pay in Great Britain 1906–79*, London: Macmillan, 1980.

Rowntree, B.S. and B.R. Lavers, *English Life and Leisure*, London: Longman, 1951.

Sabel, C. *Work and Politics*, Cambridge University Press, 1982.

Sabel, C. and J. Zeitlin, 'Historical alternatives to mass production: Politics, markets and technology in nineteenth-century industrialisation', *Past and Present*, 108, 1985.

Sandberg, C.G. *Lancashire in Decline*, Columbus, Ohio: Ohio State University Press, 1974.

Saunders, P. *Urban Politics: A Sociological Interpretation*, London: Hutchinson, 1979.

Social Theory and Urban Question, London: Hutchinson, 1981.

'Beyond housing classes: The sociological significance of private property rights in the means of consumption', *International Journal of Urban and Regional Research*, 8, 2, 1984.

Savage, M. 'Control at work: North Lancashire cotton weaving 1890–1940', Lancaster Regionalism Group Working Paper 7, 1982.

'The social bases of working class politics: The Labour movement in Preston 1890–1940', unpublished Ph.D. thesis, University of Lancaster, 1984.

'Capitalist and patriarchal relations in Preston cotton weaving 1890–1940', in L. Murgatroyd *et al.* (eds.), *Localities, Class and Gender*, London: Pion, 1985.

'Ethnic divisions in the labour market and working class politics', paper given at the Economic and Social Science Research Council Symposium on Segregation in Employment, University of Lancaster, 1985.

'Understanding political alignments in contemporary Britain: Do localities matter?', *Political Geography Quarterly*, 1987.

Sayer, A. *Method in Social Science: A Realist Approach*, London: Heinemann, 1984.

Schafter, M. 'Party and Patronage: Germany, England and Italy', *Politics and Society*, 1977.

Scott, N.K. The architectural development of cotton mills in Preston and district, unpublished M.A. dissertation, University of Liverpool, 1952.

Seabrook, J. *What Went Wrong: Working People and the Ideals of the Labour Movement*, London: Gollancz, 1978.

Searle, G.R. 'The Edwardian Liberal party and business', *English Historical Review*, 1983.

Sewell, W. *Work and Revolution in France: The Language and Labour of the Old Regime*, Cambridge University Press, 1980.

Seyd, P. and L. Minkin, 'The Labour party and its members', *New Society*, 27 Sept. 1979.

Shallice, A. 'Orange and Green and militancy: Sectarianism and working class politics in Liverpool 1900–1914', *NWLHS Bulletin*, 6, 1979–80.

'Liverpool Labourism and Irish Nationalism in the 1920s and 1930s', *NWLHS Bulletin*, 8, 1982.

Shepherd, M. 'The effect of the franchise on the social and sexual composition of the municipal electorate 1882–1914', *Bulletin of the Society for the Study of Labour History*, 45, 1982.

Shepherd, M. and J. Halstead, 'Labour's municipal election performance in provincial England and Wales 1900–1913', *Bulletin of the Society for the Study of Labour History*, 39, 1979.

Shipley, S. *Club Life and Socialism*, London: History Workshop, 1980.

Sjoberg, G. *The Pre-industrial City: Past and Present*, New York: Free Press, 1960.

Smith, D. *Conflict and Compromise: Class Formation in English Society 1830–1914*, London: Routledge & Kegan Paul, 1982.

Smith, D.G. 'The social and political significance of the Church of England in mid-nineteenth century textile Lancashire with particular reference to Preston', unpublished M.A. dissertation, University of Lancaster, 1984.

Smith, J. 'Commonsense thought and working class consciousness: Some aspects of the Glasgow and Liverpool labour movements in the early years of the twentieth century', unpublished Ph.D. thesis, University of Edinburgh, 1980.

Sowerwine, C. *Sisters or Citizens? Women and Socialism in France since 1876*, Cambridge University Press, 1982.

Stinchcombe, A. 'Bureaucratic and craft administration of production: A comparative study', *Administrative Science Quarterly*, 4, 1959.

Sutcliffe, A. 'In search of the urban variable', in D. Fraser and A. Sutcliffe (eds.), *The Pursuit of Urban History*, London: Edward Arnold, 1983.

Sykes, A. *Tariff Reforms in British Politics 1903–1913*, Oxford: Clarendon, 1979.

Taylor, A.J.P. *A Personal History*, London: Hamish Hamilton, 1983.

Taylor, P.H. 'Preston Trades and Labour Council: Its role in Preston politics and society', unpublished M.A. dissertation, University of Lancaster, 1978.

Tebbutt, M. *Making Ends Meet: Pawnbroking and Working Class Credit*, Leicester University Press, 1983.

Thane, P. 'The Labour party and state "welfare"', in K.D. Brown (ed.), *The First Labour Party 1906–1910*, London: Croom Helm, 1985.

Tholfsen, T. *Working Class Radicalism in Mid-Victorian Britain*, London: Croom Helm, 1976.

Thompson, D. 'Courtship and marriage in Preston between the wars', *Oral History*, 3, 2, 1975.

The Chartists, London: Temple Smith, 1984.

Thompson, E.P. *The Making of the English Working Class*, London: Gollancz, 1963.

Thompson, P. (ed.), *Our Common History*, London: Pluto, 1982.

Thorpe, E. 'Industrial relations and the social structure: A case study of Bolton cotton mule spinners', unpublished Ph.D. thesis, University of Salford, 1969.

Tilly, C. and L. Tilly, *Class Conflict and Collective Action*, New York: Sage, 1981.

Tilly, L. and J. Scott, *Women, Work, and the Family*, London: Holt, 1978.

Todd, N. 'A history of Labour in Lancaster and Barrow-in-Furness c. 1890–1920', unpublished Ph.D. thesis, University of Lancaster, 1976.

Tolliday, S. and J. Zeitlin, (eds.), *Shop Floor Bargaining and the State*, Cambridge University Press, 1985.

Touraine, A. *The Post-industrial Society: Tomorrow's Social History*, London: Wildwood, 1971.

Trodd, G. 'Political change and the working class in Blackburn and Burnley 1890–1914', unpublished Ph.D. thesis, University of Lancaster, 1978.

Tupling, G. *The Economic History of Rossendale*, Manchester University Press, 1927.

Turner, H.A. *Trade Union Growth, Policy and Structure*, Toronto University Press, 1963.

Urry, J. *The Anatomy of Capitalist Societies*, London: Macmillan, 1981.

'Localities, regions, and social class', *International Journal of Urban and Regional Research*, 5, 4, 1981.

Vincent, D. *Bread, Knowledge and Freedom: A Study of Nineteenth Century Working Class Autobiography*, London: Europa, 1981.

Vincent, J.R. *The Formation of the Liberal Party, 1857–1868*, London: Constable, 1966.

Walby, S. *Patriarchy at Work*, Cambridge: Polity, 1986.

Walker, W. *Juteopolis*, Dundee University Press, 1979.

Waller, P. *Democracy and Sectarianism*, Liverpool University Press, 1981.
    Town, City and Nation, Oxford University Press, 1983.
Waller, R.J. *The Dukeries Transformed: The Social and Political Development of a Twentieth-Century Coalfield*, Oxford: Clarendon, 1983.
Ward, D. 'Victorian cities: How modern?', *Journal of Historical Geography*, 1975.
    'Environs and neighbours in the "Two Nations": Residential differentiation in mid-nineteenth century Leeds', *Journal of Historical Geography*, 1980.
Webb, B. and S. Webb, *Industrial Democracy*, London: Longman, 1902.
Wedderburn, D. and R. Crompton, *Workers' Attitudes and Technology*, Cambridge University Press, 1972.
Welsh Board of Health, *The Hospital Survey: The Hospital Services of South Wales*, London: His Majesty's Stationery Office, 1945.
White, J. *The Worst Street in North London: Campbell Bunk, Islington, between the Wars*, London: Routledge & Kegan Paul, 1986.
White, J.L. *The Limits of Trade Union Militancy*, New York: Greenwood, 1978.
Whitehead's Preston Yearbook, Preston: Whitehead, 1910.
Whiteside, N. 'Welfare legislation and the unions during the First World War', *Historical Journal*, 23, 4, 1980.
Whiting, R. *The View from Cowley: The Impact of industrialisation on Oxford 1918–1939*, Oxford: Clarendon, 1983.
Wickham, E.R. *Church and People in an Industrial City*, London: Butterworth, 1957.
Wild, P. 'Recreation in Rochdale 1900–1940', in J. Clarke, C. Critcher and R. Johnson (eds.), *Working Class Culture*, London: Hutchinson, 1979.
Williams, A. *Life in a Railway Factory*, London: Tavistock, 1969.
Williams, B. 'The beginnings of Jewish Trade Unionism in Manchester 1881–1891', in K. Lunn (ed.), *Hosts, Immigrants and Minorities*, Folkestone: Dawson, 1980.
Williams, R. *Culture and Society*, Harmondsworth: Penguin, 1963.
    The Long Revolution, Harmondsworth: Penguin, 1963.
Willmott, P. *The Evolution of Community: A Study of Dagenham after 40 Years*, London: Routledge & Kegan Paul, 1963.
Willmott, P. and M. Young, *Family and Kinship in East London*, Harmondsworth: Penguin, 1962.
Winstanley, M. *The Shopkeeper's World, 1830–1914*, Manchester University Press, 1983.
Winter, J. 'Trade unions and the Labour party in Britain', in H.J. Momsen and H.G. Huring (eds.), *The Development of Trade Unionism in Great Britain and Germany 1880–1914*, London: George Allen & Unwin, 1985.
Wood, G.H. *The History of Wages in the Cotton Trade during the Past Hundred Years*, London: Sheratt & Hughes, 1910.
Wright, E.O. *Class, Crisis and the State*, London: Verso, 1978.
    Classes, London: Verso, 1985.
Yeo, S. *Religion and Voluntary Organisations in Crisis*, London: Croom Helm, 1976.
    'A new life: The religion of socialism in Britain 1883–1896', *History Workshop Journal*, 4, 1977.
    'Working class association, private capital, welfare and the state', in N. Parry et al. (eds.), *Social Work, Welfare and the State*, London: Edward Arnold, 1979.

'State and anti-state: Reflections on social forms and struggles from 1850', in P. Corrigan (ed.), *Capitalism, State Formation and Marxist Theory*, London: Quartet, 1980.

Zeitlin, J. 'Craft control and the division of labour: Engineers and compositors in Britain 1880–1930', *Cambridge Journal of Economics*, 1979.

'The emergence of shop steward organisation, and job control in the British car industry', *History Workshop*, 10, 1980.

'Engineers and compositors: A comparison', in R. Harrison and J. Zeitlin (eds.), *Divisions of Labour*, Brighton: Harvester, 1985.

Author index

References in italics are to note numbers.

274   *Index*

Subject index

Only significant individuals and firms (normally those mentioned more than once), but all place names, are indexed. (P) following a place name indicates that it is part of Preston. References in italics are to note numbers.

Amalgamated Engineering Union, 96, 98, 170, 185, 186, 230 36
Anglican Church, 3, 54, 103–10, 112, 117–22, 136, 157, 163, 189, 232 24
Ashton-on-Ribble (P), 113–14, 150, 175
Avenham (P), 103, 105, 111, 113, 114

Barrow-in-Furness, 46, 53, 54, 71, 234 49
beamers (cotton occupation), 82, 91, 149
Birmingham, 32, 45, 49, 135
Blackburn, 58, 59, 61, 65, 67, 68, 70, 135, 188
Bolton, 65, 67, 68, 69, 70, 135, 197, 237 37
bourgeoisie, 13–14, 17, 42–3, 48–9, 60–1, 66, 71, 80–1, 82, 83, 84–6, 88–9, 93, 102–3, 105, 112, 113, 118–19, 121, 138–40, 142, 147–9, 157, 185, 199
Bristol, 135, 166
building industry, 42, 70, 72, 98, 178, 191
Burnley, 54, 64, 59, 61, 65, 67, 68, 70, 90, 125, 234 50, 53

Calvert, W., 66, 88
Cambridge, 198
capacities, 39–41, 56, 58, 61–2, 64, 71, 80, 91–2, 93, 94, 98, 99–100, 112, 117, 125–6, 131–3, 136–7, 145, 150, 152, 153, 154, 155, 171, 174, 177, 188, 189, 190, 231 4
  definition of, 40
card room workers (cotton occupation), 83, 237 29
Cardiff, 35, 59
Carlisle, 35

Catholic Church, 50, 54, 110–12, 122–3, 136, 144, 158–61, 163, 194, 249 57
Cheltenham, 45
Chester-le-Street, 195
Christ Church, 108, 120–2
clerical workers, 98–9
Cliff Mill, 85, 94
Clitheroe, 147
coal mining, 30, 46, 52–3, 70, 179, 198, 232 28
Communist Party, ix, 8, 12
Conservative Party, 3, 62, 134, 136–7, 140–3, 144, 145, 146–8, 150, 155, 164, 171–3, 180, 183, 185, 189, 193
Co-operative movement, 4, 21, 23, 48, 60, 84, 101, 127–30, 137, 155–6, 191, 195
cotton industry, *see specific branches and occupations*
cotton spinning (*see also* spinners), 65–8, 84–8, 165
cotton weaving (*see also* weavers), 65, 67–8, 70, 78–80, 83, 88–9, 90–2, 181, 182
Coventry, 198
craft workers, 69–70, 74, 78, 82–4, 87, 88–92, 95, 96–8, 102, 126–7, 154–6, 175, 181, 182, 184, 189, 191, 192, 194, 198
  definition of, 42
  general significance of, 41–7, 49
culture, 1–3, 5, 9, 39, 163

Deepdale (P), 115, 141
deference, 1–3, 6, 37, 103, 140, 189

277